THE RISE OF THE
Nashville Teen

D1430262

Taylor Swift

THE RISE OF THE
Nashville Teen

CHLOE GOVAN

OMNIBUS PRESS

LONDON / NEW YORK / PARIS / SYDNEY / COPENHAGEN / BERLIN / MADRID / HONG KONG / TOKYO

Exclusive Distributors
Music Sales Limited,
14/15 Berners Street,
London, W1T 3LJ.

Music Sales Corporation,
257 Park Avenue South,
New York, NY 10010, USA.

Macmillan Distribution Services,
56 Parkwest Drive
Derrimut, Vic 3030,
Australia.

Every effort has been made to trace the copyright holders of the photographs in this book but one or
two were unreachable. We would be grateful if the photographers concerned would contact us.

Typeset by Phoenix Photosetting, Chatham, Kent
Printed in the EU

A catalogue record for this book is available from the British Library.

Visit Omnibus Press on the web at www.omnibuspress.com

Contents

Acknowledgments

Special thanks go to my interviewees:

Ashley Eidam, a child actress who played alongside Taylor in her schooldays.

Pat Garrett, the country musician who gave Taylor one of her first tastes of the stage. His music website is www.patgarrett.com and his sheepskin store is located at Route 78, Exit 19, Strausstown, PA, 19559, USA (www.sickafus.com).

Super producer Steve Migliore, whose mix of LeAnn Rimes' track 'How Do I Live' made the number-one spot on American radio, and who then went on to work with Taylor pre-fame.

An extra special thanks goes to:

Kaylin Politzer for her detailed and colourful recollections of being Taylor's best friend back in Wyomissing, Pennsylvania.

Blu Sanders, who provided his memories of songwriting sessions with Taylor in her teenage years.

Damla Taner, who attended Hendersonville High with Taylor on a dance scholarship.

Family friend Adriana Whitman. Also Mathew Lyons.

Plus all of the anonymous friends, teachers and even school bullies who declined to be named but volunteered information and quotes to give greater depth to Taylor's story.

Thanks also go to David Barraclough, Jacqui Black, Chris Charlesworth, Charlie Harris and everyone at Omnibus Press who was involved in the making of this book.

Finally, thanks to Cookie Monster for the near endless supply of chocolate cake!

Chapter 1

The Birth Of America's Good Girl

"I'm so gangsta, you can find me baking cookies at night!" joked America's number one good girl, Taylor Swift. If a rock 'n' roll star told the world she had an unlikely penchant for baking, it might well have suggested something very different from a plate of chocolate brownies.

Yet, unlike musical hell-raisers such as Amy Winehouse, whose definition of baking was more likely to mean preparing an illicit drug, Taylor was clean-cut in the extreme. While Amy's idea of a quiet night in, pipe-and-slippers style, during her short and troubled life might have meant settling down in an armchair with a crack pipe and a DVD, the closest Taylor ever came to hedonism was a midnight cereal party with her mother.

What was more, she broke the mould for a young millionaire celebrity when she reported getting home before midnight on New Year's Eve – the very same year she had reached drinking age. As for alcohol, she still hasn't touched a drop.

The music industry wasn't exactly famed for teetotal singers, but Taylor was determined to be one. She also set herself apart from other songstresses by avoiding excessive vanity. She wasn't the type of celebrity who had a plastic surgeon on speed dial. In fact, she had pledged to "grow old gracefully" and to welcome a head of grey hair when the time came, telling *Glamour*: "I don't need to be blonde when I'm 60!"

What was more, she had insisted to *Elle Girl* that, "as far as beauty tips go, there's really nothing that reads better than confidence". She felt that, rough diamond or polished gem, she would still be talented – and that how she looked on the outside could never detract from her music.

On that note, there was also Taylor's style. She was more high fashion than high exposure, more modestly tantalising than tawdry – and she was someone who was more likely to grace the cover of *Vogue* than *Playboy*. In other words, she wasn't in the game to be a sex symbol.

While other young female chart-toppers were smiling salaciously, writhing provocatively in lingerie and thrusting their hips at the camera, Taylor was dressing down in a demure outfit with an obligatory pair of country-style cowboy boots. Some of her pop peers might have turned up the temperature by resembling fetish models, but Taylor was determined for her chart domination to be a non-sexual conquest, winning people over by her music alone. She never flashed the flesh – in fact, the only type of model she wanted to be was a role model.

The irony was that Taylor was 5 feet, 11 inches of natural beauty, with blonde hair and blue eyes – but she hadn't earned the title 'The Anti-Britney' for nothing, and she was keeping her assets under wraps.

What was more, it wasn't just her refusal to hit the clubs in a see-through dress or flash her vulva as she climbed out of a car at the start of a night out that set her apart from the fallen pop princess. Taylor wrote or co-wrote all of her own songs, too. While Britney was suffering criticism in the press for not contributing to any of the numbers she sang, Taylor's conscience was clear.

Maybe so, but her parents hadn't exactly been all-night ravers either. Her father, Scott, had been a high-flyer in the banking world, first graduating from Delaware University with a first-class degree in business and then going on to found an investment banking and financial advisory company called the Swift Group. His surname was fitting, as he was scaling the corporate ladder at top speed.

Meanwhile Taylor's mother, then known as Andrea Finlay, was equally ambitious, working as a marketing executive in the finance industry. A busy career woman, marriage hadn't crossed her mind until Scott entered her life, while visiting her home town of Harris, Texas on a business trip from Delaware.

"Before she had me, she was this really big business executive that worked for an ad agency," Taylor later admiringly recalled to cable television network *Great American Country*. "I really look up to that. I respect that she had a career on her own and lived alone... and was supporting herself [financially]."

Indeed, in the late Seventies, when Andrea began her career, career women were a rare breed – and taking up traditional male professions could be seen as controversial. Sure, there were plenty of secretaries, waitresses, air hostesses and Playboy bunnies, but back then the odds were stacked against an abundance of female bankers. In fact, all the top earners seemed destined to be male.

Even by 1988, according to *Cosmopolitan* magazine in a feature of the same year, only a "tiny minority [of women] have made it through to the ranks of management – the majority work as inadequately paid support personnel".

Another *Cosmopolitan* feature asserted that women who did make it to the top alienated prospective husbands. "Most men... still have a vested interest in women being traditional and feminine," it read. "[Otherwise] who will run their homes? Bring up the children? Do the shopping? Find their socks?"

It also quoted a male model – allegedly the epitome of women's desires – as saying: "You have to be tough to get where she's got. Who wants to live with a tough woman?"

Back in the day, before feminism changed the workplace, it wasn't easy for a working woman to find a good job, let alone balance the demands of her life when she had one – so Andrea was happily married to her career.

She had no time for a man, but – a romantic at heart, like her daughter – when she met Scott, she was reluctantly struck down by the love bug. After a whirlwind romance, the two got married and moved to the small town of West Reading in Berks County, Pennsylvania, where Andrea quickly became pregnant.

Their first child, to be christened Taylor Alison Swift, was due to arrive a few months before Andrea turned 31, and gradually the corporate world became less important to her. That said, business was never too far from her mind – as soon as Andrea learned she was having a girl, she quickly decided upon a unisex name to make sure her daughter wouldn't fall prey to workplace sexism.

"She named me Taylor so that if anybody saw on a business card the name Taylor, they wouldn't know if it was a girl or a boy if they were thinking of hiring me," Taylor revealed to *The Toronto Star*.

Evidently, there was no question in her parents' eyes that the child in Andrea's womb would one day become a high-flying business woman herself – it was only a matter of time. However, their strong-minded child would turn out to have other ideas.

"My parents were in finance [so] they thought I was going to be a stockbroker and go to business school," Taylor groaned to *The Wall Street Journal*.

What was more, her father was so involved with the profession that, instead of "Bye bye", his favourite parting shot was "Buy bonds!" An impressionable young Taylor wanted to be just like her father, too. "When I was probably six or seven, I used to follow my dad around and say, 'I'm gonna be a stockbroker like you!'" she revealed. "I had no idea what a stockbroker was, of course!"

Even before Taylor had started life, it seemed as though she was destined for a world of stocks, shares and spreadsheets – but there was more genetic material in her family than just business ambition.

One of Taylor's ancestors in the early 18th century was the legendary Irish writer and satirist Jonathan Swift, most famous for his novel *Gulliver's Travels*.

Yet it was her maternal grandmother, Marjorie Finlay, who really came to Taylor's rescue. An outgoing woman with a voracious appetite for travelling, she had married an international oil worker and lived a nomadic existence, filling her spare time with a love of opera.

She sang around the world and even tried her hand at TV presenting in Latin America. "In Puerto Rico, my grandmother was the hostess of the top-rated TV variety show called *The Pan American Show*," Taylor revealed to *Wood & Steel* magazine. "[Her] Spanish was so bad that the Puerto Ricans thought she was hysterically funny! She went on to become the 'madrina' [symbolic grandmother figure] of their air force. They really loved her!"

Aside from having viewers in hysterics with her paltry command of Spanish, she was earning success and notoriety back home too. "She starred in a lot of operas and was a member of the Houston Grand Opera," continued Taylor. "I think that's where I get most of my musical ability."

Taylor herself came into the world on December 13, 1989. The number 13 might have been unlucky for some, but Andrea and Scott were delighted to welcome the new arrival.

What was more, she was turning heads almost from the moment she was born. "Taylor was maybe just a few hours old when a paediatrician said: 'She's a really good-natured baby, but she knows exactly what she wants and how to get it!'" her mother recalled. "I thought: 'What is this guy on?' but he just gave me this interesting description of her which absolutely fit her to a T!"

She wasn't only bright either – she was beautiful. Their first-born child was a natural blonde with corkscrew curls and a wide smile – and she was instantly the subject of public adoration. Even before she could sing a note, her parents would find themselves stopped in the street by passers-by eager to compliment Taylor on her beauty.

However, her quiet phase wasn't to last long. By the time she was three, her voice took over. "I would come out of Disney movies and my parents used to get freaked out because I'd be singing the entire soundtrack of the movie after hearing it once," Taylor told the *Daily Mail*. "I retained music more than anything else."

Plus, now that she could walk, it wasn't other people approaching her anymore – she was initiating contact with them. "There are videos of me walking up to strangers and singing songs from *The Lion King* when I was a baby," Taylor added to *The Philadelphia Enquirer*. Little more than a toddler, she was already desperate for an audience and to be where she felt she belonged – on the stage.

Her parents' memories were equally vivid. "The first movie I saw was *The Little Mermaid*, and my parents still tell me stories about going to see that movie," Taylor explained. "I was in the car in the back seat [afterwards] singing the words to the songs that I'd heard in the movie and they kind of looked at each other and were really confused as to how I was remembering the words after seeing the movie only once."

Taylor might have shown an early aptitude for belting out Disney tunes, but at that stage her family merely saw it as an endearing hobby. "Yes, Taylor sang, but her parents' attitude was that all kids sang," an anonymous friend of the family told the author. "They didn't really think much of it."

When her parents saw Taylor bashing away on a toy keyboard while half-singing, half-shouting 'Twinkle, Twinkle, Little Star', they didn't see a musical prodigy – they saw a normal boisterous three-year-old. Even when she was serenading strangers on the beach, running from towel to towel to impress sunbathers with yet another impromptu performance, her family still didn't believe she had an extraordinary talent – she was just their Taylor.

Keen to prove them wrong and eventually tiring of the lyrics from *The Lion King*, she started to compose her own songs, featuring words such as "I love my dolly!" and, in one case, "I can't wait to be great!" Perhaps it was a prophecy.

Together with her award-winning former opera-singer grandmother, Taylor had an opportunity to show off her singing skills in church too. The pair – devout Catholics, like the rest of the family – turned heads every Sunday when they out sang the choir. "I can remember [my grandmother] singing, the thrill of it," Taylor recalled of their times at church together. "She was one of my first inspirations."

In addition to Sunday school, Taylor would take an occasional Bible retreat course in the summer too, where she would reflect on God's teachings in rural parts of Pennsylvania. However, even there, she never missed an opportunity to sing, leading the hymns from time to time.

By now, she had also enrolled at Alvernia Montessori in West Reading, Pennsylvania, a Catholic pre-school run by nuns which contained just 56 children. The school's headmistress, Sister Ann Marie Coll, recalled:

"She was kind of shy, but not too shy, and she always liked to sing. Taylor wasn't stubborn, but she was a determined little girl. When she put her mind to something, she was very intent."

While Taylor was unleashing the power of her lungs at pre-school, her parents were trying for another baby – and, on March 4, 1993, a younger brother named Austin completed their family. Her hands now full with two mischievous children, Andrea decided that motherhood was a full-time job within itself and withdrew from professional work once and for all.

Hankering after a taste of country life, Andrea persuaded her husband to move home – and soon after, they fell in love with a Christmas tree farm in rural Pennsylvania. It had once been the property of Taylor's paternal grandfather. Located off Freemansville Road in the township of Cumru, it was just six miles away from the town of Reading on Route 625.

However, despite the blood connection, it wasn't exactly the archetypal home of a high-flying career-conscious businessman and his young family. Nearby Reading was considered to be a hotspot for poverty, unemployment, drug addiction and soaring rates of violent crime. Known throughout Pennsylvania as a troubled area, it was hardly the place to be.

And while Cumru was a much safer neighbourhood, the average household income in the township was just $40,000 (£25,000) – a tiny fraction of the Swift family's wages. Some people from outside the community sneeringly dismissed its inhabitants as "country bumpkins". Not only that, but the family would have to sacrifice their usual creature comforts to get an authentic taste of country living.

While Taylor had a fondness for "old buildings with paint chipping off the walls", her parents – both from wealthy and privileged backgrounds – might have been a little more fazed by it.

Her father also had to juggle rural life with the fast-paced world of finance – with interesting consequences. After yet another stressful day of trading on the stock market, Scott would come home to the stench of horse manure and the prospect of some DIY work around the house before cleaning out the stables. It wasn't pretty.

Yet, in spite of that, he soon warmed to farm life. "My husband and I were both professionals, we weren't farmers, but we *loved* the idea of living on the farm," Andrea later confessed to *Teen Superstar*.

What was more, a young Taylor loved the idea just as much. It was a place for her to be at one with nature and have experiences that would fuel her imagination and pave the way for prolific poem and songwriting in the future. The 665-acre Nolde Forest – a haven for hikers, bird-watchers and photographers – was close by, with pine trees stretching as far as the eye could see. Yet Taylor rarely visited – after all, she had more than 10 acres of land of her own to play on.

"Having room to run and having just the space to use your imagination and create stories and fairytales out of everyday life – I think that had a lot to do with me wanting to write songs," Taylor mused to *Teen Superstar*.

However, some inspirations were a little more gory than others. "We had barn cats and we'd go out in the morning and there'd be absolute carnage on the driveway, anything from little squirrels to birds," Andrea recalled. "Taylor would literally start to create little conversations and storylines involving all the little dead animals on the driveway!"

These mangled corpses might have sounded more like the theme for a horror novel than the subject of an innocent pre-teen girl's thoughts, but Taylor was no ordinary girl – and the farm provided her with endless entertainment.

"Her favourite thing to do was saddle up the pony for a trail ride or build a fort in the hay loft," Andrea recalled. She would also run freely in the fruit orchards, find herself pets among the woodland creatures on the farm and hitch a ride on one of the family's tractors. There would be hayrides too – both for Taylor and her friends.

Her once immaculate curls turned into an unruly mess, but she was having too much fun to care. "[At least] I grew up with all this space to run around and the freedom to be a crazy kid with tangled hair," she later reminisced to *Glamour*.

Still, she would have to make sacrifices too. Her earliest job, long before the glamour of her country-music career, was picking praying mantis eggs off the trees. Not only did the trees have to be free of them before being sold – thousands of insects hatching out on a family's Christmas tree would not be good for the Swifts' business reputation – but the insects were also useful as a form of organic pest control. Each egg case can yield up to 300 praying mantises, which – on reaching maturity – eat smaller pests such as beetles, crickets and grasshoppers. For farmers who needed pest control without resorting to chemical pesticides, it was the perfect solution. Taylor and her brother would meticulously scour the trees for egg-cases each season to earn some pocket money from their parents.

However, it wasn't all work and no play as – nestled in her countryside hideaway – Taylor quickly discovered music. The country music culture in rural Pennsylvania was virtually non-existent – but that didn't bother Taylor who, by the age of six, had persuaded her parents to buy her LeAnn Rimes' entire collection. "Le Ann Rimes was my first impression of country music," she told *The Guardian*. "I just really loved how she could be making music and having a career at such a young age."

Indeed, LeAnn had released her debut album, *Blue*, at just 13. From then on, Taylor made it her mission to learn every song by heart, which took a matter of days. When she had done that, she moved on to other big names in the genre. "I went back and learned the history," she told *Great American Country*. "I listened to legends like Dolly [Parton] and Patsy Cline – women who were the essence of country music."

At six, then, Taylor was already a connoisseur of country. Keen to follow in the footsteps of her new-found idols, she memorised song lyrics and longed to learn the guitar to try out her own tunes – but she had her family and their wildly different musical tastes to contend with first.

It was a battle of wills at home to secure her favourite radio station or select that day's soundtrack. Her grandmother, who visited regularly, would blast out her favourite opera tracks, while her mother was obsessed with heavy rock group Def Leppard. Her father, when he was around, was more inclined towards pop and easy listening – and then there was Taylor. Country had been her favourite from the start.

While still a child, she went on to see her idol LeAnn Rimes live in concert. "I saw her in Atlantic City," Taylor later told *The Seven Mile Times*. "She touched my hand! I bragged about that for about a year."

The same year that she discovered music, Taylor also began her primary education at the Wyndcroft School in Pottstown. The area was leafy, peaceful and semi-rural with a backdrop of rolling hills, yet was located just 40 miles from Philadelphia. The school was founded in 1918, a significant year, because it saw laws passed that gave American women the right to vote. The school's aim was "to provide not only for academic excellence, but for the healthful wellbeing of a child". Back in the days when measles, tuberculosis and even a simple bout of the flu could be fatal, Wyndcroft established itself as a disease-free zone by offering classes in an open-air environment.

The East Coast's bitterly cold winters might have seen children shivering stoically as they received their early morning algebra classes under an almost pitch black sky, but at least it was for the benefit of their health. As the years passed, the school expanded both in size and popularity – and, of course, by the time Taylor joined in 1996, it had plenty of indoor classrooms.

It had a prestigious reputation and was renowned for its academic excellence, but six-year-old Taylor was still reportedly head and shoulders above many of her peers. One second-grade assignment aimed at teaching sentence structure had asked pupils to write just two sentences – but Taylor handed in a three-page essay.

"She was incredibly quick-witted," one tutor, who prefers not to be named, told the author. "She would come up with these complex ideas that you just wouldn't expect from someone her age and it would leave people open-mouthed. She was always making up her own stories to entertain the class. She wasn't a show-off, but she was just genuinely excited to be learning."

Taylor's teacher added: "I had no idea that Taylor would become a singer, but I knew she would probably be famous for something. It would be an injustice if she hadn't been – she just stood out from the rest. She was very tenacious and focused, which is a very big achievement for someone in elementary school. Some of the other kids, while they were bright, had frustratingly short attention spans, but she'd always remember when you told her something. This was no ordinary child. For all her shyness on the surface, there was just something incredibly awe-inspiring and different and special about her."

By the time Taylor reached her final year at Wyndcroft, the fourth grade, she was able to read music in the treble clef, play the recorder competently and sing two-part harmonies. As well as excelling at music, she quickly made a name for herself as a talented and imaginative English student who often wrote her own short stories. One of her tutors revealed: "Even as early as first grade, she was using positional phrases unheard of from kids that age, and by fourth, she was still standing out as smart."

Taylor proved that fact by winning a national competition for the best children's poem in America at just 10 years old. When she heard about the contest, she was instantly up for the challenge, revealing later: "Poetry was my favourite thing. I loved putting things down on paper – it was so fascinating to me."

She added to *Rolling Stone*: "Poetry was the first thing that ever fascinated me about words and about writing. Poetry is what turned me into a songwriter."

During her early days of practising, she had composed some deep and meaningful poems, but decided that the one she submitted for the contest should be more light-hearted and mainstream. She was, after all, no stranger to jokey, gimmicky stories. As a child, she had avidly read the books of Dr Seuss, author of such fantastical rhymed stories as *The Cat In The Hat* and *How The Grinch Stole Christmas*. The rhyme Taylor submitted was equally fun and nonsensical.

"It was a long poem called 'Monster In My Closet'," Taylor recalled. "I picked the most gimmicky one I had… I didn't want to get too dark on them." With playful couplets such as "There's a monster in my closet and I don't know what to do/Have you ever seen him? Has he ever pounced on you?", there was little chance of that.

Yet, contrary to what the jokey-sounding topic implied, Taylor had put a lot of work into devising the winning strategy. "[I was] trying to figure out the perfect combination of words, with the perfect amount of syllables and the perfect rhyme to make it completely pop off the page," she recalled.

After winning, a thrilled Taylor became "consumed" with beating her best efforts and writing more poetry, but that wasn't all she was up to at school. Taylor was exceptionally numerate too, and even had a soft spot for sciences.

Taylor also joined her class on an overnight trip to a nature camp to learn more about science and survival in the wild. Plus, although Andrea had enjoyed her first illicit sip of alcohol at the age of 17, Taylor was enrolled in a Drug Abuse Resistance Education, which taught facts about the effects of alcohol, tobacco and marijuana on the brain and behaviour and warned children away from temptation.

It was a broad-based education, but what Taylor loved doing the most was singing and acting. She was desperate to secure the lead role for her first major school play, since the character was the only one who would have the chance to sing solo. But, unfortunately for Taylor, the character was male. Many might have given up there and then but, not to be deterred, she donned a disguise and tried out for the part.

"There was one solo, but it was a guy," she groaned in memory of it. "There was this character called Freddie Fast Talk and it was the bad guy. I didn't care, I was like: 'I will dress up like a guy, I want to sing that song!'"

Her persistence paid off. "I remember I had like a moustache," Taylor continued, "and we drew on eyebrows and I put my hair up in this hat and I dressed like a guy and I sang the solo!"

The other children might have raised an eyebrow at her gender-bending antics, but the teachers saw it as proof of her dedication to the art. "After that, her music teacher said: 'You're going to have to find another outlet for her because she just loves it!'" Andrea recalled. Luckily, Taylor wouldn't have to wait long.

The very next year, 1999, the family packed up and moved again, leaving their farm life behind them. Taylor's new home was a large white detached mansion set back from the road on a tree-lined avenue in the heart of the Wyomissing Hills.

They hadn't travelled far, but this thriving town was miles apart from the rural idyll Taylor had previously known. The new community even had a local actors' association, Berks County Youth Theater Academy

(BYTA), and, following her music teacher's advice, Andrea instantly signed Taylor up.

It was here that the former farm girl would satisfy her early hunger for being on the stage.

Chapter 2

Seduced By The Sound Of Music

When Taylor first arrived in Wyomissing, she was a stranger. "No-one talked to me," she lamented to *The Reading Eagle*. "I didn't know anybody."

While she might have moved just a few miles from her former home, it was a totally different world for her. To confuse matters further, when she enrolled at West Reading Elementary School, she found herself straddling two postcode boundaries – one of almost limitless wealth and privilege and one of abject poverty.

"The area of Wyomissing is comprised of two parts, the borough of Wyomissing and the borough of West Reading," one anonymous resident told the author. "Wyomissing is defined by its luscious park system, bordered by rich houses and mansions. West Reading, however, is an extension of the crime-ridden city of Reading, which often earns top honours in crime, murder and rape rates. The citizens of West Reading are mostly illegal immigrants and other fatherless families deprived of guidance and money. These kids are thrown into a school system along with the wealthy children of the doctors, lawyers and business owners working in the city of Reading."

According to this source, the hotspot for wealthy young girls was the King of Prussia mall, where they could shop to perfect a look of shabby chic that fitted in with their surroundings. "The most popular stores include AX and BCBG, [at] which you can pay $70 for a faded shirt that has been 'professionally aged' so that the buyer can pretend to be ghetto and poor," he said. "Kids dress to impress, often saying things like: 'Woah, man, your BMW is *so* mad ghetto!' For the cash it takes to buy the sports cars that are cruising around, you could buy and refurbish an entire ghetto."

Indeed, while some of Taylor's classmates could barely afford the bus fare to school in the morning, others were arriving in style, in cars that would cost their less privileged peers a decade's wages. "If five minutes pass in Wyomissing without seeing a BMW or a Mercedes cruising by, it's a miracle," the resident added. This was a place where the rich and the poor collided – but Taylor was firmly in the first category. Not only did she have her own room – unlike some West Reading residents who shared with their siblings – but she had an entire floor of the house all to herself.

"The Swifts' home was beautiful," revealed childhood friend Kaylin Politzer. "The stately white house had black shutters with silver moons carved in the sides and was perched on a hill overlooking the city and its surroundings. Taylor had the entire attic to herself – a floor comprised of a game room, painting room and bedroom complete with a canopy bed. I vividly remember Taylor singing along to Nelly Furtado's 'I'm Like A Bird' as I watched from that canopy bed."

She might have been on top of the world at home, but her life of luxury isolated her from her classmates, some of whom were green with envy. "Taylor found it hard to make friends," explained a Wyomissing local who preferred only to be known as Sara. "People used to call her stuck up, I guess because they were jealous. She wanted for nothing, when some of them couldn't scrape a few cents together. She was daddy's little princess and had parents who adored her, whereas some of the other kids were from broken homes. One girl I know would even fake retching when Taylor walked by. She felt Taylor's parents were so unconditionally supportive of her that it made her nauseous. Taylor also got good grades and had a perfect home life so she was an easy target for jealousy. What did she not have? She made the others feel inadequate and envious without even trying."

It cannot have helped that while the others in the class were fans of pop music, Taylor craved country – something that, for West Reading pre-teen girls, was firmly out of fashion. Perhaps in a bid to fit in, Taylor started to listen to The Spice Girls, Natasha Bedingfield and Hanson. (She had had a crush on one of the Hanson brothers, also named Taylor, since the group's first hit single, 'Doo Wop', hit the charts when she was eight.)

She even joined in with family friend Adriana Whitman in spending hours composing singing and dancing routines. "We used to belt out [TLC song] 'Waterfalls'," Adriana revealed to the author. "We also made up dances to The Backstreet Boys and Britney Spears songs and wouldn't let anyone see them until we were done!"

In spite of joining in with the mainstream girls, Taylor was still feeling like a square peg in a round hole at school. However, when she joined the local theatre association, BYTA, the group rescued her from loneliness and helped her to connect with fiercely ambitious likeminded peers. "To be a BYTA kid meant an instant welcome into a clique," fellow child-actress Kaylin Politzer told the author. "We did three productions a year and some of us also did *Theater Kids Live* – a cross between *The Broadway Kids* and *Saturday Night Live*. In those days, I spent six days a week in that rehearsal studio and more time with my theatre friends than anyone else."

Unlike most people Taylor met at school, these girls were dedicated to the world of performance and lived for the moment they could be on stage. They were disciplined, desperate for the limelight and, in some cases, so confident that they didn't even know the meaning of the word 'stage-fright'.

It was while she was at her very first audition, for a performance of *Annie*, that Taylor met Kaylin for the first time – a girl who would go on to become her best friend. "Already having been a member of BYTA for over a year, I remember feeling like a regular at that audition and I was quite satisfied with the familiarity of the process and how comfortable I felt among my peers," Kaylin told the author.

That day, she would show an uncharacteristically nervous Taylor the ropes and introduce her to the world of professional children's theatre.

"She seemed reserved and shy," Kaylin continued. "She towered over most of the kids there and was awkward and clunky in her movements, especially in the dance auditions. Not that I should be one to make such observations – I was lanky as they come at 10 years old! I can't say she made much of an impression on me that day, though our mothers hit it off straight away!"

Another girl Taylor had met at the auditions, Ashley Eidam, had similar recollections. "I remember her being a quiet, shy girl," she chuckled, "which we all know is not the case anymore!"

The musical, set in Depression-era America. follows the adventures of the eponymous young girl, whose life begins as little more than a piece of excess baggage. As a baby, Annie is dumped at an orphanage by her parents, together with a note promising that one day they will return for her. Desperate to be reunited with the parents she never knew, Annie lives most of her childhood in forlorn hope – and the play chronicles her misadventures as she waits for that day to arrive.

As a newcomer to the theatre, Taylor landed just a minor part in the production, as an 'extra orphan' in the ensemble, while the more experienced Kaylin played the part of Pepper, one of Annie's fellow orphans. It might have been humiliating for an ever-ambitious Taylor not to have scored a more prestigious role – after all, according to Kaylin, "almost everyone who auditioned was cast, even if only in the ensemble".

However, while she started off as a shy observer, standing on the sidelines, the tables were about to turn – and, before too long, she was the centre of attention at all the BYTA shows. "I used to get all the lead roles because I was the tallest person," she later told *The Reading Eagle*.

But whether she was the tallest or not, it wasn't the reason she got the starring roles, as her first major show – playing Maria, the lead part in *The Sound Of Music* – proved.

Hidden away in the Austrian Alps is the notoriously strict Salzburg Abbey, where Maria is training to become a nun. But she is unhappy there and it has become an open prison to her – until the kindly Mother Abbess suggests that she might be more suited to a life outside the convent.

Maria breaks free from its womb-like surroundings and the sheltered life it offers to become a governess for a former First World War captain in the Austro-Hungarian navy – but she must now decide whether she wants to become a woman of God or quit the convent altogether. On arrival at her new home, the Von Trapp household, she is shocked to find that the captain's seven children are well versed in military training, but know very little about affection and love.

Instead of burying their heads in textbooks, she teaches them music and, in doing so, awakens a passion for it within herself. She is also awakened by her feelings for the captain and is eventually forced to confess to herself that she is falling in love. Within months, she returns to the abbey where she had once planned to become a nun – only this time, she is there to marry the captain. No sooner have the happy couple returned from their honeymoon, however, than Austria comes under Nazi occupation and the pair find themselves fleeing over the mountains in a bid for safety.

The self-assured yet modest and demure Taylor must have seemed the perfect match for the equally modest, devoutly religious character of Maria. According to Kaylin, the role somewhat represented who Taylor was in real life. "She did an exceptional job as Maria," she explained. "It is [usually] hard to consider matching child personalities with roles in adult theatre, because most often 11-year-olds shouldn't be able to relate to the things their 20-year-old characters are dealing with… However, Taylor's wide-eyed naiveté brought depth to her character. I thought Taylor made a lovely Maria – Maria is inherently still just a child with a crazy imagination and optimistic aspirations, hopes and dreams. To exhibit these qualities, Taylor didn't even have to pretend she was someone else."

In fact, Taylor had so perfected the role that, unlike most of the children, who played their parts on rotation, she kept the lead for the entirety of the production's run, including four shows over the weekend. "In order to give more kids the chance to play leading roles, our director arranged for each of us to play a second role for the Saturday matinee only," Kaylin confirmed. "Taylor was one of the few to keep her role for all four shows."

However, Taylor was developing other musical interests, outside of BYTA, as she explained to *The Reading Eagle*. "My interest [in musical theatre] soon drew me to country music. I was infatuated with the sound, with the story-telling. I could relate to it. I can't really tell you why. With me, it was just instinctual."

With her grandmother boasting awards for her opera singing, perhaps it was genetic. But when Taylor played the leading lady, Sandy, in the Fifties-based musical *Grease* that same year, she got the chance to bring her two overlapping passions together in the one role.

The plot of *Grease* sees two teenagers, Sandy and Danny – famously played in the film version by Olivia Newton-John and John Travolta – embark on an ill-fated holiday romance. Because Sandy lives in Australia, the pair thought they would never meet again, but a change of plan means she has to stay in town and attend the same school as Danny – which is when harsh reality really sets in. Danny is as cold as ice, keen to keep his reputation intact as a smooth operator and someone who plays the field, while Sandy is soft and sensitive, preferring to wear her heart on her sleeve.

Sandy also loses points in the cool stakes by refusing to join in with her new friends' penchant for partying. A whiff of smoke from a cigarette makes her choke, she vomits at the sight of blood, she is terrified of having her ears pierced and she is staunchly anti-alcohol. In a teenage world of sex, drugs and rock 'n' roll, Danny's friends see Sandy's abstinence as lame, while she sees their antics as out of control and wayward.

Danny, who is torn between declaring his love for her and earning kudos from his school friends, eventually gives Sandy a ring, which momentarily makes her happy. However, she then storms out of his car in indignation when he tries to kiss and touch her, an action which comes in stark contrast to some of her already sexually active friends. The musical ends as the two reconcile their differences and make a relationship work between them, driving away into the sunset as a couple.

Interestingly, the role, which typecast Sandy as a prude and a spoil-sport, was not unlike Taylor's own stance towards sex and alcohol.

Taylor also shared some of her character's awkwardness. While the last few scenes see Sandy throw caution to the winds by donning leather, skin-tight lycra and bright red high-heeled sandals to seduce Danny, it is worlds apart from her usual modest clothing.

"I will never forget the work Taylor did to get down her 'walk' as the revamped Sandy at the end of *Grease*," Kaylin told the author. "Watching Taylor to learn to walk in high heels was a slow, painful and sometimes hysterical experience! Some girls aren't made for heels!"

She added: "I think we were all at an awkward stage during those years too – pre-teen girls are just plain uncoordinated. But watching Taylor wear heels during awards shows or in commercials still makes me think about her heel-walking lessons and laugh a little!"

Like her character, Taylor had been practising losing her innocence – and it was something that would certainly pay off in the future.

However, it wasn't all about learning to strut her stuff. This was the moment when Taylor would discover the pleasure of singing in a country style in front of an audience for the first time. "It just came out sounding country," she told *Great American Country* of her time playing Sandy. "It was all I had listened to, so I guess it was just kind of natural. I decided [there and then] country music was what I needed to be doing."

Unfortunately for her, the theatre company's director, Kirk Cremer, disagreed. "He worked with Taylor in private voice lessons to train her to stay on pitch," explained Kaylin, "and he tirelessly tried to extricate the 'Southern twang' from Taylor's style, often complaining at rehearsals that it just didn't work for her. He didn't want a Southern Sandy – I bet he is kicking himself now!"

Indeed, if anyone had been expecting a glamorous Broadway-style Sandy – who would wow the audience with a sexy show-girl outfit before breaking into the song 'Hopelessly Devoted To You' – they were to be sorely disappointed. By now, country was running through Taylor's veins, and – although pop and Broadway music were part of her vocabulary – those genres were never where her interests lay.

"I was totally taken by Broadway with ambitions to make it in New York. I think Taylor had the same ambition but envisioned a different stage," Kaylin confirmed. "I think she got her Southern twang from continually listening to country music. I remember she was always listening to The Dixie Chicks, Shania Twain and LeAnn Rimes. I wasn't as into it as she was, but I remember her blasting the music for me from her bedroom stereo. She knew all the words and I had no clue."

Not only were Taylor's country influences causing her to stand out, but by this point she was earning a reputation for scoring the lead roles time and time again – and on stage, she was always the centre of attention.

As in many youth theatres, there was an atmosphere of intense competition – and soon Taylor's peers were consumed with jealousy at her success. "Taylor definitely formed friendships and respect among the group, but jealousy is an ugly beast and she definitely had some enemies too," continued Kaylin. "I think there was some general nasty talk behind Taylor's back when she kept scoring lead roles among the girls who hoped to be the lead and ended up in the ensemble."

It wasn't only the fury of envious girls that Taylor had to contend with – it was their parents too. "Stage moms were often more judgemental and provocative than the kids," Kaylin added. "So it goes with the children's theatre – no mom wants to hear another child is more talented or deserving than hers."

However, even Taylor was not immune from the green-eyed monster and, to her surprise, Kaylin soon found out that her new friend often felt inferior to her, too. "I once peeked in a journal she brought over to my house and was sorry I did," Kaylin confided. "Taylor wrote an entry about our friendship and said that she was jealous, she thought our director favoured me over her. I remember feeling embarrassed she felt that way and even more envious of her beautiful poems. I was shocked when Taylor said she envied my director's favouritism towards me."

What had fuelled Taylor's jealousy? After all, Kaylin had played the lesser role of Liesel in *The Sound Of Music*, one of the captain's seven children, and, for the duration of the play, Taylor would be governing over her. However, a humiliating moment had come between them when Kaylin had switched to the role of the Baroness for an afternoon and it had threatened to destroy the show.

"I forgot one of my few entrances for the scene between just Maria and the baroness," Kaylin revealed. "I had been playing cards backstage and lost track of time. The lights came on to reveal Taylor on stage by herself. Taylor tried to save the mistake by talking to herself, articulating the thoughts Maria was supposed to express in her conversation with the baroness. It was an awkward and distressing scene for Taylor."

Indeed, not only was she put on the spot in front of dozens of people in that afternoon's audience – not to mention some of the gloating peers who envied her success and longed to see her fail – but it was Taylor who was blamed for her friend's mistake.

"When the scene was over, our director came charging to the back to yell not at me, but at Taylor!" Kaylin continued. "My mom said she remembered [Taylor's mother] Andrea's face at that moment. It was clearly my mistake and our director unfairly took his anger out on Taylor. I remember feeling guilty and ashamed that Taylor got scapegoated for no reason. But we all moved on amicably. Taylor and her mom were resilient, but they were also classy."

It helped to repair the friendship when Taylor and Kaylin were both singled out as two of a select few chosen to go further and join a group, put together by their director, entitled Broadway In Training. The group was four children whom he felt had extra potential and could go beyond the frivolous fun of a small-town theatre production, instead taking their talent to New York City and beyond.

"Taylor and I were part of the programme with just a handful of other girls," Kaylin recalled, "and he found auditions by being part of a manager website and took us all to get headshots. He also helped us select audition songs and prepare monologues. I remember getting a last call for a show called *Kid Zone*, which was incredibly exciting, but the first job Taylor and I officially landed was an independent film about a girl with a problematic family history. It was at its earliest stages when we auditioned. I remember memorising a monologue for it and Taylor was supposed to play my best friend."

It was the pair's first chance of serious stardom – but it was not to be. They made the short journey to New York together a few times to attend rehearsals, but – just when it seemed their dreams of national recognition were about to be made a reality – the film fell through due to a lack of funding. Taylor's dreams might have fallen down, but she remained positive, using her time in the city to see a couple of shows on Broadway and get inspiration for her next opportunity.

Thankfully, she didn't have to wait long. "Our director coordinated a trip for us to do a performance in Magic Kingdom at Disney World," Kaylin reminisced. "We put together a number of big dance ensembles from past shows and enjoyed a trip to Disney! I remember walking around with Taylor through Epcot, riding the Rock 'n' Rollercoaster and Tower of Terror."

While for a group of thrilled 10-year-olds, a trip to Disney World was a reward in itself, the pair enjoyed their first taste of real paid work as part of a group called Theater Kids Live. Also organised by their director at BYTA, it acted as a spin-off of the Broadway kids concert show in New York. "We were each paid about $200 for the season," Kaylin explained. "Theater Kids would sign a contract each season [about three months] and we would host one weekly show in the building's rehearsal studio. The show was composed of group musical members, solos and original skits by our director. Many of the skits were spoofs of popular TV shows such as *The Price Is Right* and *The Rosie O'Donnell Show*. As the season progressed, they became almost all skits and less songs, almost in the style of *Saturday Night Live*."

According to reviews, Taylor had shone as a "natural comedic talent". She and Kaylin were by now among the most active participants in BYTA. However, enthusiasm among the rest of the group was waning fast. Tales of cat fights, tantrums and super-sized egos had begun to dominate every project. What was more, there was increasing resentment among Taylor's peers about the prominent roles she was taking both on the local stage and beyond.

"When it became about the backstabbing and not about the acting anymore – the pleasure of putting on a performance and being praised, all of us together – that was when it was time for most people to bow out," one member, who declined to be named, told the author.

What had started out as a fun means of self-expression and a way for local aspiring actresses to take to the stage for a few hours of non-pressurised fame had now turned sour. Fortunately for Taylor, however, she had other outlets. She had begun her foray into country singing by grabbing the microphone at BYTA's after-show parties and discovering the theatre's backstage karaoke machine. Even some of the envious parents had barely been able to disguise their admiration for Taylor's sound, taking her mother to one side and whispering: "You know, your daughter really should be out there doing country music!"

According to one anonymous friend, however, Taylor was initially suspicious of the praise and compliments that were heaped on her after shows. Did her new-found fan club really think she was in with a chance – or did they simply want her out of the theatre group to make way for their own rising stars?

"I think Taylor had this idea that there was a conspiracy to push her out of BYTA to make way for the less popular children who wanted her roles," her friend explained. "When they paid her a compliment, she was very polite and gracious, but some of the moms who were saying these things really didn't want her around at all. They had to admit she was good, but then they would also talk behind her back sometimes, claiming she was getting too big for her boots."

Tensions were clearly running high. In fact, one disgruntled mother even told another at a party: "If I ever saw a form of child abuse of parents shoving their young child into the entertainment industry, it was Taylor's parents!"

Yet for her part, Taylor was quick to deny allegations about her supposedly pushy parents. Sure, she acknowledged that they had 'empowered' her, telling Country Music Television (CMT): "There are really two ways of looking at it when you're raising kids. You can either say, 'You can be whatever you want to be', and then there is actually believing it. My parents actually believed it." However, she insisted: "My parents never pushed me. It's always been my desire and love to do this. If I had been pushed, if I didn't love this, I would probably not have been able to get this far."

Due to the gossiping, any praise she received for her acting and singing was a double-edged sword for Taylor, but – whatever the motives of the other parents might have been – she now personally believed that she could cut it in the world of country. That was all the persuasion that a fiercely ambitious Taylor needed to take her passions further than BYTA and beyond a small-town stage.

From then on, she would show up anywhere there was a karaoke contest – even if it was an adults only bar. "[My parents] were kind of embarrassed by it, I guess, this little girl singing in this smoky bar," Taylor confessed to *Great American Country*. "But they knew how much it meant to me, so they went along with it."

What was more, the more time she spent performing, the easier it became. "The only way to conquer stage fright is to get up on stage and play," she explained simply to *Elle Girl* later. "Every time you play another show, it gets better and better. But when I first started singing in front of crowds… it was a little scary at first. Anything you've just started doing is going to be scary."

Taylor welcomed her peers' stage-fright survival strategies, but found that most of them failed dismally. "Once someone told me to picture the audience in their underpants," she added incredulously. "Do *not* picture the audience in their underpants. That does not work – at all!"

Evidently though, she had somehow found a formula that worked for her, because, on the surface, she seemed to her peers to be an unwavering tower of strength. Few people could have imagined that, underneath it all, the diminutive 11-year-old on that stage wasn't so supremely confident after all, that in reality she felt like a gibbering wreck.

She even had her best friend Kaylin fooled, who declared: "Taylor was a very confident girl. I think we shared a confidence and love for performing and she carried herself well on stage and off." In any case, Taylor had quickly moved up in Kaylin's estimation from the reserved girl she had met at the audition for *Annie* a matter of mere months earlier.

Yet while Taylor was hiding her insecurities well from her friends, she fell prey to self-doubt behind the scenes when her parents bought her the ultimate present – a much yearned-after 12-string guitar. Kaylin, her mother and her brother Cary were all present the day it was handed to her – and initially Taylor was thrilled. "She was very excited to show it off and get started learning chords by trial and error," Kaylin recalled.

However, her excitement was soon overshadowed by cruel comments from others at school about her tiny hands, after which she found herself fearing she would never learn to play it at all. "I couldn't motivate myself to learn because my fingers were too small," Taylor recalled to *Great American Country*. "I always had the guitar around [but just] hid it in the corner."

For a less determined child, that kind of criticism might have meant the end of their musical career – but Taylor resolved to keep on trying. Her answer to what had happened was simply to pursue her dream all the more. In fact, it was with difficulty that her parents prised her away from the karaoke circuit in the summer of 2001 for one of their annual breaks at the family's holiday home in Stone Harbor, New Jersey, a region later made famous worldwide by MTV reality show *Jersey Shore*.

As a wealthy family, the Swifts had staked an early claim on it, buying their seaside second home when Taylor had been just four years old. For Taylor, it had been a "magical" place to grow up and spend her summers, but this year she had been reluctant to leave the musical nightlife back home behind. In an effort to persuade Taylor, her mother promised that her fellow stage enthusiast Kaylin and her family could come along too – and they could chat about all things showbiz along the way.

Taylor agreed – and for a few weeks the two families had a very enjoyable holiday. "My mom let my brother stay with Taylor and Austin for an extra week that summer," Kaylin recalled to the author, "and it was one of endless activities and luxuries. By day, Mrs Swift would give us turns sitting on the back seat on their wave runner. Taylor and I would get a ride and then our younger brothers, Cary and Austin, would get a turn. I still remember the thrill of these rides – Mrs Swift would charge the waves and look for the highest ones to surge over. On one of my rides with Taylor, Mrs Swift saw a dolphin in the distance and drove up so close we must have been just three feet away from its fin. It was an unforgettable experience."

Being in the water had become second nature to Taylor after so many holidays sailing, jet-skiing and swimming. In fact, she would later comment *to Sea Ray* magazine: "[Since] the age of four, I lived in a life jacket!"

There was never a dull moment for Taylor that summer as she set about introducing her friend to the rituals that had occupied her previous annual visits. "I was there every summer, all summer for the majority of my childhood," she later told *The Philly*. "It was such an amazing way to grow up. There were so many places to explore, whether it was finding a new island in the inlet or walking to 96th Street for ice cream. I could not have had a cooler childhood!"

Kaylin was a novice to the charms of Stone Harbor, but Taylor knew how to break her in, starting by introducing her to the shore's annual celebrations for Independence Day. "We watched the Fourth of July boat parade every year religiously," Taylor later recalled. "We used to all gather together on the dock when the parades would go by and we'd shoot water balloons at them."

Taylor's holiday home was not only conveniently located right on the bay, but its position on 112th Street meant that she was just opposite the town's bird sanctuary – and she didn't even have to leave the house to benefit from it. "I had a pair of binoculars and some days I'd just stare at the window, looking for birds," she reminisced.

She had also converted the room above the family's garage into a secret clubhouse which required a password for entry. Taylor and Austin never slackened on security either – in fact, they changed the code on a daily basis. "I made a filing system with members of the club [and] everyone had a profile that I would write on tiles I found," Taylor explained. "I painted the whole room different colours and used to spend all day in there, just doing nothing but sitting in my little club – because it was mine!" she added triumphantly.

It was in this same clubhouse that same year that, unbeknown to Kaylin, Taylor secretly spent the summer penning a 350-page novel. The secret was so tightly guarded that Taylor has never revealed the details of the story – known only as *Girl Named Girl* – the characters or its plot.

There was plenty to occupy Taylor in the wider area by day – trips to the cinema, the zoo or the shopping mall among them – but, with such palatial surroundings, the most fun was to be had right at home.

In fact, for a moment, Taylor's obsession with music took second place when she and Kaylin were inspired by the area around her home to set up their own beauty products company. "During those days, Taylor and I decided to be entrepreneurs and head our own lotion business," Kaylin revealed. "We ran around Stone Harbor collecting wildflowers and plants and used a mortar and pestle in her kitchen to create a pulpy substance we tried to pass off as 'all natural' body lotion!"

Indeed, if Taylor's long-suffering mother – who later admitted her only daughter had "the potential to be exhausting" – was perturbed by the pair's penchant for collecting dead flowers and scattering them across her newly cleaned kitchen table, she didn't show it. In fact, she even encouraged the pair's eccentric venture.

However, their well-intended entrepreneurial spirit soon led to disaster when their lotion turned out to smell more like the contents of an overflowing dustbin than a 'heaven scent' perfumed body oil. "When our creations turned out not to smell as good as we had hoped, we added some help from Bath and Body Works and decided we could market them as semi-natural!" Kaylin continued. "By the end of the week, however, the crushed flowers turned the mixture into a slimy brown and we found more pleasure in making up dances to Spice Girls songs. We spent endless hours in [Taylor's] bedroom making up moves and singing along to 'Spice Up Your Life'."

So the pair's ill-fated venture ended almost as quickly as it began – but the failure simply brought Taylor's focus back to her first love, music. That was something she would never give up on. In fact, inspired by the boy who lived next door, whom the young Taylor had designs on marrying, she began to write one of her first songs, 'Invisible'.

"I swore I would marry him someday," she confessed to *The Philly* of her secret crush. "He was the son of my parents' friends. They were always at my house and their son was my age and he would always tell me about other girls he liked. I felt, well, invisible, obviously."

Like any other young girl consumed by an unrequited crush, Taylor moped a little. However, she then took her sadness and turned it into a song.

The lyrics expressed her frustration that, every time she tried to get close to the object of her affections, he would start asking her advice on someone he liked, seeing her as a friend to confide in, instead of a potential love match. "[Girls] become friends with someone because they want to get close to them and then they're stuck in the friend zone," she later lamented to *Great American Country*.

Wishing she had the courage to tell him her fantasies, she instead wrote about the fire inside him that she saw, and her belief that the girl he wanted would never appreciate all that he had to offer. Taylor felt the two of them would be a match made in heaven, if only he realised how she felt. Yet she remained invisible to him.

Another early song composed at the shore was called 'Smoky Black Nights', inspired by her summer experiences of living and loving there. Taylor had only recently reached double figures, yet in her lyrics to the song she assumed the persona of someone much older and more mature. In it, she becomes a seasoned veteran, someone who had done so much in life, yet now knows what she wants – and only has eyes and ears for her lover. In fact, by the time Taylor wrote the song, aged 11, she hadn't so much as kissed a boy, let alone had a relationship. However, her words had sincerity and conviction and, by the time she sang them around town, she had an admiring audience in her wake.

Local seafood restaurant Henny's was one of the venues to welcome Taylor in her bid to sing for all of Stone Harbor. The eatery, then located on 3rd Avenue, prided itself on offering only freshly caught produce from local fishermen. As a diminutive 11-year-old – known back then as simply "the little girl with the big voice" – Taylor serenaded strangers and friends alike as they tucked into dishes such as boiled flounder in apple sauce or devilled crab with foie gras.

Before Taylor had arrived, the best entertainment diners could hope for was a half-hearted rendition of 'Yankee Doodle Dandy' by the bartender. Against that backdrop, it was hardly surprising that many of the regulars welcomed her with open arms. To their ears, she was musical salvation.

"I used to sing karaoke for hours on end," Taylor reminisced to *The Philly*. "I used to drag my parents in all the time and all of their friends would show up and put dollars in my tip jar."

Another location where Taylor often sang was Coffee Talk, a tiny café on the edge of 98th Street. "I used to play for hours and hours in cafes like that," she recalled, "[and] when I would run out of material, I'd just start making up songs on the spot."

If she got hungry after an afternoon at Coffee Talk, she charged her batteries by tucking into a meal at the Italian Garden restaurant on nearby 96th Street. "That was my favourite place to eat," she recalled. "I loved the giant Caesar salads and the white pizza."

Meanwhile, every Saturday night, after "sneaking in" to Henny's for a hard night of flexing her vocal chords, Taylor would head over to a mouth-watering ice-cream parlour called Springer's, which could be found on the same street.

"I loved the cookies-and-cream [flavour] they have there," she confessed of her food cravings. "I've always been a huge cookie-dough fan. I remember when I was little, I used to walk in there and just stare up at all the flavours and toppings, completely frozen and unable to make a final decision. I was always overwhelmed when I went in there!"

If choosing from the vast array of ice-cream flavourings was an undertaking for Taylor, it was nothing compared to how she felt on stage – an experience she had become accustomed to over that summer. Taylor hadn't wanted to leave Wyomissing that month, being preoccupied by musical opportunities back home; but it had turned out to be her most eventful summer break yet – especially in terms of the stage.

However, as summer ended, it was time to wave goodbye to the adulation and go back to reality – and, by September, Taylor was back in Wyomissing. However, the start of the school year was marred by tragedy when, on September 11, 2001, the world as Americans knew it changed forever. America suffered the biggest anti-Western terrorist attack in the nation's history – and Taylor could only watch helplessly on TV as the footage of two aeroplanes crashing into New York's Twin Towers was endlessly replayed on the news.

The towers of the World Trade Center had been a defining landmark of New York's business district, an iconic symbol of which city dwellers had been proud. Indeed, on the very morning of the tragedy, thousands of office workers had been starting their day inside them. Terrorists hijacked two passenger jets which had taken off from Boston's Logan Airport bound for Los Angeles. They overpowered the pilots and, taking control of the planes, flew them into the towers, instantly killing thousands and utterly devastating the buildings and the immediate area.

Understandably, the Swifts were petrified. After all, they lived less than two hours' driving distance from New York and Taylor's father had numerous friends and business associates in the city. Not only were their friends in danger, but the family were scared for themselves. Could their town be next? According to some newspaper and TV reports at the time, no one could rule out a full-scale nationwide attack.

The country was shell-shocked and the air was full of fear and foreboding, but Taylor calmed her anxieties by writing poetry. One poem in particular triggered a wave of envy in best friend Kaylin. "She wrote a short but beautiful poem about September 11," she recalled. "I was moved by her words. I think she referred to the planes as birds."

Metaphors aside, Kaylin longed to possess even half of her friend's gifts of self-expression. "Of all Taylor's talents, I think her greatest gift is her ability to write," she added. "She is and always has been a skilled writer, exhibiting the insight and depth of someone years beyond her age. Taylor has an old soul and an uncanny ability to share her perceptions with the world."

Taylor enjoyed the praise, but she found herself compelled to write for more than just that reason – each time something negative happened to rock her world, she was able to put her thoughts on paper as a way of exorcising her pain. She found other outlets for her emotions too, seeking solace and escapism in the theatre group she had been part of prior to the holidays. As the world slowly started to move on from 9/11 and rebuild the wreckage, Taylor occupied her mind with the world of the stage, returning to BYTA for a starring role in *Bye Bye Birdie*.

The production, which was an award-winning show when it first hit Broadway in 1960, centres around the adventures of a flamboyant rock star on the brink of being drafted into the army. The inspiration for the play had come from 1958, when the same fate had befallen Elvis Presley, much to the distress of his ardent female fans.

Before boarding a ship bound for Germany, where he would spend the next 18 months on military service, Presley ended his adventures in his homeland on a high note, giving one lucky female member of his hysterical fan base a farewell kiss.

In the theatrical retelling, the lead character was originally named Conway Twitty. However, a real-life rock 'n' roll singer of the same name – who ironically later switched genres to become a major country star – heard of the plans and threatened to sue. This forced the producers to change their character's name at short notice to the more obscure Conrad Birdie. The army of girls who lust after this colourful character turn out to be even more formidable than the army he is about to join in Germany.

The lead female character in the musical is Kim MacAfee, a sensible woman with a steady boyfriend who harbours just one flaw – the world's greatest crush on her rock idol, Conrad. While she desperately tries to convince her partner, Hugo, that she's a one-man woman, she ends up being the love interest who Conrad chooses for his final kiss. What's more, his attraction to her threatens to be much more than a mere headline-grabbing publicity stunt.

Taylor's friend Kaylin was the student director for the production, helping manager Ronnie Cremer, brother of Kirk Cremer, to cast and organise the show and, between the two of them, they decided Taylor was the ideal candidate to portray Kim.

Casting her as the lead hadn't been a difficult decision. After all, she had already starred in several other BYTA shows and, due to her height, was able to convincingly take on adult roles. However, while previous parts had suited Taylor's character down to a T, this one couldn't have been more different from her true self.

While Kim was a sexually confident young woman whose seductive smile had won the affections of none other than the nation's rock god of choice, in real life Taylor was very unlucky in love. Just three years later, she would joke in the pages of a national magazine that she felt as if she was wearing "some kind of guy repellent".

Despite growing extremely confident in the theatre, she was painfully shy when it came to the opposite sex. Rather like Lady Gaga, who claimed she was totally content cavorting nearly naked in front of the world's TV screens, but had "no confidence whatsoever" when it came to relationships, Taylor's self-assuredness on stage wasn't translating in to romantic success in real life.

It was ironic that, while she played the recipient of a rock star's affection, envied by an entire army of fans, she was actually the polar opposite of the extroverted socialite Kim appeared to be. She was beginning to long for male affection, but wasn't nearly so lucky in securing it.

The one similarity Taylor shared with Kim, however, was that she had someone reliable in her life who she risked losing to pursue a crush on someone who seemed more exciting – and ending up with neither.

"Taylor had a loyal admirer in one of her best guy friends, Troy Ziegler," an anonymous classmate told the author. "They were close and he wanted something more; but she was seen by some people as stuck up, so he wasn't sure if she would reject him. They were both shy about relationships. It seemed like things might have been going somewhere until Taylor asked him to go for a walk with her one day and revealed on that walk that she had a crush on someone else. They tried their best to stay friends, but things were a bit awkward after that."

Unfortunately, in a double dose of bad luck, that someone else turned out to be unavailable. "Taylor and I were so young and shy when it came to boys," Kaylin explained, "but she had a crush on a boy called Corey Robinson and he chose Taylor's friend over her. I'm sure it hurt her."

Indeed, if rumours were to be believed, even at such a young age she was devastated. First Taylor had felt invisible to the boy next door she had dreamed of marrying and was forced to look on miserably as he pursued other girls, oblivious to her feelings. Then, just months later, she had spurned her only admirer so she could be with Corey, who wasn't interested in her. Despite the succession of guys she had lusted after and plotted to make hers, she had remained single – and in the end she didn't meet her first boyfriend until the age of 15.

According to Kaylin, Taylor had done a "phenomenal job" as Kim, but underneath her seductive on-stage smile, her self-esteem had reached rock bottom. There was even worse news in store when funding shortages and other issues meant that the production was downgraded.

"The show wasn't as well received as prior BYTA shows," Kaylin explained. "Because of problems renting out some of the prior venues that were technologically advanced, huge and beautiful, we had to hold the show in a very small auditorium with make-shift seats and limited stage space and resources. At that point, a number of the moms who had helped with costumes and stage crafting had had enough. That was about the time everyone was getting ready to move on."

To add insult to injury for the parents who had seen their children downgraded and forced to perform on sub-standard stages, Taylor's background meant the word "sub-standard" wasn't included in her vocabulary.

After four days of starring in *Bye Bye Birdie*, she also starred in the end-of-show party, which was held at her house in the Wyomissing Hills. All of the cast were invited and Taylor sang country music, including the Dixie Chicks track 'There's Your Trouble'. She announced to the audience there and then that she loved writing lyrics and poetry and that she thought her future was in music.

The decision to perform was innocent enough, but that was where some of her problems started. "The house was huge," confided one anonymous cast member who attended the party. "She had a games room, a working elevator and an indoor swimming pool complete with a hot tub. It was seriously like the presidential suite of some six-star hotel and I don't think many of us had been any place like that before. The auditions at BYTA were open to people from all walks of life, not just the wealthy ones, and I think there was a feeling of shock among some of them when they saw the place she called home."

It wasn't just shock – it was also envy. Confronted by a girl who not only stood out for her singing voice, but also lived in a palatial home, where every square inch seemed to be packed with elegance and opulence, was too much for some of her peers to bear. This was at a time when, particularly for some of the children who had never made it past minor ensemble roles, their dreams of being famous actresses and singers were falling apart. For these children, Taylor's multiple blessings only reminded them of the things they lacked.

There was also a feeling that certain members of the group were being singled out time and time again for special privileges, Taylor included. "I was jealous," one mother confessed. "So was everyone else. We had to watch Taylor get lead after lead in every musical and it was frustrating. But she was good, very good. Everyone knew she was going to go on to something big."

Indeed, the heads at the theatre group were no exception. For example, Ronnie Cremer – a guitar teacher, manager and music producer – was enthralled by Taylor. On the advice of his mother, who had been watching her sing at the after-show parties, he rented space in a local shopping mall and put on showcases where Taylor could perform her own headline shows. These proved largely successful and saw Taylor showered with compliments every time she spent one of her weeknights on the stage.

She was clearly gathering an audience, but if there had been complaints of favouritism amongst the others in the theatre group, they were becoming even louder now. "The environment just changed from a care-free escape to a hostile one," Kaylin later told the author of how BYTA had degenerated. "Too many stage moms and jealousy surrounding those selected for roles and to be in special programs such as Theater Kids Live and Broadway In Training just took all the fun out of it… It was just time for most people involved to move on."

Not long after, the doors to BYTA closed altogether, and the children who had been involved with the group that had been such a large part of their childhood bid it a final and fond farewell.

Sad as it was for her, Taylor by now had her sights set on a bigger prize. It might have been the death throes of the youth theatre group, but she was determined it wouldn't be the end of her – in fact, she was telling anyone who would listen that she knew she still belonged on the stage. For many of her friends it was the end – but, for Taylor, it was just the beginning.

Chapter 3

Nashville – The Place Where Country Dreams Come True

Taylor's parents were about to realise fast that their little girl wasn't exactly the average 11-year-old. For most children, Disneyland – complete with its mythical creatures and fairytale castles – was the place where dreams came true. Yet their daughter was barely interested in rollercoaster rides or meeting Minnie Mouse. For her, the promised land was not Disney, but Nashville, Tennessee.

She would later lament despairingly that Wyomissing was "about the most random place in the world for a country singer to come from" – and she wasn't joking. In small-town Pennsylvania, she felt she was alone with her obsession.

The most defining moment in her life had been the thrill of touching the hand of young country star LeAnn Rimes at a show. Yet at the time, there wasn't a single country music radio station in her area that she could tune into. While she belted out LeAnn's songs on a daily basis, the rest of Wyomissing seemed oblivious.

In spite of what anyone else thought, Taylor had fallen "hopelessly in love" with her country idols. "What cemented [country music] in my mind and made me fall in love with it was seeing three great examples of what females could bring to [the genre]," Taylor would later recall to *Rolling Stone*. "I saw that Shania Twain brought this independence, this crossover appeal; I saw that Faith Hill brought this classic old-school glamour and beauty and grace; and I saw that the Dixie Chicks brought this complete 'We don't care what you think' quirkiness. I loved what all of those women were able to do and what they were able to bring to country music."

Taylor loved everything about them from their sultry Southern drawls to their "authentic" lyrics and catchy tunes. Yet she learned more from Faith Hill than glamour and grace. It was when she came across a TV documentary about how the star first made it in the music business that Taylor's game plan first fell into place.

"She got discovered [by moving to Nashville]," Taylor exclaimed triumphantly. "So this little bell went off in my head and I automatically decided that Nashville was the place where dreams come true. The place you have to go... that's when I started the non-stop, 'Hey, mom and dad, can we move to Nashville?'"

Her parents were incredulous. Was Taylor serious? Did she really want to drop everything and move to a different state on the strength of one TV show – particularly one which she had only viewed by chance? Taylor had to work hard to persuade them that this was no whim or passing phase. "I thought, 'You know, if Nashville is the town that lets you be yourself and do things [like Faith Hill] and be different, then that's where I need to be," she recalled.

It was her mother Andrea whom Taylor approached most about her dreams. While her father had been a gentle, reassuring presence in her life, someone whom she would describe as "a big teddy bear who tells me everything I do is perfect", it was her mother who was the assertive figurehead of the family, the one who encouraged her to fulfil her ambitions.

"As I grew up, she would always just say to me, 'You can do whatever you want in life – as long as you work hard to get there. You have to work hard for every single baby-step that you take that is closer to what you want – and we will support that until you change your mind and want something else,'" Taylor told *The Independent*.

"'And when you want something else, we will be your cheerleaders in that too.'"

But Taylor didn't want anything else. All she wanted was to be the queen of country music – and the thing she had to work hardest of all for at first was persuading her mother that this really was her life's goal, despite deciding at such an implausibly early age. "This was all I wanted in life," she would later declare. "There wasn't going to be a back-up plan."

According to childhood friend Kaylin Politzer, Taylor had her mother to thank for her tenacity, assertiveness and sense of direction, too. "I remember being both in constant awe and fear of Taylor's mother," she told the author. "I remember her to be loving and encouraging, but she was also a no-nonsense woman with a fiery spirit and quick tongue... To this day, I don't know if I've ever met a more tenacious lady. She didn't need a stage to command attention!"

The archetypal modern all-American woman, there was no shortage of confidence in Andrea's life. She was assertive and ambitious – values she might have learnt during her fast-paced earlier life as a sales executive. However, beyond being a career woman, she was now a mother – and, along with her authority, she was sensitive enough to notice when Taylor was asking for something that meant a lot to her.

After months of pester power, she recognised that Taylor's hobby had turned into an all-consuming passion – and she neither wanted to stand in her way or obscure her spotlight. If Nashville was the place where aspiring country stars went to fulfil their dreams, then it was Nashville where she would have to take Taylor.

The trip came as no surprise to Kaylin or her family. "My mom told me some of her most fond and vivid memories of the Swifts was when Andrea said to her: 'I'm taking Taylor all the way!'" she revealed to the author. "My mom said she wasn't surprised in the least when they went to Nashville. She knew Andrea wasn't kidding around."

"I made it really clear," Andrea later related to *Teen Superstar*. "'Okay, if this is something you want, you've got to do it.'"

After months of being, in Taylor's words, "absolutely obnoxious" and pestering her parents relentlessly for a trip, she finally got her way. One school holiday, she produced a four-track demo tape of herself singing karaoke versions of her favourite songs. It was heavily influenced by her recent background in musical theatre. There was 'There's Your Trouble' by the Dixie Chicks and 'One Way Ticket' by LeAnn Rimes – both songs that she had belted out at BYTA's after-show parties – and 'Here You Come Again' by Dolly Parton. Finally, the tape ended with a re-worked country version of 'Hopelessly Devoted To You' from the musical *Grease*, which she had played the lead in the previous year.

Taylor emblazoned the front cover of the tape with a picture of her face and the simple words "Call me". On the back, it had her telephone number and email address. While it might have sounded more like a prostitute's calling card in a phone box, in reality the affair was much classier. Armed with the demo she hoped would change her life, she and her mother hired a rental car and headed to Nashville.

Taylor loved the city at first sight. She was in her element, driving around looking out for the musical landmarks that could give her a golden ticket of opportunity. She started back-seat driving, shouting at her mother to stop the car every time she saw an appropriate place to hand out her demo. As her mother cruised down Music Row, she would prompt: "That's Mercury Records! Pull over! I need to give them my demo tape!"

"I'm not a stage mom," Andrea told *Teen Superstar*. "I didn't sign up to drive her into the music business, so I would walk her to the front door and wait for her. She went to every place on Music Row."

Unfortunately, an inexperienced Taylor hadn't taken much time to perfect her sales pitch. "I was like, 'If I want to sing music, I'm going to need a record deal. So, I'm going to get a record deal,'" Taylor told *Great American Country*. "I really thought it was that easy."

She added: "[I'd hand] my home-made demo to the receptionists at all the labels. I'd say, 'Hey, I'm 11 and I want a record deal. Call me!' How did that work out for me? It didn't."

Initially she returned to Pennsylvania on a high, waiting with bated breath for the phone to ring. However, her lofty ambitions didn't quite go according to plan. "I think I had like one person call me back," she winced. "He was so sweet, just kind of telling me, 'You know, this is *not* how you do this.'"

It might have worked for R&B-soul superstar Mary J Blige, who had been discovered after handing out tapes of herself singing karaoke; but, even with a talented singer, the odds were usually stacked against success with this method. "There are thousands of girls going up and down Music Row who are gorgeous and have amazing voices and can sing higher and louder than me," Taylor continued.

Not to be deterred, she simply went back to the drawing board to work out a strategy that would distinguish her and set her apart from the myriad other girls trying to make it who craved stardom in exactly the same way. "I didn't realise [at first] that there were hundreds of people in Nashville trying to do exactly what I was trying to do, and that everybody had the same dream," she explained to *Teen Superstar*. "I thought, you don't just make it in Nashville. I've got to really work on something that would make me different."

It was a light-bulb moment for her, something that would define how she saw her desired career. Something that wouldn't dishearten her but only make her game-plan stronger. It crossed her mind that, while her rivals might also have CDs of themselves singing well-known country classics, how many of them could also write their own songs? She wrote lyrics and melodies already – and then there was the guitar, which had been left abandoned in a dusty corner ever since she had been taunted that her hands were too small to get to grips with it. It was time to take on the disbelievers. Now, more than ever, it was time to pick it up and start playing.

"I realised that I needed to find a way to have a fighting chance of making it, so I started writing songs [in earnest] and playing the guitar," she explained. "I actually learned on a 12-string, purely because some guy told me that I would never be able to play it, that my fingers were too small. Anytime someone tells me that I can't do something, I want to do it more."

She was desperate to prove her detractors wrong, but was nervous about taking the first step. Yet a fearful Taylor's prayers were answered when a computer repairman called at the house and offered to get her started. "In this magical twist of fate, the guy who my parents had hired to come fix my computer [taught me]," she marvelled. "I'm doing my homework and he looks round and sees the guitar in the corner and he looks round and says: 'Do you know how to play guitar?' I was like, 'Ah, no.' He said, 'Do you want me to teach you a few chords?' After that, I was relentless. I wanted to play all the time."

A typical 12-year-old in one regard, Taylor needed little persuasion to be distracted from her homework. She would daydream at school each afternoon, longing for home time, before coming in, racing through her work and finally being reunited with her beloved guitar. She practised until her mother called her for dinner and, when she had finished eating, she would be straight back at it.

"The first song I ever wrote [on the guitar] was 'Lucky You' and it was about this girl who dares to be different," Taylor recalled. "At that time I was describing myself."

However, she wasn't just different in the way she hoped – as a survival strategy to attract the record companies – but she was also seen as unusual by her classmates. For a 12-year-old longing to be accepted, standing out isn't always a good thing. In fact, in Taylor's case, it was a recipe for unpopularity.

She had just moved from West Reading Elementary School up to Wyomissing Junior High, where she began her secondary education, and she stuck out like a sore thumb. While the other girls in her class were only just making a transition from Barbie dolls to boyfriends, and were far from even considering their ideal career, Taylor was already focused on music. "Music was so necessary for me to be happy," she recalled later. "I would practise guitar for hours and hours every day until my fingers were bleeding."

She was like a junkie with an addiction – once she started playing, she couldn't break the habit. She would stumble into school with bandaged, swollen fingers each morning, which didn't exactly help her to blend in. "My mom had to tape my fingers up and you can imagine how popular that made me," Taylor joked. "'Look at her fingers! So weird!'"

Meanwhile the closest most seventh graders would get to understanding her point of view was dancing to the latest chart hits at a disco – and 'country' wasn't a word in their musical vocabulary. Destiny's Child was in fashion, while Shania Twain – with hits like 'Man, I Feel Like A Woman' and 'That Don't Impress Me Much' behind her – was definitely not.

What was more, her cruel classmates were even less impressed by her than they were by Shania. "In a high school that houses seventh through twelfth grade, kids are forced to grow up fast or they get eaten alive," commented childhood friend Kaylin. "Taylor's proclivities for songwriting and country music didn't mesh well at all with the status quo."

"All the girls at school were going to sleepovers and breaking into their parents' liquor cabinets at the weekend," Taylor confirmed later to the *Daily Mail*, "and all I wanted to do was go to festivals and sing karaoke music."

What was more, when the weekend came, that was exactly what she did. "I was [considered] weird [because] I would play singer-songwriter nights instead of going to parties," she mused. "I think it's weird to go to parties and get drunk when you're 12 – but whatever!"

Another area that would see Taylor divided from her classmates was her poor sporting performance. Being on a sports team was usually an instant invitation into the 'cool' clique – but, for Taylor, it wasn't to be. One of the girls she had been close to, Courtney Hamsher, had excelled at football and later went on to play semi-professionally. But when Taylor followed in her footsteps by trying out for the basketball team, it was a humiliating disaster.

"Everybody thought I'd be good at basketball, but then I tried out and it was like, 'Oh'. I was awful!" Taylor confessed to *The Ottawa Citizen*.

She might have been swift by name, but – unlike her younger brother – she certainly wasn't swift by nature, and she hated running. She would later admit that she "wasn't fast at anything" and would rather be playing a game of Trivial Pursuit. Her failure didn't go unnoticed by classmates either. "Her coordination was terrible," remarked one to the author. "She was tall, yeah, but she was clumsy with it. She had two left feet. She was one of the last people anyone would want to pick for their team. It was so bad that there'd actually be titters going round the class when she made a really bad shot."

What was more, she grew apart from Kaylin – the one person who had understood her passion for performance. It turned out that she too had switched to sport. "Unfortunately our friendship dissolved with the theatre group," Kaylin recalled. "I often regret not making more of an effort… The end to BYTA was not an amicable one and most kids and parents left with bad tastes in their mouths. I gave up theatre for field hockey and track and tried desperately to make 'school friends' [instead of theatre friends] in an effort to move on.'

Where did that leave Taylor, who had no intention of leaving her dreams behind? As an increasing number of her classmates began to taunt and tease her for liking "that dumb country music" she began to face social isolation. She spent every evening on her guitar, which was something her peers just couldn't relate to. She was also one of the first in her class to have a mobile phone and, whenever a melody came into her head, she would pull it out to make her own impromptu voice recording. To many, this alone made Taylor an irredeemable 'freak'.

While Taylor's focus might have helped in the quest to earn herself a record deal, when she was trapped in a class full of ruthless 12-year-olds it was definitely to her detriment. "The kids at school would make fun of me [for liking country]," she told *Teen Vogue* of those days. "They didn't think I was cool or pretty enough, so they stopped talking to me."

This period gave birth to a relentless bullying campaign, driving Taylor out simply by refusing to speak to her. From then on, it was a lonesome existence for her. She would sit down at a lunch table with a tentatively hopeful smile, only for all her peers to instantly get up and move away. She would join in a lively conversation only for the entire group to stop talking altogether and eye her in icy silence.

While they scarcely acknowledged her presence to her face, they had plenty to say behind her back. Catty whispers in corridors became commonplace. Each time she walked past, there was smirking, sniggering or, even worse, roaring with laughter at some undisclosed joke. That joke, almost invariably, was on Taylor.

She was a high achiever at school, so she was a 'nerd'. She was unlucky in love and inexperienced with boys, so she was a 'prude'. Her shyness saw her described as 'aloof' and 'stuck up'. Her hair was curly and at times unruly, unlike the glossy, poker-straight manes of her more popular peers, so she was branded 'ugly'. And that was just the beginning – when Taylor's pursuit of music led to her biggest public appearance yet, things really came to a head.

Through her father's connections with a marketing manager for the local Philadelphia 76ers basketball team, she landed an opportunity to sing the national anthem on April 5, 2002 to over 20,000 fans. The rowdy sports crowd couldn't have expected someone so young to serenade them, dressed in a bright red headband and matching sequinned top, embroidered with dozens of miniature American flags.

Young and girlish in appearance, she was the total antithesis of the sports world – until, of course, she opened her mouth and started singing. She went on to describe it as "an awesome experience" and one that she would never forget – not least because it saw her exchange words with a chart-topping celebrity at the side of the stage.

Ironically for someone whose musical diet was almost entirely country, her first compliment from a high-profile figure came from someone whose work was the polar opposite of her own – gangsta rapper Jay-Z. Their backgrounds couldn't have been more different – while Jay-Z had hustled for survival on the tough streets of Brooklyn, New York, running the daily risk of falling victim to gang warfare, Taylor's upbringing had been one of wealth and privilege beyond the young Jay-Z's wildest dreams. At one point, he had barely been able to afford food; in stark contrast, Taylor's early life had been filled with trips to the theatre and holidays abroad. While his tunes mirrored his street upbringing, seeing him rap about "bitches" and "hoes", Taylor had erased profanities from her vocabulary altogether, reprimanding her friends if a cuss so much as passed their lips.

In spite of their many differences, however, Taylor and Jay-Z patently had one thing in common – a naked ambition to succeed on stage. Plus, as far as the showbiz world was concerned, a compliment from Jay-Z was about as awe-inspiring as being namechecked in the Bible.

"Jay-Z was sitting court-side and gave me a high five after I sang," Taylor recalled fondly to CMT. "I bragged about that for, like, a year straight."

His validation of her only encouraged Taylor to try harder. "Every single weekend, I would go to festivals, fairs and karaoke contests," she continued. "Any place I could get up on stage." Not every show was as glamorous as the auspicious 76ers game – and most of her audiences were unknown Pennsylvanian teenage revellers – but that didn't stop Taylor from trying. In fact, she thrived on any kind of attention.

Years later, when taking a trip down memory lane to her 76ers game performance live on BBC's *The One Show*, a shamefaced Taylor blushed: "I look petrified! Oh my God, I was terrified! I'm from Pennsylvania, so I think I was really nervous because I knew all my classmates were watching."

She was frightened about how her already hostile classmates would react to the sight of her succeeding and, as it turned out, her fears weren't unfounded. The next morning, her photograph was emblazoned all over the local newspapers, together with a write-up of the game – and her bullies wasted no time in taunting her over it. "It caused a not-so-fun day for me the next day at school," she grimaced in memory of it.

Singing the national anthem had been a standout moment for her, both good and bad. It was undoubtedly the biggest show she had played in her life, but instead of being congratulated by the girls in her year, they made her life a living hell. Jay-Z might have loved her, but no one at school seemed to want anything to do with her.

"My worst time of the day was going to pick Taylor up from school," her mother recalled, "because I'd have to hear about the ostracising."

Saddened by the rejection, Taylor decided to try some retail therapy and, in a last-ditch attempt to befriend the girls who blanked her, phoned to see if they wanted to join her for a shopping trip to the local Berkshire Mall. Predictably, she would be disappointed.

"That memory is one of those painful ones you'll never fully get over," she recalled. "At that point I'd been shunned from the group for whatever reason and I was still desperately trying to be included. That evening, I called them up, they each said no, and Mom said: 'You know what? If you want to go to the mall, let's go together.' And we ran into this entire group of girls who had told me they were busy that night."

"I remember what happened next like it was yesterday," her mother told *Elle Girl*. "Taylor and I walked into a store and these six little girls who had all claimed to be 'really busy' were all there together."

Taylor was on the brink of tears, confronted by her classmates' deceit – confirmation that she would never be friends with them – but her mother came to her rescue. "In situations like that, my mom has always known exactly the right time to run away," Taylor continued. "There are situations where you have to encourage someone to be tough, then there are times when you should just run. So we got in the car and drove to the [King of Prussia] mall that's an hour and a half away, but is a better mall – and we showed them in our own little way. We had a great time."

The experience, tearful as it had been, was a defining moment for Taylor. It made her realise that, her mother aside, she was her own best friend. Not only that, but the trauma distanced her enough from her desire to break into the cool posse, and be accepted by them, to allow her to focus on herself and her music again. She was now free to be selfish. Rather than trying desperately to fit in, she became defiant about her right to be herself. Instead of hiding her penchant for country music like a shameful secret, she wore it like a name badge. She was proud of her voice, knowing it would make her a success some day.

The cruelty of her peers saddened her for a few seconds, but it ultimately strengthened her resolve to do things on her own terms. After all, if her so-called friends were fickle enough to pick her up and drop her over her choice of music, she wasn't so sure she wanted to know them anyway.

More to the point, their disdain for her had made Taylor want to succeed all the more, because she now had something to prove. She might have been the school's biggest social outcast, but she was also determined to be recognised as its biggest talent one day, too. She was going to show the popular crowd that they were wrong to write off her friendship.

Of course, being brave enough to stand on her own two feet meant that Taylor would endure moments of intense loneliness. "I would go to school a lot of days and not know who I was going to talk to," she told *The Toronto Star*. "That's a really terrifying thing for someone who's 12."

However, Taylor was now immune to it. She sat by herself at lunch and in classes. She wrote short stories – and not just in English classes – and sometimes doodled lyrics to pass the time. She started to embrace being by herself instead of feeling sorry for herself and turned her pain into music.

"I dealt with a bunch of different kinds of being alone," she explained to the *Daily Mail*. "There's being alone because no one talks to you. There's feeling alone when you walk up to a table at lunch and you're not welcome to sit down. There's standing on a stage at a local festival with your acoustic guitar that's as big as you and some kid from your grade screams obscenities at you. It's school. It's what everyone goes through at some point. And the only thing that got me through really tough days was writing songs about it."

The complex emotional events of school life became Taylor's own private psychology lesson. She became a silent observer – a voyeur of a life she no longer belonged to – and, ironically, the very people who reduced her to tears began to inspire her creatively. Who was laughing now? "If they weren't going to talk to me," a determined Taylor recalled, "I was going to watch them and watch how they talked to each other. Then I wrote songs about them. I could take what happened that day that was horrible and write a song about it and make it good."

Perhaps then, this tough life lesson had been a blessing in disguise. An idyllic life with dozens of close friends might have lulled her into complacency and taken her focus away from the music she loved so much. She might even have found herself conforming to the status quo to maintain a coveted spot in the cool group, and letting her passion for country music and her real identity take a back seat in the process. Instead, her exclusion meant she was drawn to it all the more.

What was more, Taylor found – like Coldplay, Amy Winehouse, Leonard Cohen and many other artists before her – that she was at her most creative when she was unhappy. "I would sit there on those lonely days and say: 'It's OK, because I can write a song about this later,'" Taylor explained. "I've carried that mantra with me since. Anytime I feel pain, rejection, heartbreak, I subliminally say to myself: 'I can write a song about this and then it will feel better.'"

One of the first songs she wrote about life at school was 'My Turn To Be Me', an ode to the pains of peer pressure. The girls she knew were in their formative years and hadn't found themselves yet, but they were already dividing up into cliques. There was the wild-child group, where girls who hadn't yet reached their teens took to heavy smoking and sharing bottles of vodka every weekend. These girls were also among the first in school to lose their virginities. Wyomissing was packed with wealthy young women looking to break out of a small-town lifestyle and find some excitement. Yet it was clear that a devout Catholic like Taylor, whose church preached chastity and drug abstention, wouldn't be joining in.

Then there were the hardcore fashion icons, who lived and breathed *haute couture* and – even at 12 – were rarely to be seen without the latest copy of *Vogue* under their arms. While some girls were busy sneaking an illicit cigarette at break time, this crowd spent lunchtimes hunched over a Chanel compact in the bathroom. Unlike the hell-raisers, they spent weekends in Philadelphia's priciest malls. Their wardrobes were colour coordinated, high fashion and, in some cases, obscenely expensive.

These shopaholics probably knew the layout of their favourite clothing stores better than their own homes and they looked down their nose at anyone who failed to measure up in the fashion stakes. Wearing a shade or style that the style bibles defined as passé had the same effect on this crowd's friendships as a bad case of leprosy. It went without saying that Taylor – who had frizzy hair, cared little for make-up and was scarcely seen without her casual blue-denim jeans – was seen as a fashion failure.

She didn't mesh well with the sports crowd, either. From the tennis court to the treadmill, those girls never stopped training. Every lunchtime was occupied with sports-team activities and anyone who wasn't a basketball player, a gymnast or, at the very least, a cheerleader, was automatically disqualified. The butt of jokes for her poor co-ordination, Taylor didn't stand a chance.

So it was five-inch skyscraper heels for the party girls, elegant two-inch designer sandals for the fashion pack and trainers all the way for the sports teams. Already, there were so many cliques and Taylor didn't belong to any of them.

'My Turn To Be Me' was a song of defiance against feeling obliged to fit in. She was fighting against the pressure to conform and asserting that all she really wanted to do was sing.

The song talks of the people who tried to change her and asks, if they liked her, then why couldn't they accept her for who she was? It also tells of a time when she came into school one morning to find cruel comments about her scrawled across a wall for everyone to see. At first she had tried desperately to be the person her classmates wanted her to be and had allowed them to mould her into somebody she wasn't, believing it could bring her acceptance and happiness.

But ultimately she couldn't keep up the façade. Every time a little bit of who she was shone through, she had to read obscenities about herself on the wall at school. Yet her anger at being rejected gave her the confidence to rebel and be who she wanted to be all along. By taking hold of the reins, she was letting her spirit free. Writing 'My Turn To Be Me' exorcised the pain she felt and allowed her to move on a little.

The same was true when she put pen to paper for a track that would later become world famous: 'The Outside'. "I was a complete outcast at school and never fit in, never felt like I belonged, [so] I was writing exactly what I saw," Taylor later revealed to *Entertainment Weekly*. "I was writing from pain," she recalled: "I've always felt so lucky because I've never needed an escape like drinking or drugs – music has always been that escape for me."

While Taylor had promised she wouldn't turn to alcohol to dull the pain of never being accepted, she was equally unlikely to resort to the bottle to look cool. "Popular girls in school start partying when they're like 12," she commented of her Wyomissing upbringing. "I had to choose between being popular and not messing my life up."

Instead of binge drinking and boyfriends – and the inevitable perils to which that combination would lead – Taylor remained shy, single and determined to make a success of her music. One of the pre-teen girls in her class was sighted shopping for pregnancy tests the same year Taylor wrote 'The Outside' and 'My Turn To Be Me' – but, married for now to her music, that wasn't a risk she would be facing herself.

Music provided not just a form of therapy but an opportunity to make sense of what her bullies were doing and why. For months, she felt like a square peg in a round hole. But was she really a social outcast and a 'geeky kid' whom everyone despised – or was there a different reason for people's attitudes?

One of Taylor's tormentors solved the mystery when she anonymously revealed to the author: "We treated Taylor like crap, but you know why? We were absolutely downright jealous."

Consumed with envy as one of the school's star pupils not only scored some of the highest grades, but also appeared in their local newspapers and was showered with adulation for her singing, her classmates became increasingly insecure. With a string of onstage appearances at such a young age, Taylor was clearly top dog in the success stakes, but there was one way they could still hit her where it hurt – by ostracising her.

"Her star shone so brightly, it eclipsed all the rest of us and made us feel inferior," her bully continued. "Excluding her was one way we could get our power back."

She added: "We didn't necessarily all want to sing, but a lot of us liked the idea of being famous and I know we at least all wanted to feel special. Taylor took that away from us. She was always the topic of conversation. She was a very sweet girl, but when she would talk non-stop about getting a standing ovation for her singing, or her mom supporting her all the way, we couldn't stand it. When we heard about her singing, we'd say that she was stuck up and thought she was better than everyone else – but when I look back, it was probably us that feared she was better than we were."

Little did Taylor, whose self-esteem was now bruised and almost rock bottom, imagine that her classmates' taunts were motivated not by dislike but by jealousy. She only knew that when she tried to share each new achievement with them – for example, taking delight in learning a new song or securing a lead role in a local musical – they would respond badly.

"We were like something out of that film, *Mean Girls*," her tormentor continued. "We'd talk about how Taylor was stuck up and up her own ass. We'd make fun of her voice and the way she walked and called her a spoilt princess behind her back. I guess we were a bit resentful that her mom would put her entire life on hold to make her daughter happy and we didn't feel like our own parents would do that for us. She was on some kind of fast track to success and we couldn't relate to it. We had no idea what we'd be doing in 10 years' time – it was Taylor who had it all planned out. When you're an insecure young person, that's not easy to face."

Taunting Taylor salvaged the self-esteem of her schoolmates and masked their feelings of inadequacy, so they took pleasure in it. Her bully revealed: "We'd say, 'Look how she walks in like she's better than everyone else!' and, because she liked the Dixie Chicks, our nickname for her behind her back was Dipsy Shit. Taylor got used to the fact that when she turned up, the rest of us would roll her eyes. She did have friends but not many, so she was a fairly easy target. If we wanted to be mean about her, we knew most people would be up for a joke at her expense and at that age we didn't have much of a conscience. We left Taylor out to make ourselves feel strong, like at least we were superior socially. It was stupid and I regret hurting her. I admit that we made her life a misery, but she was so darned good at everything that it made me feel pretty good at the time to see her upset."

Her tormentor then apologised for the past, confessing: "I realise now that by being spiteful to her, no one was winning. We were just making her as miserable as we were ourselves. I think we were young and immature and couldn't handle it right, so our emotions took over and it made us feel better to shun this perfect girl and keep her out of our circle. It was wrong and I'd like to apologise to Taylor for what we did. I hope she realises we were just being dumb and that we crossed the line. She didn't do anything wrong – it was us that was the problem. I just hope that time has turned a page on it. And I'm genuinely pleased for her these days."

Taylor isn't the only one to suffer at the hands of jealous peers. For budding singers, it seems commonplace. Beyonce, then a child prodigy, wrote in *Soul Survivors*, the autobiography of her band Destiny's Child: "Some people can't handle it when their friends become successful. They're only comfortable when you're struggling. It's probably because they're just not happy with themselves. Instead of them trying to grow along with you, they want you out of their life. But that's how you find out who your real friends are."

For Taylor, it underlined how her tally of 'real friends' was very low – and the die for her junior-school years in Wyomissing was cast. However, one of her friends mattered so much to her that she inspired her to write a song. 'Me And Britney' was a heartfelt recollection of happier times when she felt loved and wanted, focusing on her loyal friendship with fellow Wyomissing resident Brittany Maack (although Taylor changed the spelling of her first name for the recording to give her privacy). Even after her friend moved to Memphis, Tennessee, they remained close – and the song was a way for Taylor to reach out to her across the miles that lay between them.

Another early track, 'Used To Fly', was a soundtrack to her schoolyard exile. Despite battling loneliness and depression, Taylor didn't want anyone to see her cry. By admitting her sadness privately, the song allowed her to expose her vulnerability without seeming weak in front of those who would become her enemies.

While she might have been holding back the tears in 'Used To Fly', there was no such self-restraint during 'In The Pouring Rain'. Taylor hadn't spoken much, even to her closest friends, about the betrayal she experienced when her crush, Corey Robinson, had started dating a girl whom she had once considered a close friend. Instead, she vented her frustrations in a song. Her poetic side was revealed when she used the pouring rain as a metaphor for her tears of heartbreak. She might not have felt comfortable baring her innermost feelings to Corey himself, but the song did the trick.

Each song she wrote was confessional – the musical equivalent of writing in a diary – and blood, sweat and tears were invested in every single one. At that stage, as much as she wanted to be famous, she wasn't simply writing songs to be conventionally successful – she was doing it purely for self-expression.

That said, she would never miss any opportunity to perform her songs in front of an audience, as the determination of her father secured her several shows supporting the Pat Garrett Band. In the world of country music, Pat was regarded by many as the genre's 'best kept secret'. In his earlier days, he and his four bandmates – consisting of his wife and three close friends – had been a huge success throughout America. Pat had placed six singles on the *Billboard* chart and performed with country legends such as Loretta Lynn and Johnny Cash.

He was a respected veteran in the industry and appearing alongside him would give Taylor the level of exposure she craved. What was more, she already had a history with him – he had secured her a slot at the local Bloomsbury Fair the previous year, too.

"Taylor's dad is a persistent cuss," Pat joked to the author, "and he kept after me to use Taylor to open a few of my shows. Being the lovely guy that I am, I rehearsed a couple of tunes with her, so she would look good performing live on our shows."

One of these shows had been at the Knoebels Amusement Resort in Elysburg, Pennsylvania in June 2002. For Pat, it was just another show – he had been playing the same venue annually for several years by that point. Taylor, on the other hand, was absolutely petrified. Her hands were shaking, her knees were knocking and there was a tremble in her voice – but, when she took to the stage, she managed to mask her fear and join in with the onstage banter. "I said: 'Hey Taylor, come talk with me a bit and tell everyone your name again,'" Pat recalled. "She said, 'I'm Taylor.' I said, 'Tell everyone how old you are.' She told me she was 12. I said, 'You're 12, wow, I couldn't even find my shoes when I was 12 – now get out of here because you're getting more applause than I am!' Just kidding with her. Did I think at that time she would be one of the most popular stars in America or the world? I had no clue. She was a cute little girl I was happy to include on our portion of the show – especially since the audience really liked her and so did I.'"

But Pat was no stranger to Taylor's singing voice at that point – he had been working with her for the past two years. He owned two country music clubs in Pennsylvania – one spacious outdoor arena called the Pat Garrett Amphitheater and another small bar named the Pat Garrett Roadhouse. Both were family-run ventures, but while the amphitheatre saw well-known acts perform, the Roadhouse was an informal setting for amateurs.

The latter hadn't been running for long and was in need of some publicity. That was when Pat had a eureka moment – a country music version of talent shows like *The X-Factor*. "To build the business, we started doing karaoke," Pat told the author. "That was accepted by the public, but when I got the idea of having the karaoke stars open shows for the big classic country stars we had appearing at the amphitheatre, the Pat Garrett Roadhouse became a very popular place. Thus began the Pat Garrett Karaoke Concert. You know, it's almost impossible for an unknown to get to appear on the same bill as a big name. So I made it possible, because I owned both places."

Potentially, this was a chance for a complete newcomer who had never so much as sung in public before to win the prize. The only criteria was that the judges liked their voice enough. Even for those who weren't huge fans of the genre, it was an irresistible opportunity – and after adverts appeared in local newspapers such as *The Reading Eagle*, people tried out from all over the state. Everyone from dedicated singers already building their careers to novices out to have a good time would be there – and Taylor was up against some tough competition.

To boost her confidence, Pat introduced her as the next big thing, not for a moment realising that it was only a matter of time before the shy looking, diminutive girl in front of him made the big time for real. "Ladies and gentlemen, here's someone who's going to be a big country star one of these days!" Pat called as she went into her first song.

"It was the first time I got to hear Taylor sing," he reminisced. "She was a cute 10-year-old golden-haired little girl who had some poise and a bit of stage presence. She introduced herself, 'Hi, I'm Taylor and I would like to sing a country song for you.' And that was the beginning with us."

The format for the competition included a karaoke night every Thursday for 16 weeks. "At the end, we had a sing-off, with radio personalities from our areas as judges and the 16 contestants would do their thing," Pat recalled. His wife Suzy hosted the shows, while judges included representatives from Reading radio station WRFY FM – Y102 Rock Hits.

Taylor was an instant hit with local audiences and automatically earned bonus points in their eyes for entering at her extraordinarily young age. She was the polar opposite of the type of contestant an adult might expect to compete against. However, she wasn't the only one in her age group to try out.

"There were quite a few people out there who are very good singers, good enough to make a career out of singing," Pat said. Back in those early days, he had been sceptical about the quality of Taylor's voice, believing it needed to be more polished. Consequently, the first few times she entered, Taylor had been disappointed – so much so that she made the one hour's drive back to Wyomissing in floods of tears.

However, the early failures didn't deter her for long. According to Pat, armed with a large group of family and friends, "she came back and continued to come back". The strength of her ambition was impressive. "She had an insatiable drive," he marvelled later. "Her dad showed me this ring notebook and the only thing she had in this notebook was her signature – she was practising her autograph!"

He might have laughed incredulously, but this meant the world to Taylor. She was convinced that one day, sooner or later, she would be the headline act up on stage and her work would see her besieged by autograph hunters. Some people dismissed her ambitions as childish fantasies or laughed them off as delusional – and she certainly couldn't expect much support from her schoolmates.

But Taylor's persistence paid off. She made it to the finals, along with two other hopefuls, and the prize was to open for country-music veteran Charlie Daniels. Daniels had begun his career in Nashville in the 1950s, just when the city was beginning to build its reputation as the place to be for the genre. He went on to play bass on no fewer than three Bob Dylan albums, worked as a session musician for Leonard Cohen and – a couple of years before the contest – had composed the score for feature film *Across The Line*. He was probably best known for his big 1979 hit, 'The Devil Went Down To Georgia'.

Some of his work had been controversial though. One song, 'Simple Man', seemed to be an anthem in praise of vigilante justice. Another, 'In America', was a defiantly patriotic response to the Iran Hostage Crisis of 1979-1981; within weeks of the terrorist attacks of September 11, the song had been renamed 'Fuck Bin Laden' and was circulating widely on the internet. Despite the controversy, however, Charlie was a Grammy Award-winning singer and someone Taylor was desperate to share the bill with.

Taylor won the sing-off that time and shortly afterwards was preparing for her dream show, opening for Charlie Daniels. Yet she had a reality check when she heard her stage time would be 10:30 a.m. and the star of the show was nowhere to be seen. He was scheduled to play no fewer than 10 hours later – and very few of his fans would even get to see Taylor.

Keen to prove herself nonetheless, Taylor returned to singing the national anthem – and this time in earnest. "It occurred to me that the national anthem was the best way to get in front of a large group of people if you don't have a record deal," she later told *Rolling Stone*. "So I started singing the national anthem everywhere I possibly could... I would sing it at garden club meetings. I didn't care. I figured out that if you could sing that one song, you could get in front of 20,000 people without even having a record deal. So I sang that song many, many, many, many times."

One day, she was invited to perform it at the US Open Tennis tournament in Flushing Meadow, New York. This time, by a stroke of good fortune, a talent spotter from a major entertainment agency was in the audience – and Taylor immediately caught his eye. The agent, by the name of Dan Dymtrow – who would later go on to manage Britney Spears – approached the entertainment director at the tournament, desperate to be connected with Taylor.

In turn, the director requested more information about her, without specifying a reason. Oblivious, her father – ever the proud parent – sent a 'cheesy' home video. "My dad put together this typical 'dad video' type of thing with the cat chewing the neck of my [guitar] and stuff like that – and sent it to her, not knowing that she was going to send it to Dan Dymtrow," Taylor later recalled to *Wood & Steel*. "Dan called and asked us to come down and play for him in his office, so I brought my first 12-string down and played some songs for him." Dan's instantaneous reaction? "I want to work with you guys."

Taylor finally had a manager – albeit an informal one at that stage – and was going places with her music. Yet geographically, she was still stuck in Pennsylvania, in a school full of bullies. What was more, she hadn't got the first clue about how to clinch a record deal.

However, it wasn't too long before Taylor's father dropped in to visit Pat Garrett again at his sheepskin store in Strausstown – both to share the good news about her management and to ask him how best to channel his daughter's rampant ambition. Pat's answer was instant. "Scott said, 'What can I do with this girl of mine?' I said: 'Well, in Hershey they make bars, in Detroit they make cars and in Nashville, they make stars! Move to Nashville!'"

That was the answer Taylor had been looking for. She wasn't arrogant, but she already knew by that point that she could impress small-town audiences and be the best in show in Pennsylvania. The problem was that this wasn't where the country music scene was located – and the only way to test whether she could cut it among the professionals was to go back to Nashville. With the type of naïve optimism that only a child yet to reach their teens possesses, Taylor resumed, "absolutely tormenting my parents on a daily basis to move there".

"She now felt Nashville was her only chance," one former friend revealed to the author. "She didn't want to be a big fish in a tiny pond, she wanted to try for survival out there in the ocean and see if she could still shine!"

Taylor's parents weren't prepared to just get up and leave, though. Even Pat himself hadn't expected them to follow his advice. "Telling people that usually gets them out of my hair," he joked to the author.

"Most people are not able to pick up their entire lives and move, because they have jobs and houses and family in a certain area and it would be a hardship to move."

Taylor might have been as free as a bird and ready to fly, but her father, with an extensive business history, had decades worth of excess baggage. All logic and common sense pointed towards staying in Pennsylvania.

It was going to take more than sheer pester power to change their minds, so Taylor took some time out from the one-woman Nashville awareness campaign and began to bury her head in books instead. She became an avid reader to get her through the lonely lunchtimes at school. The trouble was, everything she picked up seemed to remind her of her beloved Nashville.

She loved *To Kill A Mockingbird*, Harper Lee's harrowing tale of racism in small-town Alabama, because she was "a fan of anything written from a child's perspective". However, the setting for the story was tantalisingly close to the state of Tennessee. What was more, Alabama's civil rights history and controversial legacy of slavery made its background strikingly similar. As she read through the pages, in spite of the dark subject matter, she felt her heart aching for Nashville.

She also became a fan of Shel Silverstein, a satirical cartoonist, songwriter and poet turned children's writer. He was an unusual candidate for the devoutly religious Taylor's affections, as he was full of bawdy jokes and had started off as an illustrator for world-famous men's magazine *Playboy*. He had written a monthly column entitled 'Shel Silverstein Visits…', which saw him jet to various locations around the world – notably including a New Jersey nudist colony. On returning to his home town of Chicago, he would write up his adventures and pair them with illustrations for the monthly cartoon strip.

Next he began to write poetry and lyrics with mischievous storylines, such as 'The Smoke Off', about a competition to see who could roll a joint fastest. Profane, highly sexed and extremely counter-cultural, he didn't seem an ideal addition to Taylor's reading list. Even some of his children's books were the subject of complaints from parents for encouraging bad behaviour. But Taylor was a fan nonetheless.

Before long, however, reading his work only brought her back to what mattered to her the most – the music. Shel had written a number of country music classics, including 'One's On The Way', performed by Loretta Lynn, and 'A Boy Named Sue' and '25 Minutes To Go' – the latter about a Death Row inmate's final moments – performed by Johnny Cash. Both of these artists had made their fame in – you guessed it – Nashville. Taylor had been longing to go back and try her luck a second time – and now everything she laid her eyes on seemed to be a teasing reminder of the city. That was when it hit her – if she couldn't be writing songs *in* Nashville, she could be writing songs *about* Nashville.

So Taylor sat down one morning and, within hours, had poured out her love story. A common Shel Silverstein technique was to attribute feelings and actions to animals and inanimate objects, even though neither category could talk. For example, in his popular children's book *The Giving Tree*, Shel talks of a tree's affections for a young boy and its gift of leaves to him.

In her own song, Taylor took a leaf out of his book by attributing feelings to her cat Eloise, when she accompanies her on a journey to her family's old Christmas tree farm. While they both enjoy their trip down memory lane, she realises Nashville has replaced childhood attachments to the farm and that, while life in Pennsylvania made for a pleasant past, it's Music City where she sees her future. The song, simply named 'Tennessee', was designed to tug at the heart-strings – and, indeed, her mother soon saw what was in her heart.

"As a parent, there's no bigger pain than watching your child being rejected by her peers," she told the *Daily Mail*. "But it made me realise, if she was ready to sacrifice being accepted and having friends for the lonely experience of writing songs in her bedroom and singing on weekends, it must mean a lot to her."

Indeed, in Taylor's head, she was already on a fast track to country music fame – and attending a school she hated was her biggest obstacle. She was waiting for her parents to remove the roadblock – and how could they say no to their daughter's request when it was delivered in a song?

Seeing how set she was on success, they wondered if it might be time for another brief visit. Finally, they agreed to take a road trip and Taylor was headed right back to Nashville, the place where, just like in the Disney movies she had been raised on, dreams really did come true.

Chapter 4

Singing For Survival

Nashville was, for Taylor, the mecca of the music world – indeed, it wasn't called Music City for nothing. Every artist whose CDs she had ever coveted or singled out as special had worked there, and – in some cases – made their fortune there. But the music industry was one that, as Pat Garrett had warned her father, chewed up vulnerable, naïve young artists and spat them out. It wouldn't be the first time Taylor had fled in floods of tears after failing to win yet another sing-off. Could she really make it here or would she be left lamenting the teardrops on her guitar? She had no way of knowing for sure what the future held, but she also knew the only way to find out was to try.

Since the 1950s, Nashville had made a name for itself as the home of country music, the place where everyone with ambitions in the genre came to record. The industry might have faltered a little when Elvis Presley first arrived in town to record hits such as 'Heartbreak Hotel' and America fell under the spell of rock 'n' roll; for a while it seemed as though the country music industry had been forgotten in the excitement. Indeed, over the years Nashville had continued to diversify and, decades later, was even home to rap and rock stars such as Kings of Leon, Young Buck, Paramore and Ben Folds – all of whom had lived or recorded in the area.

But the city's roots were still resolutely country. Every year it was home to a host of annual events to celebrate the genre, such as the Country Music Marathon where over 25,000 music lovers from around the world showed their support with a bracing run. Then there was the four-day CMA (Country Music Association) Music Festival every June – the only major gathering in America devoted exclusively to the genre – and the nationally televised CMA Awards in the city's Bridgestone Arena.

It was a veritable paradise for country music enthusiasts, and the first thing Taylor did on arrival in the city was to take a tour of all the legendary landmarks in country history. Some of her teenage classmates might have headed, mouths watering in anticipation, for Jack Daniels' Distillery – but not Taylor. She was ready to take on Music Row.

The famous street was lined with record-label headquarters, shops that sold vintage and out-of-print records, and meet-up hotspots where pressurised talent scouts and busy record executives took their liquid lunches. However, by far the most famous attraction was the internationally renowned RCA Studio B.

This tiny, single-storey recording studio had seen the production of over 35,000 songs, including more than 200 performed by Elvis Presley alone, and had played host to veterans such as Hank Williams, Roy Orbison and Johnny Cash. It had also seen its fair share of dramas – back in 1967, Dolly Parton had been so anxious to get there for a recording session that she crashed her car at breakneck speed into the side of the building.

The studio hadn't been used professionally for years, but it was packed with history, boasting the very same grand piano that Elvis had used back in 1956, as well as a collection of old-school tape machines tucked away in the corner. Audio guides were narrated by the likes of Dolly Parton and Patsy Cline. Guests could take a guided tour and, if they reserved in advance, even follow in their idols' footsteps and book their own recording session there. The price tag was much lower too. Recording a country album for real would set you back more than $300,000; here you could belt out a casual rendition of the Elvis classic 'Are You Lonesome Tonight?' without the need to remortgage your home.

Just a few doors down from the iconic Studio B was the Country Music Hall Of Fame and Museum (it has since relocated to a $37 million premises not much more than a mile away in downtown Nashville). Even from the air, the museum needed little introduction – the building was shaped like a bass clef, while back on ground level its windows took the shape of piano keys. If its exterior seemed to be devoted to music, that was nothing compared to the sights within. It was packed from wall to wall with hundreds of historic video clips and vintage costumes worn by the celebrities of the genre. Plaques hanging from the walls honoured the forefathers of country such as Johnny Cash.

It was a country music lover's treasure trove. However, it was the dedication by author Garrison Keillor that warmed Taylor's heart the most – and it seemed to speak to her personally. "Country music is still devoted to the lyric and to the telling of stories, which people love and people need," it read. "Country music artists took what they heard around them, material that was in the air and that has common currency and they made something entirely new. This is a museum that preserves their memory so that they can continue to inspire creators in the future. It's also a museum that honours the people who their music was made for. Those people are all of us, people who've ever been lost or confused or sad or felt excluded."

Not only had Taylor felt at first-hand the pain of social exclusion, something the sounds of her favourite country artists could soothe, she had been feeling inspired as a lyricist too. Seeing the words of her favourite songs scrawled across bar napkins and hung up around the museum proved to her that ordinary people who wrote a diary or composed lyrics at home while strumming on a guitar could rise from their humble beginnings and go on to top charts all over the world.

What was more, singers like Trisha Yearwood and Kathy Mattea, who had gone on to become big stars, had started out as humble tour guides at that very museum.

Not just a casual observer, Taylor was in Nashville to succeed as a songwriter – and these exhibits made her feel that anything was possible. "When I first came, I didn't know anything about how the music business worked, I didn't know how to build connections, I didn't know where to start," Taylor admitted to *The Useless Critic* in recollections of those early days. "It has always been my mantra to… remember that if you try hard enough you can achieve anything, even if you are an unpopular, geeky kid from Pennsylvania who has never quite fit in!"

Yet this city was Taylor's starting point – and it wasn't a bad place to begin. Just a few doors down from the museum was the Ryman Auditorium, a 2,000-seat theatre which had been the home of the famous Grand Ole Opry show from 1949 to 1974. This legendary weekly showcase for country music had been host to such greats as Hank Williams, Patsy Cline and the Carter Family over the years, but when it moved to its own custom-built premises, the Ryman Auditorium continued to welcome artists such as Sheryl Crow and The Dixie Chicks to its hallowed stage. The venue was known as the Mother Church of Country Music, the place where it had all begun. Keith Urban had claimed, "There's no place I'd rather play", while Marty Stuart declared it "the Vatican of country music". But artists of all genres idolised the venue, with Coldplay calling it "the best theatre in the world".

Meanwhile, about 10 miles northeast of downtown, in Music Valley, stood the new Grand Ole Opry House, a 4,400-seater music venue with backstage tours offered daily. Its wax museum boasted life-size statues of costume-clad country stars, while next door housed a shopping mall. Within it was the Gibson Bluegrass Showcase, a working factory where Taylor could peer through the glass and watch the mandolins, banjos and guitars she had always drooled over in shop windows going through the production process.

Elsewhere in town was the Wild Horse Saloon, a venue blaring out traditional country music and offering free dance lessons to punters; the Douglas Corner Café, where Katy Perry had played while pursuing a gospel career pre-pop fame; and the famous Bluebird Café, which regularly held open-mic music nights for would-be country stars. Meanwhile, the Gaylord Opryland Hotel, with its simulated rainforest canopy walkways and boat rides in the lobby, was the number-one place for music fans to stay in town.

It was certainly the ideal place for Taylor to recharge her batteries after a day of touring the city. Seeing Dolly Parton's early showreels and running her fingertips over the same piano keys that Elvis Presley had once played had whet Taylor's appetite for success — and it was soon time for her to get back down to business.

She was no longer a starry-eyed wannabe. From now on, Taylor would be pounding the pavements with a sense of purpose — she was scouting for a record deal. However, she soon found it was not nearly as easy as she'd hoped. She had been lulled into a false sense of security at home in Pennsylvania, where many fellow singers had taken to the stage purely for fun. In Nashville, the competition was both fierce and relentless, and everyone seemed desperate for a deal: she was up against a whole new level of talent. What was more, making it in Nashville was so tough that authors had even penned survival manuals for those intent on carving out a career there, warning how it wasn't for the fainthearted.

After another long day of trudging hopelessly from one record label to another, Taylor's morale was at an all-time low. The glamour and glitter had definitely faded. It was then that she heard the words she had been dreading: "Tell her to go back to school and come back and see me when she's 18." That one sentence left her patronised, belittled, humiliated — and, for a split second — ready to give up.

After all, despite her talent, she had few of the attributes of the average fame seeker. She was neither as hard as nails nor as impenetrable and emotionless as the wax statues she saw of her idols in the city's museums. She thought the playground insults of her bullies had been painful, but that was nothing compared to the moment a music executive — who held a position of power in the industry — had dismissed her dreams. With just one sentence, he sent a starry-eyed Taylor plummeting back down to earth — and the infant stages of searching for stardom were anything but glamorous. However, fortunately for Taylor, she had her parents as her cheerleaders when all else failed.

Reminding her that even Jay-Z had already sung her praises, Taylor's mother told her: "You've had hundreds of people tell you they love your voice, and now you're going to give up just because one person doesn't see your potential? If that guy was right, you wouldn't have been singing at the Phillies game. God might have closed one door in your face, but He did that for a reason. He still has plans for you. Trust in Him that another one will open."

Taylor listened and took heart. "Basically all of the record companies went, 'Ah, how cute. She's just a little kid,'" Taylor grimaced to *The Telegraph*. "They also said, 'Give up your dreams. Go home and come back when you're 18.' I chose not to hear that. I wasn't prepared to accept that I wasn't a relevant artist until I was 18 and so I just kept coming back."

By this point, her mother was driving a 13-year-old Taylor to Nashville every month to meet as many agents, songwriters, producers and label bosses as they could convince to see them. She was willing to repeat the arduous journey for the entire five years until Taylor turned 18 if she had to.

Taylor began to get interest eventually – but it was the wrong kind. Some labels saw her youth as a novelty for their team's marketing department to exploit. They saw a photogenic, cute, camera-friendly young girl with the voice of an angel – someone who could make headlines on account of her early start in the industry. But Taylor suspected they were only interested in marketing strategies and media campaigns, while she wanted someone who would look beyond her age to what she could do behind a microphone.

"I've never wanted to use my age as a gimmick," Taylor later clarified to *Entertainment Weekly*. "[I've] never wanted it to be the headline, because I want the music to win."

Other labels expressed an interest in working with her when she was a little older because they saw a future currency in her good looks that – at her tender age – couldn't yet be withdrawn from the bank. They wanted someone to bring back sex appeal to the world of country.

Taylor was wary of that kind of angle, especially after one of her favourite bands, the Dixie Chicks, had posed naked. After a controversial period during which they attracted strong criticism for their public disapproval of the 2003 war in Iraq and denounced then President George Bush, claiming they were ashamed that he was from Texas, The Dixie Chicks had chosen to diffuse the tension in an unusual way. Consequently, the May 2003 edition of *Entertainment Weekly* was emblazoned with the three of them stark naked, their modesty covered only by ironic slogans that denounced them as "traitors", "Dixie's sluts" or "Saddam's angels" or extolled them as "proud Americans".

Taylor wasn't about political statements, shock tactics or flesh-flaunting: she wanted the music to speak for itself. As much as she loved The Dixie Chicks for their sound, she didn't want to follow in their footsteps and find herself, a few years on, reclining, legs spread, on the front cover of a music magazine with only a carefully placed acoustic guitar to hide her goodies. Even worse, in her eyes, was the prospect of posing for *Playboy* to boost her career. A traditional girl at heart, Taylor just wanted to write songs about love.

She came into the business because she had "so many songs I wanted people to hear" and one of those early songs, 'My Turn To Be Me', had already made the message clear. She wanted to be successful on her own terms, no one else's – and she wasn't prepared to compromise her ideals to get a front-row seat in the queue for a record deal.

Some had accused so-called "pop tart" Katy Perry of compromising herself to become famous. She'd started off as a squeaky clean gospel singer who wrote ballads about her commitment to God but, within a couple of years, had switched to songs with shock value. Early unreleased efforts included stories of seeking a sugar daddy and bathing in champagne to promote an album. After making it big, she'd posed topless for magazines and married Russell Brand – a comedian and actor, but also someone whose main profession up until then seemed to have been heroin-smoking hell raiser and – according to the tabloids – serial shagger. It left people wondering whether Katy was an angelic teenage girl reading her Bible, her hands clasped earnestly in prayer, or a scantily clad sex symbol willing to do anything to make the headline news. Even at 13, Taylor knew this wasn't a debate she wanted the masses to be having about her.

In Taylor's eyes, the main option being offered to her seemed to be to wait a few years so that she could be transformed into a sex symbol who also happened to be a singer, a fact that would be rather an afterthought for the leering audience she envisaged herself being marketed to. As she had given up a social life at school and endured months of taunts and teasing to pursue her dreams, that option – one that differed so greatly from her own ambitions – wasn't one she felt prepared to accept. She needed to go back to the drawing board. As much as she believed an artist should come across naturally and she rejected premeditated formulas for success, it was time to outsmart those major labels and devise a marketing strategy of her own.

Canadian country and folk music veteran Gordon Lightfoot had said of musical success: "You don't have to be the best, you just have to do the most." Taylor hoped to break the mould by succeeding on both counts and, to do that, she needed more onstage experiences. Using a mixture of her parents' help and Dan Dymtrow's connections, she started to play concerts anywhere and everywhere.

"I was so driven because I didn't expect that anything would just happen for me," she later told *Cosmo Girl*. "That doubt fuelled me to work harder. My attitude was the opposite of people who are like, 'It's gonna happen for me, it's gonna happen for me.' My mantra was always, 'It's not gonna happen for me. Go out and play that show or it's not gonna happen.'" And, of course, that was exactly what she did.

In February 2003, she performed the national anthem in Philadelphia to support the Reading Royals hockey team at an all-important match. Then, in April, she landed a slot at the Florida Music Festival in Orlando as a headline performer for the AMP Radio VIP party. In May, between visits to Nashville, she sang at the Berks County Chamber of Commerce annual dinner, and in June she had an audience on regional radio as a pre-game entertainer before a Reading Phillies game. Throughout June, she played four more shows, from garden parties in Nashville to performances at her local Reading Hospital to cheer up sick patients.

Whether it was a song at a charity event to raise funds for cancer, a rendition of the national anthem for a party, or even taking to the stage at a formal business dinner, she performed wherever there was an audience willing to listen. Taylor learned to cast her ego aside, regardless of whether the crowd was small and humdrum or whether classmates or drunken revellers were heckling her. If it gave her something to add to her CV or it gained her exposure to record labels, it was all worthwhile.

Taylor Swift wows with more than just her model looks as, in her quest to become the first teenager to truly take on country, she attends the 2006 Academy of Country Music Awards – the first ceremony of many. JEFF KRAVITZ/FILMMAGIC.INC

Taylor raises her guitar in the air triumphantly at the 2007 Academy of Country Music Awards in Las Vegas.

The pre-teen Taylor Swift. WENN

Taylor arrives at the ceremony with her supportive mother, Andrea, in tow. FRAZER HARRISON/ACMA/GETTY IMAGES

Behind the scenes: a backstage reveller captures Taylor in action. JASON SQUIRES/WIREIMAGE

Taylor poses by the pool for a 2008 *US Weekly* cover shoot. Strip away the glamour and she could almost pass for a sweet and innocent high school student, but the naiveté in her eyes belies her status as a platinum-selling artist. JASON MERRITT/GERRY IMAGES

aylor with beau Joe Jonas and his brothers at the 2008 MTV Video Music Awards. She would defend him that night after comic Russell rand publicly taunted his virginity pledge, but the relationship ended after a 27 second phone call. KEVIN MAZUR/WIREIMAGE

addy's Girl: a family girl at heart, Taylor – with her father, cott takes time out from filming a show at the CMT studios in ashville. RICK DIAMOND/GETTY IMAGES FOR CMT

Taylor performs at the MTV Studios in New York's Times Square for an episode of TRL, her trusty guitar strapped to her back. GARY GERSHOFF/WIREIMAGE

A flashback to the past: Taylor sings the National Anthem to kick off a 2008 Philadelphia Phillies basketball game, recalling her early fame-hunting days when she'd perform the song repeatedly to blag a place on the stage. JOHN MABANGALO-POOL/GETTY IMAGES

Taylor takes to the stage for a 2009 performance on NBC's *Today* show, filmed in New York. BRYAN BEDDER/GETTY IMAGES

It's all smiles from the audience as Taylor sings at the 2009 Country Music Association Awards, armed with just an acoustic guitar.

The starlet continues to wow the audience during the 44th annual Academy Of Country Music Awards All-Star Jam in Las Vegas.

Meanwhile, she reviewed her approach. Her three favourite country acts of the moment were Faith Hill, The Dixie Chicks and Shania Twain. These weren't bad role models to have. After all, Shania Twain's second album, *The Woman In Me,* had gone 12-times platinum and her 1997 follow-up, *Come On Over,* became the best-selling album ever by a female artist, not to mention the best-selling country album of all time.

At the time Taylor was scouting for a record deal, Shania was almost the best-selling artist in Canada – second only to Celine Dion – and she went on to sell almost 80 million albums. Both The Dixie Chicks and Faith Hill had also enjoyed the success of multi-platinum-selling CDs, with scores of number-one singles in both the country and main stream charts between them.

However, as accomplished as these artists were, Taylor knew it was important not to simply present herself as replicas of them. "When you are trying to shop for a label deal, never use the phrase, 'I sound just like [another famous artist],'" she later explained. "Don't say that to the labels. They'll say, 'Well, we already have those big-name artists, so we don't need to sign you.' Young artists [should] try to sound original so [they] don't sound like anyone else."

That brought Taylor to the next part of her marketing plan. Nashville's Country Music Museum had taught her how to distinguish between cajun, country, rockabilly and honky tonk – but how did she want to sound herself? There had been many cross-over attempts over the decades – including attempts to match country with elements of rock, pop and soul, with artists like Bob Dylan, The Rolling Stones and Gram Parsons getting in on the act. Artists like Shania Twain had increasingly melded mainstream pop into her songs, while new genres within country – such as the ludicrously named truck-driving country – were being introduced all the time.

As for Taylor, she wanted to be all of these elements and much more besides. She wanted to make a definitive country album containing a whole spectrum of influences, but above all she wanted to make music that was real, honest and from the heart. After all, hadn't Nashville native Harlin Howard claimed that "country music is nothing more than three chords and the truth"? And Howard was an authority on the subject: his own successful country career had spanned several decades.

Taylor's first ever track, 'Lucky You', had been just that – a three-chord work of emotion. While Taylor had later cringed with embarrassment, claiming that the track had made her sound like "a chipmunk", it had given her an inkling of what type of music was meaningful to her. She wanted it to be simple, truthful, raw and honest – an authentic insight into people's emotions and lives.

"My definition of country music is really pretty simple," she later clarified to the *Daily Mail*. "It's when somebody sings about their life and what they know, from an authentic place – and you know, a lot of country artists sing about topics in their life that are authentic. One guy will write about how he grew up on a farm and fell in love and raised kids on that same farm. Some people sing about how, when they get sad, they go to the bar and drink whiskey. I write songs about how I can't seem to figure out relationships and how I'm frustrated by love."

Taylor knew writing about love from a young teen perspective would reach out to other girls struggling with exactly the same feelings. She wanted to share her fears, heartbreaks and joys with like-minded people, knowing that she and her audience would understand each other. Taylor wasn't interested in being a loftier-than-thou superstar – after all, her descriptions of low-key love affairs in small rural farming communities couldn't have been more different from the glamour of fame and fortune – but it was these "simple folk" that Taylor admired and was inspired by.

Singing relatable songs about love could set her apart from some of the other hopefuls – but, even better, she could write them too. Add to that her age and she was becoming someone quite unique.

Taylor's writing skills were especially important to her because, without those, she felt she was at risk of being replaced by another generic attractive young singer at any time. "I didn't just want to be another girl singer," she later explained *to Entertainment Weekly*. "I wanted there to be something that set me apart and I knew that had to be my writing... I wanted a record label that needed me, that was absolutely counting on me to succeed."

Another advantage that Taylor had on the road to success was the love and support of two involved parents, both of whom were willing to devote time and money to getting her noticed. Most importantly of all, they believed in her, regardless of her youth and inexperience. "I think people should never, ever put an age limit on what someone can accomplish," Taylor declared defiantly to *Great American Country*. "My parents, ever since the day I was born, have empowered me."

With their business acumen, her family were also able to channel Taylor's teenage fantasies and convert them into realistic goals, together with action plans on how to achieve them. One way that they helped her emotionally was by reminding her not to be disheartened by other people's criticism.

"I don't think anyone at Wyomissing Junior High thought she was going to make it," childhood friend Kaylin Politzer told the author. "When she talked about moving to Nashville, most people thought she'd gone crazy," added another friend, Sara. On top of that, there was the most humbling criticism of all – the type that came straight from the mouths of record executives.

However, her parents insisted that no matter how good she was or how much she might appeal to the masses, there were always going to be some people who would despise her. There was nothing she could do about that, but it was important for her not to believe that it vetoed her chances of success.

For instance, one of Taylor's favourite CDs was Shania Twain's fourth album *Up*, released the previous year in 2002. It sold over 20 million albums worldwide, but not everyone was a fan. For example, sarcastic critics claimed that the sentiment expressed in her opening song, "It's about as bad as it can be," was a good way to describe the entire album.

Yet the sharp-tongued columnists' comments were nothing compared to the harsh putdowns of the public. One *Metacritic* user raged: "This is the ultimate in disposable, plastic, sugar-coated music", while another joked: "Barbie-doll looks, boring hooks – don't buy. Waste of money." Finally, a third reviewer, clearly dissatisfied with his purchase, ranted: "Not one memorable track. Next time she should sing over the sounds of garbage disposal in the background. It would be so more fitting. A broken toaster is worth more than this stinking heap."

It was the type of condemnation that would make even a singer with the skin of a rhinoceros flinch – and yet Shania was having the last laugh. Not only did her album go straight into the *Billboard* charts and remain there for four consecutive weeks, but it made her the world's only female artist to have three albums in a row achieve diamond status in America. So a few disgruntled critics disliked her – but she was laughing all the way to the bank.

The Dixie Chicks had also released a new album in 2002, entitled *Home*, which promptly went 11-times platinum. *All Music* claimed that they had delivered "the best country album yet released" that decade and declared the CD an "instant classic". Yet *Rolling Stone* awarded it just two stars, sneering: "They are incapable of shaping a song."

Clearly, not even best-selling artists were immune from a media backlash, let alone a public one. Just as Taylor's mother had warned her, she wouldn't be liked by everybody and she couldn't please all of the world all of the time. The put-downs could be eye-wateringly aggressive –and yet that was all part and parcel of being a country artist – having negative comments splashed across a national newspaper for all the world to see. One thing was for certain: the music business was not for the faint-hearted.

Yet the Swifts did their best to protect their thin-skinned daughter. They realised that it would be easy for the average would-be superstar, as yet without money or success behind them, to become disheartened every time they heard a playful putdown or a snide remark. Their advice to her was to keep on going. According to Pat Garrett, her parents' support was invaluable both in her future success and even in winning his karaoke contest. "There were a couple of other guys and gals who did a great job of singing and maybe could have gone on to be something in the music business, but Taylor had some things they did not," he explained to the author. "One was her writing ability, another was her charisma, but the most important thing in her career in my estimation was her dad and mom."

He added: "They were 100% behind her and there is nothing like having somebody to support anybody trying to be in the music business. It's a tough business, somewhat ruthless – it chews people up and spits them out. Crushes your ego and it makes it hard to continue, especially when you don't have a lot of money and have to work at something else to support your music habit. Taylor had this support. I guess she realises how valuable her dad was in encouraging her, making contacts for her along the way… It was a family team effort. But I think if it wasn't for dad pushing and mom going out with her meeting radio and interviews, she might still be in Wyomissing singing around here – or not?"

Taylor also credited her family with preventing her from giving up at the first demoralising comment. "I know I'm so lucky that I've got two perfect parents," she later agreed. "I'm really good friends with [*American Idol* contestant] Kellie Pickler, whose mom abandoned her. I look at my mom, who's been there for everything and I think, like, if I'd been in Kellie's situation, I probably wouldn't have made it."

Not only did she regard her mother as her "best friend", she also knew she could rely on her to keep her focused. "She's been the person who's not afraid to whip me into shape," she confessed to *Elle Girl*.

In fact, it was her mother's recommendation that she took pen to paper, as she had done so many times before to write a song, but this time the aim was to hone and fine-tune her feelings about what she wanted from the music business and convert it into a short mission statement. It would help her to compartmentalise her aims into a few short sentences about what she wanted to achieve, thereby making the goal closer and easier to attain.

Taylor thought about all the things that might set her apart from the other hopefuls and clarified them into writing. For instance, she knew she took influence from the greats, but her songs also had their own added twist. She knew she had more exposure and concerts under her belt from working on the karaoke circuit than many would-be singers twice her age had notched up. She also knew that she had the support and backing of a loving family – a green-light for labels, as it indicated she had guidance and was unlikely to squander her time. Finally, she had a collection of pre-written songs. That was when she had the idea of combining the last two factors. She could start recording high-quality demos with renowned producers, combining her writing skills with her father's financial ability to pay for the recordings.

Taylor instantly started working on some last-minute songwriting sessions – all about relationships. She might have been young – in fact, she hadn't even had her first boyfriend yet – but that didn't prevent her from writing a whole catalogue of songs about love. She wasn't writing about the love affairs she had experienced but rather the ones she wanted to experience. "You can draw inspiration from anything," she later insisted to *The Washington Post*. "If you're a good story-teller, you can take a dirty look somebody gives you, or if a guy you used to have flirtations with starts dating a new girl, or somebody you're casually talking to says something that makes you so mad – you can create an entire scenario around that. You don't have to date people or be married to people to write songs about them."

Consequently, although her early song efforts, about a range of different boys, might have made her look like the middle-school slut, in reality her only crime was a gift for story-telling and a colourful imagination.

Armed with both, Taylor wrote 'Honey Baby', about trying to extricate herself from an addictive love affair but failing miserably. Then came 'For You', an ode to a lover who's sweeter than candy and deserves her thank-yous for being there, followed by 'Mandolin', about a mystery man who has caught her eye at her local bar by making beautiful music on a red mandolin.

'Love They Haven't Thought Of Yet' tells of a romance so unique that the pair connect like no other couple have ever done before. 'Don't Hate Me For Loving You', meanwhile, is a heart-felt tale of a guilty crush. 'Your Face' is the story of a love long since lost, whose happy memories she is praying will never fade.

Yet Taylor isn't always sweet and innocent – when the opposite sex betrays her, the revenge vocals start flowing. 'Matches' is Taylor's fury-filled ode to a cheating partner who she feels deserves to see their romance burnt down to the ground.

Meanwhile, 'Sugar' talks of a perfect romance between a young southern girl from Music City and her irresistible other half, while 'Better Off' describes a boy none of her friends approve of.

In 'That's Life', a spurned Taylor demands, in the world-weary guise of a woman twice her age, to know why exactly love hurts. The heartfelt content almost belies Taylor's lack of relationship history.

However, one song that does give a clue as to her inexperience is 'Spinning Around'. It is interesting to compare it to Kylie Minogue's song of the same name: while Kylie's version is about a love affair that left her in a trance, Taylor's song is all about the potential of one. Looking into her crush's eyes might be like looking into another world, but the object of her affections is too self-absorbed to notice her charms.

Meanwhile, 'This Here Guitar' is about a different kind of love affair – one with a battered, bruised, but in Taylor's eyes beautiful, guitar. Cracked and worn, it has seen far better days, but while its previous owner discarded it as trash, to her it will always be treasure. Like Amy Winehouse's 'Cherry', a song released the same year, 'This Here Guitar' describes a deep bond with the instrument – one so strong that it becomes a best friend.

When life lets her down, her guitar stays around. Its strings sound out the emotion she feels but doesn't dare to tell anyone. It might be a mere coloured lump of wood to anyone else who sees it, but to Taylor it's her number-one confidante – she even stops to wonder what it has seen before and where it has been. She has learned to rely on its ability to soothe her sorrows, knowing that, unlike people whose actions are variable, music is the one consistent force in her life that will never disappoint her.

While she was on the subject of disappointments, Taylor also penned 'Point Of View'. She knew that her classmates ridiculed country music, but it was the greatest pleasure in her life – and one that she was ready to sacrifice any number of friendships for. While some saw Shania Twain's tracks as tuneless caterwauling by a plastic faux-Barbie, Taylor firmly believed her to be both beautiful and talented. What was more, while Taylor's Wyomissing-based peers saw her as a hopeless nerd who would never fit in, would she come across the same way in the south? Her parents had already advised her that no one in the world could be liked by everyone. Even the most popular or beautiful girl in school wouldn't match everyone's tastes.

And, as invisible as Taylor felt to the male population right then, she reassured herself that one day she would be the missing puzzle piece that completed some man's jigsaw of life. In the meantime she was using the song to ponder on why people had so many differing points of view.

Whether it was music, art, love or good looks, there was no universal answer to what was good and what was not. Who was right, or did personal tastes defy categorisation? With all of this in mind, Taylor vowed never to change herself. In 'Some Girl', she explored her down-to-earth nature that was here to stay. Unlike Lady Gaga, who claimed she was "never in jeans", Taylor lived in jeans – and she wasn't afraid to admit it. She would stay a simple country girl who sang every morning and kept a diary to express her feelings – and she would never change.

It was with the promise to be herself that Taylor took to the studio with producer Steve Migliore to record her first fully professional demo. Steve had started out with a modest production business which he ran from a makeshift studio at the back of his parents' Philadelphia home. Together with his friend Michael, he charged $25 an hour to produce and mix songs for then unknown artists. When he befriended a music attorney who introduced him to all the major labels, talent combined with power and his studio was transformed from a backyard business to an award-winning enterprise. Steve quickly earned his credentials – within three years, his remix of LeAnn Rimes' 1997 single had hit number one on the *Billboard* adult contemporary chart. At the time, Steve was so broke that he was flipping burgers in a food court for a living. Among his first words when he found out were: "Does this mean I have a career?"

First, the song had made the top spot on KTV Radio, when he received a call to break the news. "The station's phone lines lit up with 60 requests to play the remix again in less than a minute," Steve recalled to *Musician Wages*. "The following week, the remix went to number one on *Billboard*... my world flipped!"

"I quit my job so that I could sharpen my skills in the studio," he continued. "I ended up getting five more records that month from that same label and others. One of them was my remix for Brian McKnight's

'Anytime', which broke records as the first remix to replace and remove the original hit from the radio."

Meanwhile, 'How Do I Live' went three-times platinum, selling over three million copies in the USA alone. It remained in the *Billboard* Hot 100 Chart for 69 consecutive weeks, while it entered the Top 25 Country Singles Chart in June 1997 and remained there for five-and-a-half years. It became the highest selling country single of its time – a record that wouldn't be broken until 'Love Story' – by a certain Miss Taylor Swift – hit the charts 12 years later.

In the months that followed, Steve – once penniless – was bombarded with offers of work from major labels, making 40 successful records in the first year alone. By the time Taylor and her parents walked into Philadelphia's legendary Sigma studios six years later – which had seen Madonna, David Bowie and Whitney Houston sing there – he was already a fully fledged producer, mixer and sound engineer. They were looking for an established producer to work with them and Steve wasn't exactly running short on hits.

Those in the know called him a behind-the-scenes genius, while *South Jersey* magazine asserted: "When it comes to the music industry, Steve just might be the biggest name you've never heard." Yet Taylor had heard of him, and the signs pointed to the two of them being perfect musical partners.

Taylor was the same age that LeAnn had been when 'How Do I Live' first hit the airwaves. Initially the song had barely scratched the surface of even specialist country radio stations, but with a few tweaks, Steve transformed it into an up-tempo track with a catchy beat that sailed straight to the top of the nation's charts, mainstream pop or otherwise. He seemed well versed in retaining a track's country roots while giving it a beat that would coax the mainstream public into a listen, too, delivering a traditional theme with a commercial twist. Making a song universally popular without sacrificing its original country flavour was the goal for Taylor – and Steve looked like the man to fulfil her plans.

Not only that, but – unlike the label heads who had patronised Taylor in the past – Steve wasn't about to dismiss her for her age. In fact, he too had known music was his calling at an early age. "I knew from the time I was about seven years old that I was going to do this for the rest of my life," he later told *Musician Wages*. "I considered giving up, but at the same time, when I turned on the TV, I see these people doing what they want to do. What makes them different from me? I am just as good as anyone else."

Now Taylor was at a similar life-stage and Steve saw something in her that reminded him of his youngest self. Unlike his predecessors, he was willing to look for her potential. He didn't have to look far, either. Although he had worked on music for Akon, Beyoncé, The Backstreet Boys, Usher, Britney Spears and Wyclef Jean, he believed that Taylor might top them all.

"[While] they are all exceptional at what they do, Taylor is definitely on her own level," he told the author. "At 14 she already exhibited signs of creative genius. She learned to play a 12-string guitar in a few short months and wrote close to 100 songs within a year's time. The day we met, she played 12 songs back to back with no break and we recorded them live to get a feel of what we had to work with."

Steve was pleased both with her voice and with her sense of direction. He wasn't looking for a manufactured artist with lists of pre-programmed PR spiel in the space where their brains should be – he sought someone who already knew what they wanted to achieve. He told *Musician Wages*: "I really like working with artists who have a vision and don't just come into the studio and sit there all day waiting for you to figure out who they are and what they should sound like. After all, they are called 'artists', so they should know how to create their own art. The producer is there to guide them and to help them achieve that vision."

For Steve, Taylor had been a model pupil, heading to the studio with a string of her own songs. She hadn't been afraid to direct him during the production process either, telling him how to interpret her lyrics so that he could create the right feel for her on the backing track. "We discussed [the lyrics] so that I could understand the kind of emotion the songs needed to convey."

The two found it easy to connect artistically. At 30, Steve was old enough to have years of experience in the industry, but still young enough to have a youthful outlook on the topics Taylor covered in her songs and to be in tune with the ideals of teenage romance. Her lyrics were a little mature for her age, while Steve remembered the first flushes of young love, and they met somewhere in the middle.

While Taylor had written numerous new songs, it was her younger efforts that she was the most fond of – and so the pair reworked 'Smokey Black Nights', written at age 11, and 'Lucky You', written at age 12.

"'Lucky You' is an up-tempo song about a small town girl who feels she has a lot more to offer the world and she wants to break out of the shell or vacuum of her life and show everyone what she's made of," Steve explained to the author. "'Smokey Black Nights' sounds and feels earthy like it was just a soundtrack about what home feels like."

He added: "I wasn't a country music producer, but I tried my best to give the tracks as best a country feel as I could. After I created the musical beds for the two songs, we spent the rest of the week solidifying the lyrics, melodies and arrangements and then we recorded Taylor's vocals. I even jumped in the booth for some background harmonies. She was gracious, pleasant and a joy to work with."

The feeling was mutual, with Taylor praising his sensitive interpretation of her lyrics. She was now that bit closer to her perfect demo – and, as an afterthought, she added 'American Boy'.

This song depicted the world of a wealthy all-American character for whom there is no such word as 'impossible'. Growing up saw him idealise both his parents, but in Taylor's story the rose-tinted glasses are for real – nothing in the world can destroy the hopes and dreams of a traditional American boy.

Within the lyric lies a thinly disguised reference to Taylor's own world, with the character living on Grandview Avenue, rather like her own childhood street, Grandview Boulevard. Perhaps the song was a tribute to her younger brother, Austin?

'American Boy' became the lead track, while 'Lucky You' and 'Smokey Black Nights' followed. After adorning the demo CD with pictures of her face, Taylor returned to Nashville and handed out copies to anyone influential in the industry.

However, with her previous track record of failing to impress the music moguls, she wasn't holding her breath for an immediate response.

While she waited, she looked into enrolling herself in a ten-day summer camp, the Britney Spears Camp for the Performing Arts. She was a country girl at heart, while Britney was pure pop, but Taylor idolised her nonetheless. Back then, Britney was still a good girl who had yet to go bad, and had even pledged to save her virginity until marriage. Her style was clean-cut, family-friendly pop – and it was something Taylor had a soft spot for.

Britney's camp, a 100% free charity venture, seemed like the ideal place for a crash course on the fame game. The problem was it was already overflowing with applications. Each year, the children would receive a personal visit from mentor Britney herself, whose money had gone into setting the enterprise up. In August 2002, the same month that Taylor had performed at the US Open, she saw photographs of Britney strolling hand in hand with underprivileged but musically talented children, mentoring them through their personal battles, and that was all the persuasion she needed to want to get there herself.

But, desperate for a glimpse of their favourite star and the opportunity to learn about fame from someone who, in many young girls' eyes, had practically invented the word, her fans were flooding the admissions office. What was more, of these starry-eyed fans, priority was given to disadvantaged children wanting to practise the performing arts – those who wouldn't otherwise have been able to afford it. Taylor didn't belong in that category, but her parents were willing to make a donation to the camp's funds to help her earn a place in that summer's group – and to seal the deal even further, Taylor agreed to perform there.

Taylor would be sitting alongside "economically disadvantaged students from every setup [who] in many cases have never spent time out of the city" – a new experience for her in itself. Plus, with her knowledge of the stage, she would have some of her own ideas to bring to the table, too.

She arrived at the camp in Cape Cod, Massachusetts. Live shows from talented performers filled the evenings, while the days were an opportunity for the audience to put into practise anything they had learned. There was an array of masterclasses on offer, including a writing workshop where guests could create their own lyrics and sing them in front of the group, with teachers and peers offering instant feedback.

Any good entertainer has to think fast to entertain an audience on demand, so the Fill In The Blanks classes saw students thrown into the spotlight without a script. Forced to improvise, it was a tough test intended to develop razor-sharp, lightning-fast wit. There were also on-site video production workshops where the children could direct, shoot, edit and star in their own promotional videos, and music production classes where they learned the basics of professionally recording a CD.

Other behind-the-scenes lessons covered lighting, set design and show production to give a glimpse of how the average pop star's glitzy stage shows were put together, while the more flamboyant students flocked to acting classes, trying their hand at anything from Shakespeare to modern drama.

The less confident children made their way to audition workshops, which taught self-presentation and encouraged them to develop their own sense of swagger: confidence was key. Besides that, there was tap dancing, jazz, hip-hop and modern dancing, drumming techniques and even masterclasses for would-be stand-up comedians. Taylor knew where she wanted to be, though, and spent most of her time singing.

Catty critics had commented that Britney Spears, who was widely criticised for miming, was more in need of singing lessons than the children she was mentoring, but Taylor loved the classes and the opportunity to meet her idol. What was more, she was right on time, because just a year later Britney completely cut her ties with the organisation she had founded, making 2004 her final year at the camp.

Taylor's mother had been concerned at first, fearing that her daughter would be booed off-stage by pop purists. "She wasn't sure how the kids at that camp would embrace a country singer," an anonymous friend of the family confided to the author. "She wasn't always so sure it was the right career move for Taylor."

However, she needn't have worried. One teacher at the camp, Ashanti Floyd – tellingly nicknamed the Mad Violinist – had a performance history spanning hip-hop, rock, gospel, classical and – one of Taylor's favourite country genres – bluegrass, and he was just 21. Other instructors on the course had dabbled in professional opera, rap and cabaret ventures, making the camp a truly mixed bag.

When Taylor returned from camp, she was delighted – if a little surprised – to find that super-producer Steve Migliore was still singing her praises, talking to anyone who would listen about the talented young girl he had met.

"I was excited about her abilities," Steve explained to the author. "I was telling everyone around that time that I had just started working with this young, super-talented girl who wrote really catchy songs and who I believed was going to blow up. At that time her talents were still raw as she didn't have much studio experience yet, but we were all super impressed with what she already demonstrated. Her natural storytelling ability was already apparent. It was awesome."

As it turned out, he wasn't the only person who thought so. The demos had reached the attention of RCA Records, the same label that had signed Elvis Presley in the Fifties and then gone on to add pop icons such as Christina Aguilera to their books almost half a century on. RCA was a major presence in the music world, with a formidable reputation for releasing albums by some of the biggest names around.

The endless frantic trips to Nashville came to an abrupt halt in September 2003, when Taylor finally struck gold and landed a development deal. The words of her hopeful father said it all: "Celebrityville, here we come!"

Chapter 5

On A Rocket To A Dying Star

The same month that Taylor landed her development deal, she began eighth grade – and she wasn't looking forward it. It would be her fifth year in a row of dodging bullies and her second year of having virtually no friends at all.

Yet Taylor was now triumphant – all those lonely evenings she had spent writing songs had paid off. She had a year to impress RCA and perfect her material, after which – if they liked it enough – they would give her the green light to release an album. Even better, Taylor's parents had promised that, at the end of the school year, they could move to Nashville for good.

"Now I'm really pleased that I was miserable in school," she revealed to *The Telegraph*. "After all, think what might have happened if I'd been happy – I could still be in Pennsylvania!"

She had her bullies to thank for some of her best material too. One of her first songs about social alienation, 'The Outside', made it onto the 2004 edition of *Chicks With Attitude*, an annual Maybelline-sponsored CD aimed at giving young female newcomers with talent a springboard to success.

"'The Outside' talks about the very reason I ever started to write songs," Taylor revealed later. "It was when I was… a complete outcast.

I was a lot different from the other kids and I never really knew why… I think every person comes to a point in their life when you have a long string of bad days. You can choose to let it drag you down or you can find ways to rise above it. I came to the conclusion that even though people hadn't always been there for me, music had. It's strange to think how different my life would have been right now if I had been one of the cool kids."

It wasn't the only song she would record as a teenager about the girls who seemed to despise her. Inspirations came to her all the time – and in the most inconvenient places. While Taylor was willing time to move faster so that she could leave Pennsylvania permanently, she took to daydreaming and doodling at her school desk. "In class, the teachers did random notebook checks and you can imagine their surprise when there was algebra on one side of the page and song lyrics on the other," Taylor joked to *Teen Superstar*.

But it wasn't time wasted. By April 2004, Taylor's talents had impressed music moguls so much that she was offered a paid position at music publishers Sony ATV as a songwriter – the youngest the company had ever had. It was time for Taylor to upgrade her enemies to "frenemies", knowing that – while they might have seemed monstrous at the time – without them, she might never have felt the urge to record her first song.

The following month, Taylor put in an appearance at the Bitter End nightclub in New York's trendy Greenwich Village – once the home of Jimi Hendrix – to celebrate. Within months of that performance, school was out for summer – and, in Taylor's case, for good.

The usual cliques in the corridors gathered to whisper about her, their voices laced with scorn – but this time the topic of conversation was her move to pursue a career singing "that dumb country music". Suffice it to say that, inside the school gates, few people were supportive. When she left, barely a single person stopped to say goodbye. However, Taylor wasn't looking back either – she was already on her journey.

The last stop before she hit the road was a visit to Pat Garrett's sheepskin store, to thank him for the opportunities he had given her and bid him a fond farewell. "Scott said, 'Well, we're going!'" Pat recalled to the author. "I said, 'Where are you going?' He said, 'To Nashville!' 'Oh great,' I said, figuring they would be taking a trip for a week or two. 'How long for?' He said, 'For the rest of our lives!' I said, '*What!*' He said, 'But isn't that what you told me I should do?' I said, 'Yeah, but no one ever listens to me!'"

Yet Scott had listened – and they were on their way. What was more, unlike most teenagers switching schools, Taylor would be pre-announcing her arrival in a national magazine. Her mentor, Dan Dymtrow, had been scouting for work for Taylor when he heard about an advertising campaign for upscale casual fashion brand Abercrombie & Fitch entitled 'Rising Stars'. The promotion matched up-and-coming talents with the retailer's autumn range of clothing. It was a two-way publicity stunt, and it was clearly mutually beneficial – the stars would share the spotlight in a 19-page spread for glossy fashion magazine *Vanity Fair*.

"Dan sent the company a press kit and they immediately called him back and were like, 'Yeah, we want her on the shoot,'" Taylor told the *Nashville City Paper*. "I was just thinking, I'm not cool enough for this. I mean, it's Abercrombie & Fitch!"

It was a fair assumption. Abercrombie was the brand that many of the cooler-than-thou classmates who had snubbed her had worn. It was the ultimate revenge bid, the ultimate farewell present to her haters. Yet, cool credentials aside, she felt she might not have been sexy enough and, confronted with her first major dilemma, she started to panic.

Famous figures of the fashion world often seemed almost inextricably linked to sex appeal. The Abercrombie campaign was to include hunky male models with bulging biceps and, at times, open shirts, while some of the female competition would be scantily clad and willing to run through a repertoire of raunchy poses. It wouldn't have been the first time that a girl under 16 had been invited to do a risqué photo shoot, even if it caused moral outrage. As for *Vanity Fair*, even its perfume adverts often displayed closely intertwined bodies in poses that left little to the imagination – readers could fill in the obligatory husky bedroom voices. After all, sex sold.

Then there were the expectations of the modern music world. As a singer, Taylor wasn't immune from the pressure to dress provocatively. Britney Spears had recently transformed from a pig-tailed school girl with PG13 fantasies of true love and marriage to a toxic temptress who dressed in crimson-coloured PVC catsuits. Meanwhile, clean-cut Christina Aguilera had gone from being from a virginal genie in a bottle, not ready to release herself, to a "Dirrrty" Delilah in leather chaps. Surely then, rising stars in a fashion magazine had to have sex appeal? Could a devoutly Catholic Taylor participate without compromising her strict moral code?

"Taylor's reaction to landing the campaign was two-fold – first she was screaming with excitement, then she was worried sick," one friend told the author. "She was worried that they'd want her to show off more than she wanted to."

Even if the shoot turned out to be tasteful, Taylor was anxious not to be known as "that pretty girl" who posed in magazine advert campaigns. "She was saying she was a singer and songwriter, not a model," her friend continued. "She didn't want the look to end up more important than the message and I don't think she liked the idea of being put out there as a beauty."

After some soul-searching, she decided that, although she was anxious to make it in the music business and the campaign was the perfect way to get noticed, she would either take part without compromising her ideals or not at all.

As it happened, she needn't have been worried. She was provided with casual clothes – blue denim jeans and a short-sleeved white top – and the only accessory she had to sport was an acoustic guitar. Her long curls were flowing loosely but there was no hint of sexuality – in fact she was depicted as a heartbroken woman, wiping a fake tear from her eye with a handkerchief. That was much more the look that Taylor was hoping to achieve – it even expressed the emotions of her songs. Readers with a keen imagination could visualise the teardrops pouring onto a forlorn Taylor's guitar.

In July 2004, the magazine hit the newsstands, featuring a full-page photograph, plus a passage introducing who she was and why she was one of the hottest new additions to the music scene. It read: "After I sang the national anthem at the US Open last year, a top music manager signed me as his client. Now I have a record contract with RCA and I'm moving to Nashville with my family. I write all of my own songs and my roots are in country. I love the sound of fiddles and mandolins ringing in my ears and I love the stories that you hear in country ballads. I sometimes write about teenage love, but I am presently a 14-year-old girl without a boyfriend. Sometimes I worry that I must be wearing some kind of guy repellent, but then I realise that I'm just discovering who I am as a person. Right now, music is the most important thing in my life and I want to touch people with my songs."

As she had hoped, Taylor's 'Rising Star' mission statement managed to preserve an innocent, virginal image, while reinforcing that the main message was her music. Mission accomplished, Taylor then accepted an invite to the official *Vanity Fair* and Abercrombie & Fitch party held in New York at the Hotel Gansevoort on July 14. Taylor appeared in a purple faded-effect top with the Abercrombie logo emblazoned across it, a pair of the brand's jeans and a couple of plain plastic bracelets. There wasn't a trace of make-up on her face and, while she was willing to endorse the clothes she wore, she was determined that revellers' memories of her should be musical ones.

The publicity campaign for Taylor's move to Nashville was moving into fifth gear – and the final pieces of the puzzle fell into place when the family found their ideal home. It was a spacious detached property located in the small-town suburb of Hendersonville, just a few minutes drive from the hustle and bustle of central Nashville.

"We stopped at the dock on the way up to check out the house," Taylor's father Scott told *Sea Ray* of their first viewing. "I looked down the cove towards the lake, imagined my Sea Ray [boat] tied up there and said, 'I'll take it!' [My wife] said, 'Don't you want to see the house first?!'"

They almost didn't have to. Old Hickory Lane, which overlooked a scenic lake, had been the street of choice for many a country star in the past from Roy Orbison to Johnny Cash, the latter of whom had lived it up in a luxurious 18-bedroom mansion. Property here didn't exactly come cheap, but it was the price of fame – and one Scott and Andrea were willing to pay.

While her parents organised the paperwork, Taylor was off to intern at the CMA Festival. That day, as a newcomer to living in Nashville and a virtual stranger to the city's showbiz scene, she experienced being on the outside looking in all over again. While she rushed around clutching a clipboard, the big-name celebrities she hoped to rub shoulders with one day barely noticed her. To them, this lowly intern was invisible. "I remember just feeling like if there was ever a chance that one day people would line up to have me sign something of theirs, then that would be a really, really good day for me," Taylor would later recall. For now she might be on the bottom rung of the ladder, but she was climbing fast.

The feelings of isolation faded away once she had enrolled in school, beginning her freshman year at Hendersonville High School. From the first day an anxious Taylor arrived, she found herself an instant ally in the shape of classmate Abigail Anderson.

Abigail was a champion swimmer with aspirations of also becoming a journalist, but, like Taylor, she never quite felt like she fitted in. What was more, the two were both hopelessly unlucky in love, a stroke of bad luck that saw them share a bitterness for happy-ever-after endings.

"We were the ones in the back of the class saying negative things about *Romeo And Juliet* because we were so bitter towards that emotion at that time," Abigail explained. "We just really connected – we were obsessed with [the film] *Napoleon Dynamite* and ever since then we have been inseparable."

Taylor had even opposed the emotion of love in her darkest moments having penned songs such as 'Matches', where she tried to burn the emotion down, but now she wasn't alone in her fury; she had a like-minded friend who agreed with her.

Napoleon Dynamite appealed to Taylor because it centred around an eccentric and sometimes lonesome high school student like herself. Napoleon was a perpetual daydreamer, spending his school hours doodling mythical creatures such as 'ligers', a cross between a lion and a tiger. She liked the light-hearted comedy so much that she adopted the characters' accents as her own.

"Me and Abigail always talk with Minnesota accents," Taylor later explained to *The St. Petersburg Times*. "Everyone thinks we're weird. When I was in ninth grade, I didn't talk in any other voice except *Napoleon Dynamite* the entire year!"

She left her classmates incredulous. Beyond that, Taylor was a science buff – an instant ingredient for unpopularity – and one of her favourite items of clothing was a T-shirt emblazoned with the chemical elements of the Periodic Table. Added to which one of her closest friends, along with Abigail, was a boy named Paul who was obsessed with *Star Wars*. Consequently, Taylor still saw herself as hideously unpopular, but at least now she had friends to share her predicament with.

"[Abigail and I] kind of came to the conclusion in ninth grade that we were never going to be popular," Taylor confided to *The LA Times*, "so we should just stick together and have fun and not take ourselves too seriously."

The Minnesota accents were one example of that. Plus whenever there was a school dance, while the others would max out their parents' credit cards on expensive dresses and tuxedos, Taylor and Abigail would opt out. Instead of dancing the night away, they casually gossiped at each other's houses and filled up on chocolate ice cream. "[I don't want to] go out and get drunk," Taylor explained to *The Telegraph*. "I remember at school trying to cheer up my girlfriends who were crying in the bathroom after some party, when they couldn't remember who they'd made out with the night before... I don't ever want to be that girl in the bathroom crying."

Taylor may not have had a penchant for partying – in fact she was more likely to have a date with a DVD – but, in spite of that, she quickly found herself a boyfriend. Alas, she and senior year student Brandon Borello were passing ships in each other's lives, with Taylor arriving in town just weeks before Brandon was due to leave to go to college. It was a fleeting relationship, but in Taylor's eyes it was still worthy of a song.

Within a week of enrolling at Hendersonville High, she had penned 'Our Song' for him and publicly entered it into the school's talent show. "[Brandon and I] didn't have a song, so I went ahead and wrote us one," Taylor told *Great American Country*. "I wrote it in like 15 minutes. I wanted a song that would make people tap their feet."

It certainly did that – but little did she know that, a few years into the future, it would be lighting up the number-one spot on the country charts for six weeks running.

In the meantime, Taylor made a name for herself with the talent show, which saw strangers stop her in corridors to rave about her "incredible ability". People's perceptions of her also began to change. "When I first met her, I thought that she was kind of selfish and mean, but she knew about books," classmate and scholarship dance student Damla Taner told the author. "That was my first impression, then I got to know her better and I realised that she wasn't selfish, just a little bit excited. She was so nice to everyone."

She was right about one thing – Taylor definitely knew her books. In fact, she once shocked classmates by writing an impromptu thriller after her gym class. "One day, she just sat down and started to write," Damla explained, "and 20 or 30 minutes later she was reading a short story about a killer who fell in love with the Duke's daughter in England in 1891."

Taylor made an explosive impression on her classmates in chemistry too, when a fit of temper over a failed experiment sent the contents of her test tube flying across the room. "I will never forget that," Damla chuckled. "We should've mixed some acid and base and then it should have turned a blue-purple colour. I was sitting on Taylor's left-side desk and she was doing it like she really knows what she's doing and she mixed them and... nothing happened. She mixed it again and then she just lost control and started shaking it. Then it turned purple and she was like, 'Yes! *Yes!* I did see it, I did! Yes! Ha – what happens now?' While she was saying those words, the mixture started to rise up and boil all over her dress and my desk. Most memorable thing in my life ever with her!"

Whether she was drenching herself with chemicals or writing unlikely love stories and bloodthirsty murder mysteries, Taylor was certainly making an impact on her new friends. However, unsurprisingly, the thing that stood out most about Taylor was her love of music.

She would hastily excuse herself from lessons and rush to the toilet to record a verse that had just popped into her head, or hum a guitar lick for future reference. She also whipped out her mobile phone for an impromptu voice recording, no matter where she was, which perturbed some of her fellow students.

"It was a little awkward for us sometimes when she just sang to her phone and played the air drums, air piano or air guitar," Damla continued. "But I know why now!"

Taylor was also able to show off her voice more formally at the school's theatre productions. History repeated itself when Taylor won the role of Maria in the class performance of *The Sound Of Music* – just three years after playing the same role back in Pennsylvania.

For the first time, Taylor was beginning to enjoy school life – but then a bolt of unlucky lightning struck twice. First, she broke up with Brandon, who was leaving to pursue college. He left amid rumours that he had cheated on Taylor less than two weeks after they first got together. Within days of discovering his alleged infidelity, Taylor had a call from RCA – and it was bad news.

"Basically there were three things that were going to happen," Taylor later explained of her deal with the label. "They were going to drop me, or shelve me – that's kind of like putting me in cold storage – or give me a record deal. The only one of those that you want is the record deal."

Keeping her in development had meant that the label was happy to pay for her to record demos and to offer her mentoring and resources, but – perhaps surprisingly, given their financial investment – they weren't commiting to releasing any of her material afterwards. They would simply monitor her progress until they felt she was ready. Taylor had felt she was ready years ago, but, when RCA phoned, they revealed they were unhappy with her performance and planned to shelve her for at least another year. She knew what she had to do.

"After a year of development, we just decided that we wanted to look round, so we walked," she told *Entertainment Weekly*. "It's not a really popular thing to do in Nashville, to walk away from a major record deal – but that's what I did."

Taylor had been unhappy for several reasons. Firstly, she wasn't keen on singing other people's songs, but RCA refused to let her record her own. "I had so many songs I wanted people to hear [so] I did not want to be on a record label that wanted me to cut other people's stuff," she continued. "That wasn't where I wanted to be."

She was also alarmed at the prospect of being held back, when she had a catalogue of her own creations ready to go. "I genuinely felt I was running out of time," she added. "I'd written all these songs and I wanted to capture these years of my life on an album while they still represented what I was going through."

Finally, the atmosphere at the label was stifling to Taylor. She couldn't relate to songs she hadn't written and she felt insulted that the company didn't have any confidence in her own. She wanted to work with a label that believed in her abilities as much as she herself did, if not more so.

Taylor liberated herself from her contract and hit the road, relieved that at least she had her Sony songwriting job to fall back on. What was more, now that she lived around Nashville, she was able to take advantage of their facilities every day.

"It was a really weird existence," Taylor recalled to *Entertainment Weekly*. "I was a teenager during the day when I was at school and then at night it was like I was 45. My mom would pick me up from school and I'd go downstairs and write songs with these hit songwriters."

Taylor was happy to team her lyrics and melodies with a producer's technical skills – provided that they treated her as an equal and gave her some input into the music that they were writing. However, she guessed correctly that, at her tender age, she was going to have to work doubly hard to convince the writers she was working with that she deserved to be there at all.

She wanted to be a co-writer, enjoying an exchange of ideas with talented people, but many of those that she met were three times her age and extremely sceptical of handing the reins down to a 14-year-old, no matter how enthusiastic.

"I knew every writer I wrote with was pretty much going to think, 'I'm going to write a song for a 14-year-old today,'" Taylor told *The New York Times*. "So I would come into each meeting with five to 10 ideas they were solid. I wanted them to look at me as a person they were writing with, not a little kid."

It was a smart defence. Yet time and again, Taylor struggled with people's perceptions that she was the face of the song, instead of the brains behind it.

On one memorable occasion, Taylor sang a guitar lick to an unnamed producer the way she felt it should sound on the song – and he was instantly dismissive. "He said: 'Little girl, you know I am the producer and you are a little girl who is here to sing this song. So why don't you do what you do and I'll do what I do?'" Taylor recalled to *American Way*.

She recoiled, too timid to question his response, but then vowed that would be the last song they ever worked on together. "I would always be polite about it, but I would know that I never needed to work with that person again," she continued. "I never wanted to be known as a spoilt brat, but I never wanted to be working directly with someone who didn't believe that I had any musical intuition [either]."

According to Taylor's mother, this was far more than the demands of a precocious teenager determined to get her own way – she genuinely had a sense of how every aspect of the song should sound. "When she writes her songs, she hears them in her head," Andrea revealed to *The LA Times*, "and she knows where she wants the mandolin to come in, or what guitar lick should be there."

From then on, Taylor would have to divide the writers she met into two teams. "Basically, there are two kinds of people – people who see me as an artist and judge me by music," Taylor explained to *Great American Country*. "The other kind of people judge me by a number – my age, which means nothing."

That wasn't the case with Texan songwriter Liz Rose, who described herself as "open-minded" from the start. She was cerebral, like her young workmate, once declaring that her favourite instrument to work with was her brain, but she wasn't a dominant personality in the studio. For her, it was all about accessing someone's innermost feelings and thus working together with the singer to apply them to the song. "Whoever I'm in the room with, I pick their brain and make them spill their guts!" Liz joked to *Music Row* magazine. "I'm there to help artists say what they want to say."

Although she was lending a helping hand to develop the songs, Liz also gave Taylor space for creative freedom and self-expression. During the moments when Taylor was heating up in the kitchen, she preferred to step back. "She's incredible!" she recalled later. "I just stay out of the way!"

Taylor threw herself into writing with Liz, producing dozens of songs – most of which were never officially released. In 'Stupid Boy', Taylor rebels against her fate as a partner's plaything, feeling that she had misjudged his love. She endures a pain so strong in the aftermath that she feels almost compelled to rip her heart out. It was times like these that inspired Taylor to speak out against Shakespeare from the back of her English class, feeling that true love would never be hers. Similarly in 'Never Mind', a boy who isn't acting right loses out on her love before a romance even begins.

Taylor's taking no prisoners again in 'R.E.V.E.N.G.E', in which she spits out each letter of the word with formidable fury. However, she seems to have recovered her old-school game of romance in 'Perfect Have I Loved'. Here she reminisces on time spent together, including hilarious moments getting hopelessly stuck when her loved one's truck submerges in the creek. She suggests that if the two of them swear by the moon never to part, then there is no barrier to growing old together.

In 'All Night Diner', Taylor questions whether she is worthy of all that the man in her life has to offer, believing that without him to inspire her, she would be nothing.

Then 'Ten Dollars And A Six Pack' features someone Taylor's fallen for, but her infatuation falls on deaf ears when she talks of him to her family and friends and it becomes the ultimate tale of a forbidden affair. She's fallen deep, but, to her horrified loved ones, the news is on a par with evangelical Christian Katy Perry bringing home notorious womaniser and self-confessed heathen Russell Brand for tea – something just isn't right. In the song, Taylor describes the lengths she would go to in persuading people her man is the one for her – but to no avail.

"I don't remember all the demo songs I hear," one anonymous studio worker revealed, "but this one stood out. So many songs are written around here and so many end up in the trash – it's all about experimenting to find what fits. If it's a new artist, they're usually trying to develop an identity as a singer that's unique to them, so in those early stages I wouldn't take much notice of individual songs.

"But this one dealt with something almost everyone goes through at some stage, whether you're 13 or 60. Imagine you're a multi-cultural couple who are serious about each other, but you're of different faiths and your parents don't approve, or an old-fashioned country boy is taking a stripper home to his parents and telling them this is the woman he wants to marry. Or a girl's bringing a guy 10 years older, plastered in tattoos and with a string of infidelities behind him, into her life. But love doesn't discriminate on looks, age, religion or colour. Sometimes love just happens – and that's what this song was about."

However, in this story, Taylor, who was betting on him being the perfect man for her, has to face 'I told you so' taunts when she takes him to a bar, only to find him constantly eyeing up other girls. With reluctance, she has to admit that her friends were right – and that she owes them $10 and a six pack of their chosen poison.

Less complicated love stories included 'Made Up You', a tune where dreams and reality meet in the middle. As Taylor gets to know the person she has fallen in love with from afar, she discovers the fantasies she has built up in her mind of him are coming true and that he really is everything she's imagined.

'Check Out This View' describes beautiful scenes such as the waves of the ocean crashing against the bay, but reveals that the joy of seeing them is bittersweet as no view could be more beautiful than the eyes of the guy she has just broken up with.

Meanwhile, 'You Do' is an ode to the type of passionate love that almost becomes a sickness, where the victim can't eat, sleep or think straight and the memories of a kiss make their hands shake in anticipation.

Yet all good things must come to an end, as she discovers in 'Perfectly Good Heart'. She subjects her first love to an inquisition, asking why she wanted to break her heart and inflict its first scar. Before the break-up, Taylor threw herself passionately into relationships, but this betrayal has left her afraid to love at all. In between berating herself for not seeing the signs of an ending and the distance in her boyfriend's eyes, she asks how she can get back to the unblemished girl she used to be, before someone stole her innocence.

The majority of Taylor's songs were about romantic relationships, although she did occasionally veer from the subject. For example, 'Gracie' tells the story of a childhood leukaemia victim she knew. By the age of five, hospital had already become Gracie's second home. This was Taylor's way to reach through the darkness and penetrate the girl's world with a song.

Then, in a rare moment of anger, Taylor's in fight mode, slipping on her boxing gloves to take on a pretty but talentless prom queen she knows. While her rival aspires to be a singer because it's fashionable to be famous, Taylor has been one from the beginning. The mystery girl, who longs to be the centre of attention in any way she can, is no match for her. She hints that, even with handwritten lyrics scribbled in a notepad and an old guitar in a beaten-up old case, she still overshadows her flashier rival. Music wins out over beauty eventually, when Taylor demands to know where the pageant queen's crown will get her in the singing stakes. She challenges her to strip down to her real self, join Taylor in an empty room and see who wins the battle then.

According to one of Taylor's close friends, the girl she had in mind had used sexual favours and good looks to seduce her way into the music industry and had slept her way to the top. "If it's the girl I think it is, she was totally shameless," Taylor's friend revealed to the author. "She was ruthlessly ambitious and she used her looks to disguise the lack of any real talent. Anywhere she got, she got there by sleeping with somebody, or promising that she would. If she could win someone over that way, it made her feel powerful. She was mean and spiteful – the type of girl who would throw her own mother under a bus to get what she wanted. All Taylor was pointing out, I think, was that – in her sad world – she never realised it was talent that was really important."

Most of Taylor's songs were composed with Liz Rose, although she did have some successful writing sessions with other producers, such as the Warren Brothers. Brad and Brett Warren even sang background vocals for her on 'That's When', a demo about a commitment-phobe who dangles his girlfriend on a string while he decides whether he wants to be with her. While the song was thematically similar to Katy Perry's 'Hot And Cold', it lacked the pop hook of that tune, remaining true to its country roots.

By this time, Taylor was starting to become a small-scale legend at her publishing company offices and had definitely proved herself musically. Before long, unannounced visitors were knocking on her door demanding to write with her. Everyone wanted a piece of the action with the girl who, despite being younger than many of her counterparts' sons and daughters, was said to have a lightning-fast songwriting speed and an impressive grasp of relationship topics.

One of her many admirers was Blu Sanders, a local songwriter who – taking a proactive approach – propelled himself to the front of the queue. "She was writing with someone else and I stuck my head in the room and told her I wanted to write with her," Blu revealed to the author of that first meeting. "In songwriting, everyone's looking for someone young and good to latch on to in hope that they do well and you can be part of it as it grows. Taylor was writing around town, so people knew about her and that she had something happening."

By the time they first started working together, Taylor hadn't even reached her 15th birthday. However, her reputation was already beginning to precede her. Blu had high expectations – in fact, she had him feeling "intimidated" by her lyrical prowess from the first verse.

"If I remember correctly, she came in with the first couple of lines which I thought were some pretty heavy lyrics for a 14-year-old," Blu recalled incredulously. "I was a bit intimidated, frankly. Guy in mid-thirties with confident teenage co-writer. People like to bash young, successful artists. Attribute it to their label, marketing, the target market, but Taylor was the real deal. I know first-hand that the girl at a young age, before her first record ever came out, was more driven and focused than I've probably ever been. When I was 15, I was kicking the soccer ball around, not writing songs!"

Despite their differences in age, they soon found a winning formula with which to work together. Taylor offered the first few lyrics of the track, while Blu began to experiment with some alternative tunings and the pair also collaborated on suitable melodies, until eventually the framework of a song came together.

However, Taylor knew what she wanted in some regards from the outset. "I remember throwing chorus ideas to her and she was certainly not afraid to say no to things she didn't like," Blu explained.

When the track took shape, it was called 'Is This Really Happening?' and it became an ode to a love affair that seemed almost too good to be true. "It's about being in a relationship or a moment with someone and it's amazing and you sort of have to pinch yourself and wonder if it could be as good as it seems," he added. However, while Blu connected instantly to her as a writer, he wasn't so sure how to relate to the teenage optimism that flowed through her work. "The challenge in writing with someone else is making [the lyrics] mean something to two different people with completely different lives," he revealed. "I'm a jaded 30-something. If I had to guess, I'd say a teenager has more of those moments than I do. Maybe I need to rethink my approach!"

Despite spending several hours on the track, it was never recorded in the studio with a band – instead it seemed destined to remain an acoustic demo forever. The irony was that, just like the song Taylor had been picturing, the love affair was more of a fantasy than a reality and never really got off the ground.

"I still think the song stands up on its own," Blu declared. "I love the lyrics and I love the melody and I actually thought it was going to make her first album. But then I'd be [speaking to you] from my beach house, instead of my brother's air mattress, if it did."

One early song that was destined to go on to greater things, however, was an early version of 'Teardrops On My Guitar'. Taylor had been hoarding many of her compositions, becoming so attached to them that she couldn't bear to let them go. However, on the recommendation of Sony, she considered pitching some of her songs to big-name artists – a way to quickly build up credibility, money and fame.

'Teardrops On My Guitar' instantly came to mind for a potential sale. The track exorcised Taylor's pain about an unrequited crush she had on part-time semi-professional wrestler Drew Hardwick, a tall, dark, handsome student at her school. "I used to have a huge crush on this guy, who would sit there every day talking to me about another girl – how beautiful she was, how nice, smart and perfect she was," Taylor lamented to Country Music Television. "I sat there listening, never meaning it any of the times I said, 'Oh, I'm so happy for you.'"

Drew had seen Taylor as a confidante, a sounding board for him to wax lyrical about his glamorous new girlfriend. He had no idea Taylor was secretly falling for him – and, as his relationship with the other girl deepened, she began to think he would never see her as potential dating material at all. "I guess this is an example of how I let my feelings out in songs and sometimes no other way," Taylor continued. "I love this song because of its honesty and vulnerability."

Reluctantly, Taylor decided to offer her beloved track to The Dixie Chicks, substituting the word "you" for "Drew". When they turned it down, she reclaimed it for herself and shelved it for future reference. Then, before she had the chance to try to sell any other songs, there was a development in Taylor's own career when Scott Borchetta came into her life.

Scott had started life in Southern California and, when growing up, had been a player on the Hollywood scene. As someone who fronted several rock groups in his youth, he seemed an unlikely candidate to be involved in the country scene. Yet, by 1981, he had left his fast-paced rock 'n' roll lifestyle behind and had a yearning to settle in Nashville.

He began his musical career there as a lowly mailroom worker on the lowest rung on the ladder, whose job was to sort through the endless stream of post and distinguish the main important packages from those destined for the trash. It was hardly a thrill, but, by 1996, he had worked his way up enough to join the major record label DreamWorks, a start-up company owned by Hollywood movie moguls such as Steven Spielberg.

That company had a country division, DreamWorks Nashville, and it was at his office there that Scott invited Taylor for a meeting. He had heard that she shone as a song writer and, when she whipped out her guitar and gave an impromptu performance for him, he wasn't disappointed. DreamWorks Nashville was about to close and Scott was on the lookout for new artists, hoping that he could set up a brand new label of his own.

Within weeks, his contacts had arranged a showcase for her at the Bluebird Café so that he could test her in front of an audience, and in November 2004 – just a month before her 15th birthday – Taylor performed there. The small, 100-seater café was tucked away on a quiet street, so unassuming that even those looking for it might accidentally walk right past.

But those in the know kept the place packed to the rafters. On an average night, press photographers, award-winning song writers, record-label bosses and talent spotters mingled, all with the hope of discovering the next big thing. If the crowd was lucky, big-name artists like LeAnn Rimes might be seen, trying to blend in with the punters.

The club had a history of spawning famous artists – Kathy Mattea, Garth Brooks, Faith Hill and Kevin Chesney had all started out there. It had also provided the setting for River Phoenix's last film, *The Thing Called Love*, released in 2003 and also starring Sandra Bullock.

The venue had certainly received its fair share of attention – but while it might have featured in national newspapers and major films, it wasn't all about the celebrity. Its website claimed: "Any given week, we have film crews, national photographers and celebrity visits, but it is always the music that people remember and the songs that keep Bluebird devotees 'shushed'."

These were bold words – now the club had a reputation to uphold and a responsibility to live up to its promises. It had to ensure the audience was silent with admiration, not covering its eyes in collective horror. Thus, those planning to play a showcase had to take part in a stringent audition procedure, judged by an intimidating panel of both Bluebird staff and other professionals in the industry. Founder Amy Kurland had claimed that all it took was 60 seconds for a listener to be won over by a song – or, on the other hand, to become bored enough by it to switch the radio station.

Based on that philosophy, nervous entrants were given just a one-minute slot to impress the judges. What was more, there could be no percussion or backing tracks – it would be a purely acoustic performance. This format was designed to show off their voices at their clearest – or, alternatively, reveal their every weakness. However, most of Taylor's demos had started off in an acoustic format and she had practised way more times than she could remember, so she had no shortage of confidence.

Taylor realised she had made an immediate impression on Scott, later commenting: "Out of all the people in the room, he was the only one who had his eyes closed and was totally into the music."

And when Scott did open his eyes, he was looking around frantically to survey the reactions of the competition. He had his eye on Taylor, believing she had the potential to be something big – but he knew very well he wasn't the only one who noticed her earlier. "There were several other record companies in the room," Scott later told CBS, "and I'm looking round going, 'I hope none of these other guys are getting it.'"

Feeling he had to act fast before Taylor was snapped up by a rival label, Scott called her within days. At first his plan was thwarted when he was confronted with a recorded voicemail message explaining: "Hey, it's Taylor. I can't get your call right now, but call back like 100 times and I'll get back to you."

Barely repressing his frustration and impatience, Scott tried again – and eventually got through to relay his clandestine message. "He was like, 'I'm going to be doing something and I need to talk to you in person because I don't trust the phone,'" Taylor recalled to *Great American Country*. "And I was like, 'If you don't trust the phone, there has got to be something going on that I want to know about!'"

The mystery surrounding the meeting appealed to Taylor's sense of adventure. When she found out he was about to set up a new label and wanted to make her his very first signing, she was flattered, excited and "absolutely blown away". However, the label was to be a small, independent one – it had no links to a large corporation and, compared to the giants in the business, his financial backing was miniscule.

In spite of these inauspicious beginnings, Scott was praying his new venture could provide meaningful competition to the major labels on Music Row. However, the statistics at that time suggested that fewer than two out of ten music business ventures prospered, so the odds of getting off the ground, let alone surviving, were uncertain.

Taking a chance on a tiny label that had yet to release a single CD was a huge risk for an unknown singer. That said, Scott told Taylor he respected her vision and wanted her to come into her own as an artist – something which, after the fiasco at RCA, was a very appealing proposition for her. "Obviously, creative control is the most important thing for me," Taylor would later tell *The LA Times* wryly, "or I wouldn't have left the biggest label in Nashville for a label that didn't have any furniture."

So Taylor was in – after all, what did she have to lose? She accepted, joining Big Machine Records as Scott's very first signing.

Chapter 6

Named And Shamed

It had started out like any other day in the life of a typical American teenager – textbooks, timetables and early morning gossip. But Taylor was no ordinary school girl – and today, it wasn't her best friend sitting beside her, but a magazine journalist. While Abigail Anderson's biggest fear that day was getting caught out for not memorising her Latin verbs, Taylor's was trying to live up to her new moniker as Nashville's next superstar.

She had barely put her books down for fashion class when a voice crackled over the intercom, summoning her to reception. From there, she and her mother would jump into a car and start the journey downtown faster than a Ferrari on a race track. Once she left the safety of the school gates behind, she would be subjected to the scrutiny of the press, the public and a full camera crew, but it was all for a purpose. Today she was officially signing to Big Machine Records, and she was the star of the label's first ever press conference.

According to classmates, her day's absence from school meant little. "She'd just have been scribbling lyrics at her desk anyway," one joked. "She was on the brink of the biggest opportunity of her life – would you be paying much attention in class?" Indeed, after years of searching for the right label, she had found one which signed her without hesitation – but tensions were running high for both parties.

It had been a risk for Taylor to sign up to a record company that didn't yet formally exist, at a stage when it was nothing more than an idea in her employer's head. Yet for Scott, who already boasted over 20 years of experience in the industry and had a reputation to protect, expectations of success were higher and the risks were even greater. "He broke two rules," one local record executive told *Blender*. "Taylor was a teenager *and* she was female."

In an industry that catered predominantly to the musical urges of much older listeners, bringing Taylor in was breaking the mould. What was more, a large number of those listeners were female – and statistics showed that they often preferred to have crooners of the opposite sex on their radar.

Even worse, one national music magazine, *Entertainment Weekly*, had suggested without irony that no one under the age of 25 with any cool credentials would even consider buying a country album. It wasn't looking good for Taylor's campaign.

However, she firmly defended her right to be a young, successful female country artist who broke the boundaries, telling *Entertainment Weekly*: "All the songs I heard on the radio were about marriage and kids and settling down. I just couldn't relate to that. I kept writing songs about the guy who I dated for a couple of weeks and who cheated on me, about all the things I was going through. There was no reason why country music shouldn't relate to someone my age if someone my age was writing it."

Taylor would prove that sentiment correct when her debut became the first female-fronted album in the USA written or co-written by the singer to sell a million copies. However, right now, before she had so much as sold a single song, she had a lot to prove – and some of Scott's peers openly thought he was insane.

"People would look at me cross-eyed [when I told them I was signing Taylor]," he confessed to *The New York Times*. "I would feel like they were deleting me from their Blackberry as I was telling them!"

Scott was sacrificing his credibility by the second and risked making himself a laughing stock with his new teenage protégée if she didn't deliver – but he still believed she was the "full package".

The press conference was a success, seeing Taylor switch from her school uniform into a figure-hugging yet modest little black dress. She posed for photos with her new team, armed with an acoustic guitar – all she felt she needed to make it to the top. Scott celebrated the launch with champagne, while Taylor stuck to soft drinks – but once the elation had died down, that was when the real work began.

Now Taylor had something to prove – both to the non-believers and to the existing fans she had attracted who were relying on her not to let them down. She was now balancing a full curriculum of lessons with rushing into the studio after hours, spending evenings planning her grand entrance into the music world.

It was time to start sourcing potential material for her debut album – though she had no shortage of tracks to showcase. "I've been very selfish about my songs," Taylor later confessed to CMT. "I had this dream of this project coming out for so many years that I just stockpiled."

She had a catalogue of dozens of acoustic tracks to choose from, but most of these failed to make the cut. However, Taylor and Scott also looked at the contents of two promotional CDs she had released a little earlier in the year, on tiny independent label Majorly Indie. These had been used to make her music known to radio stations and had been released just prior to signing with Big Machine Records, so they contained some of her most recent material.

One track, 'Superstar', explores the inferiority complex Taylor has developed following a crush on a musical legend. Her affections are complicated by the fact that, as a would-be singer herself, she doesn't only want to be with him – she wants to be him too and experience the fruits of his success at first-hand. While hundreds of girls scream his name at the front row of his concerts, Taylor longs to be singled out but realises it's impossible, as she sees herself, in sharp contrast, as far from special.

She sings herself to sleep with the sounds of the superstar humming through her headphones, but when she wakes up, she laments that he will already be in another new location. As he races from one city to another, it is as if time has stood still for an unhappy Taylor, as she wakes up in the same place where she has always lived, clutching his photograph and dreaming of bigger things. She mourns that there will be no real-life romance because she is just one of his many admirers – and not only does she lack her fantasy man, but she lacks his fame too.

The track seemed relevant to audiences, as many teenage music fans might have had a similar experience of feeling insignificant in comparison to their gregarious idols. However, in the end, it wouldn't make the cut.

Taylor explored her melancholic side further on 'We Were Happy'. Here she talks about a teenage relationship that has run its course, describing how, at its height, the pair sneaked into the circus without paying, watched sunsets by the lake and took long walks in the dark. The couple had even talked about marriage, buying his father's farm and living together forever – but their plans ended in failure. This track exorcises some of the disappointment about what could have been.

'Your Face' is another song about the aftermath of the same relationship. Keen to capture the memories and keep them alive forever, Taylor fears that even these may be slipping away with the passage of time. All she has left to prove he ever existed is his photograph – and even as she looks at it, she questions whether he was ever there at all.

Next, 'The Cure' sees Taylor desperately in love, wishing that she were ill so the object of her infatuation could be the remedy. Another song, 'Sweet Tea And God's Graces' – which had been considered potential single material – talks about a girl who crashes and burns after a tragic affair. Taylor concludes that she loved too deeply, and she has learned to keep a harder heart – but it's still tender enough to make her cry. Taylor had to be ruthless and give these songs the chop, too.

Many of these songs were either composed during dark times in her life or looked back to when she was heartbroken, friendless and struggling to get a career off the ground. Now that she had a record deal and life was a little easier, the atmosphere captured on the tracks no longer reflected how she was feeling. She decided it was time to move on – but she did save a few tracks from her promo CDs, including 'Our Song', the upbeat number she had written for Brandon Borello, her first boyfriend at Hendersonville High.

Ironically, it was one song she had never intended to release publicly. However, months after she had performed it at the school talent show, her classmates approached her and started singing it. "They'd only heard it once," Taylor recalled to *Great American Country* incredulously, "so I thought, 'There must be something here!'"

If the hook was catchy enough to be memorable to them months on, then she felt it was special enough to take a chance on. "You really can't go wrong with the banjo," she recalled later.

Despite being one of the first songs to make the track list, Taylor was determined that it should be the last track on the album as a subliminal message to her listeners. "I wanted it to be last, because the last line of the chorus is 'Play it again'," Taylor joked. "Let's hope people take it as a hint to go ahead and play the album again!"

Out of her older tracks, Taylor also selected 'Teardrops On My Guitar' and 'The Outside' for the album, as well as another song that she wrote as soon as she moved to Nashville, 'A Place In This World'.

Although Taylor's parents had never pressurised her to find fame, instead casually presenting their new life cross-country as "a move to a nice community", she had been terrified of failing. She had an action plan, but there was nothing predictable about carrying it out and each day became an mystery. However, when the daily hustle began to get her down, Taylor did what she always did when confronted by emotions she couldn't handle – she wrote a song.

"It was tough trying to find out how I was going to get where I wanted to go," Taylor explained. "I knew where I wanted to be but I just didn't know how to get there. I'm really happy ['A Place In This World' was added to] the album because I feel like I finally figured it out."

An unlucky-in-love Taylor then penned a track called 'Stay Beautiful', about her former love interest, Corey Robinson, who had chosen her friend over her back in Wyomissing. She also wrote a song about the girl he dated instead, Angelina, listing all the ways she would never be able to compete with her more glamorous rival, but again it wouldn't make the cut. In her eyes, however, not dating Corey turned out to be the best move she ever made.

"After hearing my songs, a lot of people ask me, 'How many boyfriends have you had?' and I always tell them that more of my songs come from observation than actual experience," joked Taylor. "In other words, you don't have to date someone to write a song about them... This song is about a guy I thought was cute and I never really talked to him much. But something about him inspired this song, just watching him."

Taylor also played the silent observer in 'Cold As You', taking a step back from a boy and, removing the rose-tinted glasses from her eyes, quickly discovering that he isn't worth defending. "It's about that moment when you realise someone isn't all that you thought they were, and that you've been trying to make excuses for someone who doesn't deserve them," Taylor explained. "Some people are just never going to love you."

She finally takes solace in the knowledge that while he's as cold as ice, her heart will always be warm. Another comfort was that, not only could she exorcise her demons with a song, but each failed relationship or burst of outrage was an inspiration and a potential commercial opportunity.

Taylor would also build a reputation for herself as a formidable girl, someone not to be messed with unless the offender wanted to end up named and shamed in a song. While the best the average woman scorned could provide in the way of revenge was a cruel Facebook taunt, Taylor was taking public humiliation to a whole new level. A past partner's secrets could be unveiled worldwide and their legacy would last a lot longer in a song.

"The cool thing about being a songwriter is, whatever you go through, you can write a song about it and turn it into something good for your career," Taylor later chuckled to *Blender*.

'Picture To Burn' was another example of the perfect revenge. "This song is the angry song on my album," she told CMT. "I think girls can relate to the song because basically it's about just being mad – and it's okay to be mad after a breakup or after something goes wrong with a relationship. It's just like completely, brutally, honest."

The fieriness calmed down a little with 'Mary's Song (Oh My My My)', a dedication to an almost life-long relationship between the couple who lived next door. As someone whose longest relationship at that point had been just two weeks, she took comfort in seeing that long-term relationships really were possible to sustain.

"I made this song about a couple who lived next door to us," Taylor explained. "They'd been married forever and they came over one night for dinner and were just so cute. They were talking about how they fell in love and got married and how they met when they were just little kids. I thought it was so sweet, because you can go to the grocery store and read the tabloids and see who's breaking up and cheating on each other (or just listen to some of my songs!). But it was really comforting to know that all I had to do was go home and look next door to see a perfect example of forever."

Later, when Taylor would be mixing with showbiz crowds and having her heart broken by promiscuous fellow musicians, she would need that reminder all the more.

Another song, 'Tied Together With A Smile', addressed something she believed to be the biggest enemy of teenage girls in America – "insecurity". It's a true story about a friend who wears a deceptive smile that hides all kinds of agonies underneath. She is promiscuous and seductive, but she's looking for affection in all the wrong places. She is the object of envy for miles around, but when she looks in the mirror, she doesn't consider herself pretty. Worst of all, she's been making herself sick.

"She's absolutely beautiful," Taylor elaborated. "She goes to beauty pageants and wins everything. Girls want to be her and guys want to be with her. I wrote this song the day I found out about her eating disorder. It completely blew my mind and this one was tough to write, because I wasn't just telling some sad story – this one was real."

Ironically, due to her beauty, she was the last person Taylor expected to come down with bulimia. "That is one of the moments when your heart kind of stops," she admitted to *Glamour* of hearing her friend's revelation. "How can somebody that seems so strong have such a horrible, horrible weakness? Something that is killing her."

Taylor didn't intend her song as a lecture – instead it was a gentle gesture of support to let her know that, no matter what she went through, she wouldn't judge her. After a few chats with other friends, Taylor persuaded her friend to seek help and, by the time the song was produced, she was well on the way to recovery. What was more, unlike the cheating men whose identity Taylor made no effort to disguise, she had protected her friend's dignity by declining to name her.

Another new song was 'I'd Lie', a story about being friends with a boy she secretly wanted to date. Her feelings are shrouded in secrecy and, when he asks if she loves him, she defensively lies.

Since the positive reaction to 'Our Song', Taylor had started to seek out her friends' feedback on all of her newer songs, streaming them on the internet or playing them in person to classmates in her bedroom or gathered around a camp fire. Her friends were a vital connection between her and the music-buying public and, until her songs hit the airwaves, they were her only source of public opinion. Taylor's target audience was first and foremost teenagers like herself, so when 'I'd Lie' was universally approved by the Nashville crowd she listened and scheduled it to appear on her album.

However, just days before the final mastering of the album and hours before the sleeve was due to be printed, she made a terrifying discovery – her then boyfriend Sam had cheated. With a cry of "Stop press!" she brought the CD's progress to a standstill.

"It was something really, really dramatic and crazy happening to me," she later revealed, "and I needed to address it in the form of music." By the next day, 'Should've Said No' was recorded and 'I'd Lie' had been lifted from the album to accommodate it.

Later, Taylor reflected: "Just being a human being, I've realised that before every big problem you create for yourself, before every huge mess you have to clean up, there was a crucial moment when you could've just said no. This is a song I wrote about a guy who never should have cheated on me."

Changing the track-list at the very last minute was just one of the signs that Taylor was going to take Scott Borchetta out of his comfort zone. But she had already demanded that the album be produced by an inexperienced, virtual unknown who had never been part of an official album before.

Scott's heart was in his mouth, but Taylor knew what she wanted and, to her, taking charge of her album was a much more thrilling prospect than traditional teenage acts of rebellion such as drinking alcohol. "It's true that I've never had a burning desire to rebel," she confessed to *Entertainment Weekly*, "but... I've rebelled against people trying to push me around in the recording studio. To me, that's much more exciting than going out and getting drunk."

Nathan Chapman had been a promising demo producer who'd yet to have his big break, with a shabby makeshift office just behind the Sony studios. He was anything but a safe bet. However, following an introduction to Liz Rose, Taylor had been working with him for over a year. "I started out with this demo producer who worked in a little shed behind this publishing company I was at," she revealed to CMT fondly. "I'd always go in there and play him some new songs and the next week he would have this awesome track on which he played every instrument and it sounded like a record."

Taylor was delighted with the results but inevitably, once she scored her record deal, things started to change. "All of a sudden, it was, 'OK, we're going to use this producer,'" she continued. "So I got to record with a bunch of really awesome producers in Nashville, but it didn't sound the way that it did with Nathan."

Putting forward a producer without a single album credit to his name, whose former workplace had been a tiny shed, wasn't exactly the conventional way to impress a new label, but Taylor was insistent. Although her favoured producer had only ever made demos, her boss finally caved in, telling her: "OK, try some sides with Nathan."

According to Taylor, that was when "the right chemistry hit" and the album began to take shape. While the production was underway, she was also giving the public their answer to a question they never knew they had asked: Who is Taylor Swift?

The answer began, ironically, with someone else's name: her début single was all about country artist Tim McGraw. What was more, he was one of the top-selling artists of his genre in the world.

"We put that out deliberately so people would ask, 'Who's this new artist with a song called 'Tim McGraw'?" Scott Borchetta revealed.

Indeed, while a track with Tim's name attached to it was no guarantee of success, it was at the very least guaranteed some attention.

Tim, an established singer more than 20 years Taylor's senior, whose father had been a footballer for teams such as the Philadelphia Phillies, was a household name among country fans. He is married to fellow country veteran Faith Hill and, between them, they have sold over 64 million albums – a number equivalent to the entire population of the UK.

Tim's last eight albums had debuted at number one on the *Billboard* Country Chart, while Faith's last three had shot to the top on both the country and the mainstream charts. The two had quickly become the king and queen of their genre, and there were few contenders able to challenge the throne.

Meanwhile, Tim was setting out to dominate not just the charts but the world, starting by threatening to run for the position of governor in his home state of Tennessee. When not in the news for his chart performance, he was featured for his increasingly outlandish antics, once being arrested on suspicion of stealing a police horse in Buffalo, New York. Several weeks later, in a parody of the incident, his wife had stormed on stage in a police officer's uniform to take him into custody.

Now, just two months before the release of Taylor's first single, he and Faith were embarking on a joint tour that would become the most lucrative in country music history. The Soul2Soul II tour sold over a million tickets and grossed $89 million for just 73 nights, a feat that made pop giant Madonna's schedule look as small-scale as a concert at Hendersonville High. A wealthy, powerful and high-profile couple, they were to country what Beyoncé and Jay-Z were to R&B and hip-hop – and their names were synonymous with success.

Cunningly, Taylor was now about to take on Tim's entire fan base. Not only would a song with his name on it attract instant curiosity, but there was also a chance his followers would come across it accidentally as they trawled the internet for tracks by their idol.

However, she did risk inciting Tim's wrath with this technique – not least because she would be securing free publicity from it. Amy Winehouse had once tweeted, "Rihanna, you owe me!" when her pop rival had released a song called 'Rehab', which shared its name with a song by Amy. And when Katy Perry gushed that Scarlett Johansson had inspired her to write 'I Kissed A Girl', the actress had jokingly demanded a share of the royalties. Whether Tim would be amused, flattered, indifferent or just plain furious remained to be seen.

One thing was for sure – few listeners would have imagined that 'Tim McGraw' had been penned by a teenager in a moment of boredom during a painfully long algebra lesson. Like Britney Spears in the video for her debut single, 'Hit Me Baby One More Time', Taylor had been sitting in class, impatiently sneaking looks at the clock and daydreaming, before waiting for the bell to ring so that she could start singing. Yet, while Britney was an actress depicting a fantasy in the video, for Taylor the scenario was real life.

"The idea for this song came to me in math class," she explained. "I just started singing to myself, 'When you think Tim McGraw'… After school, I went downtown, sat at the piano and wrote this with Liz Rose in 15 minutes. It may be the best 15 minutes I've ever experienced."

It might have been a teasing marketing strategy to make fans of the biggest star in the genre sit up and take notice, but Taylor's love of Tim McGraw was genuine. She had been thinking of things that would remind her ex-boyfriend Brandon of her after he left town, and one of Taylor's trademarks was that she loved every song in Tim's back catalogue. Her ultimate favourite, and the one she had in mind when penning the track, was 'Can't Tell Me Nothin'' from his 2004 album *Live Like You Were Dying*.

According to co-writer Liz Rose, the instant Taylor had turned up at the studio, she had known "exactly what she wanted". However the loss of Brandon affected her so deeply that after the initial recording, she shelved the song for months, finding the memories too painful to relive. "It's thinking about a relationship you had and then lost," Taylor later explained. "I think one of the most powerful human emotions is what should have been and wasn't… A lot of people can relate to wanting something you can't have."

However, she was unable to hide it from Scott Borchetta for long, who – within seconds of hearing it – declared: "That's your first single!"

A puzzled Taylor responded, "Oh… so that's how that works, then!" It had taken some persuasion to convince her that the song had commercial potential, but she eventually relented – and the single was released on June 19, 2006.

This would be Scott's opportunity to prove to the non-believers that taking a chance on such an unconventional country singer had paid off – and, fortunately for him, the song's popularity spoke for itself. "From the moment 'Tim McGraw' hit the channel, she began to amass an audience that traditional Nashville didn't know or didn't believe existed – and that is young women, specifically teens," claimed Brian Philips, vice-president of CMT.

Indeed, internet forums were crammed with young female listeners who enjoyed the song. Plus, thanks to maintaining a connection with her followers by streaming some of her songs online prior to their release, Taylor already had a growing digital fan base. By the time 'Tim McGraw' was released, she had accumulated more than two million hits on her MySpace page. The song would also be downloaded more than half a million times in just five months. Slowly but surely, this started to translate into CD sales, with the track reaching a peak of number six on the *Billboard* Country Chart and number 40 on the mainstream chart.

The promo video was attracting some attention too. Taylor had personally cast a tall, dark-haired actor called Clayton Collins in the role of her love interest, due to his similarity to Brandon. She also added some authentic country style to the set – for instance, her ex-partner drives a vintage pick-up truck.

The video dealt with the impact a song can have on emotional memory – as soon as her ex turns the radio on, it triggers flashbacks to the moments he and Taylor shared, which was exactly her intention. "The video deals with the haunting power of music and how hearing a song years after it was first popular can have such an emotional appeal," Taylor elaborated.

The promo proved popular, receiving a nomination for 'Number 1 Streamed Video From A New Artist' in the CMT Online Awards that year. However, she lost out to Lindsey Hawn, whose track 'Broken' won the trophy instead.

But Taylor was working to increase her popularity every minute, taking to the road on a city-by-city radio tour that would keep her occupied for half of the year. Unlike in Britain, where cracking the principal national station, Radio 1, guarantees airplay throughout the country, artists in America must win over each station individually, which makes launching a new singer a painstaking and at times expensive process. Most artists would spend six weeks visiting stations personally, but Taylor had vowed to spend a whole six months meeting every single person who could be instrumental in shaping her career.

"I love it when people want to meet me," she explained, "because I want to meet them! Early on, my manager told me, 'If you want to sell 500,000 records, then go out there and meet 500,000 people.'"

Scott also gave Taylor some home truths about how hard it was to get radio play, but his advice only spurred her on to try harder. "I told her, 'They don't like to put new artists right on the air,'" he recalled. "She responded, 'Then that's the goal, isn't it?'"

She would sweet-talk a producer into paying her a compliment on her music and, as soon as she scored one, would blushingly thank him before suggesting a live broadcast there and then. "I mean, checkmate!" Scott laughed incredulously. "It was so adorable, you couldn't say no. It was deadly."

Taylor was discovering her womanly wiles and putting them to good use – and her intensive meet-and-greet tour with the stars also helped her to cross over into pop territory. "I walked into their radio stations as a 16-year-old girl with a song named 'Tim McGraw'," Taylor told CMT, "and I don't think it gets any weirder than that. The fact that they opened their arms and embraced me, I will never, ever forget them as long as I live. Country radio is where my base is and I love them so much, [but] the fact that pop radio stations are playing my songs is amazing to me. I am so blown away and thankful for it."

However, Taylor would have to make some sacrifices to fully embrace success – starting with school. She withdrew herself from Hendersonville High and enrolled at Christian distance-learning college Aaron Academy, which sent her assignments by mail. Although Taylor had hit 16 and was legally entitled to abandon education altogether, she was keen to complete school. So the pattern began of studying in the back of cars as she traversed almost every state in America.

Then, weeks after Taylor resumed studying full-time, she was invited on tour with fellow country artists Rascal Flatts, who were promoting their platinum-selling album *Me And My Gang*. "I've always been such a fan of their music and it means the world to me that they were the first major artists to take me out on the road," she told *Elle Girl*. "When I was 16, I barely had a single out and they believed in me enough to let me open up shows with them."

While Taylor was sharing the spotlight with six other headlining acts each night, she still appreciated the exposure – and her enthusiasm didn't go unnoticed by the media. "Awesome. Energetic. Entertaining. Fantastic. Absolutely incredible!" raved About.com of the Toronto show on November 1. "Taylor Swift was just 16 years old [but] now, after seeing her perform, I'm quite sure she'll be in the business for many years!"

She made an immediate impact with the audience, too, successfully urging them to hold their mobile phones in the air during 'Tim McGraw' so that the illuminated screens looked like "Georgia stars" in the sky. She also earned extra brownie points by honouring every single autograph request after the shows. "I'm still in the 'Oh my gosh, this is really happening' phase!" she joked. "I still haven't been able to grasp the fact that if I sign a piece of paper, it might mean something to somebody!"

Throughout the tour, Taylor wore a trademark lucky pair of red cowboy boots with a skull and crossbones logo emblazoned on them – but, while the dress code remained the same, little was predictable about each five-song set. One minute she was an innocent, inexperienced schoolgirl exclaiming that she had just been an ordinary student a few months earlier, and the next she was a vengeful man-eater, ready to declare war on those who had wronged her.

That war started with the release of the album. Taylor promoted the CD concurrently with the tour, performing on *Good Morning America* on October 29 to celebrate the first day of sales. In a matter of days, the phone started ringing. A string of Taylor's victims came forward, petrified that she would go a step further than just a song and reveal their secrets live on prime-time TV without disguising their identity.

However, Taylor was unrepentant. For example, she might not have named the cheating boyfriend who inspired 'Should've Said No' in the song itself, but she customised the lyric booklet, capitalising letters in each song to pick out relevant words – in this case, 'Sam, Sam, Sam, Sam, Sam'.

"I encoded [his] name over and over," Taylor chuckled to *Women's Health*. "It was only his first name but everyone [who knew him] figured it out. I'd get texts from him. He was scared out of his mind I'd crucify him on a talk show. All I could think was, 'Well, you should've said no. That's what the song is about.'"

Much to his horror, she was making no promises not to go ahead and spill the beans further. Her explanation? "I like to have the last word."

Her ode to wrestler Drew was equally unsubtle. The selected capitals in the lyrics for 'Teardrops On My Guitar' revealed the phrase "He will never know" – although he certainly did when the album hit the shelves. Within days, he started bombarding her with texts, phone calls and voice messages – all of which Taylor ignored. Having poured her heart out on CD, she felt too embarrassed to face him – plus, as far as she was concerned, she had said it all in a song.

She would later invite a *Blender* journalist on a tour of her old neighbourhood, complete with her ex-boyfriends' houses, pulling her car over at Drew's place to reveal: "I took my prom pictures in that backyard [but] I've totally moved on."

Other shout-outs to boyfriends were slightly more subtle – for example, the encoded lyrics for Brandon's songs were simple: "Can't tell me nothin'" in an ode to the 'Tim McGraw' track and "Live and love" for 'Our Song'. The reference to Corey Robinson – the boy she nearly dated – was virtually undetectable, merely name-checking a café that the pair had visited called Shake 'N' Bake. However that didn't save Corey from teasing. Everyone knew he had inspired the song.

"It became an on-going anthem that followed Corey around in classrooms, sporting events and parties long after Taylor's departure to Nashville," revealed childhood friend Kaylin Politzer to the author.

Even those who hadn't directly been named or implicated were feeling nervous. In fact, every adolescent male who had ever offended her seemed to be quaking in his boots and questioning just how much he had hurt her. After all, the girl he feared had announced that "a letdown is worth a few songs and a heartbreak is worth a few albums". With this in mind, Taylor's past loves – many of whom had been tracked down on MySpace by furious fans, swords drawn – were wondering what the next revelation would be.

Her fame was growing and she was becoming increasingly loose-lipped and honest at the same time – for those in her way, it was a deadly combination. Where would Taylor's relationship diaries end up next – a gossip magazine? A national newspaper? Or – even worse – prime-time television? Were they destined to be forever known as the boys who enraged Taylor Swift? Future partners might do well to remember her dark warning: "If you're horrible to me, I'm going to write a song about you and you're not going to like it. That's how I operate." After all, Taylor's best weapon was her mouth – and she had a microphone!

Chapter 7

A Fairytale Romance Gone Bad

Taylor's début might have frightened the life out of the guilty parties who knew her, but it was now flying its way up the charts and she was enjoying her newfound fame. Ever since Avril Lavigne had rejected her record label's early attempts to market her as Faith Hill Junior, the world of country had been missing a young female singer. But now, according to the majority of reviewers, Taylor was perfect to fill that gap. Her age had once been a problem, but *Pop Matters* now saw it as a selling point, declaring, "16 years old, blonde, willowy and undeniably gorgeous, Swift is every marketing man's wet-dream girl."

However, she wasn't to be written off as the archetypal blonde beauty either. *About.com* praised her "uncanny ability, especially at such a young age, to write a compelling narrative", claiming that it was "hard not to be pulled into her pain" and that "her breathless voice is nothing less than captivating".

An even bigger coup for Taylor was when the website compared her favourably to her biggest idol – the very woman who first inspired her to pick up a guitar – claiming: "Country music has not seen a phenomenon like Taylor Swift since Shania Twain broke through in a big way back in 1995."

All Music, meanwhile, described Taylor as a "seasoned pro", two words the public wouldn't normally expect to be used to describe a girl in her mid-teens. Its review continued: "[Her] considerably strong voice straddles that precarious edge that both suggests experience far beyond her years and simultaneously leaves no doubt that she's got a lot of life to live. It's a fresh, still-girlish voice, full of hope and naiveté, but it's also a confident and mature one. That Swift is a talent to be reckoned with is never in doubt."

By the time she joined veteran singer George Strait's tour in January 2007, completing 20 dates as his support act, her media reputation was near flawless – but Taylor still described the experience as a "pinch-myself moment". She went on to win over fans with mammoth signing sessions that lasted until the early hours of the morning. What was different about Taylor from some of her counterparts was that, while others found their thrills in binge-drinking cocktails and partying the night away, she preferred to spend her time offering out autographs and meeting fans.

The following month, on February 24, her second single, 'Teardrops On My Guitar', was released – complete with a video and Drew-look-alike Tyler Hilton playing a starring role. Keen to keep it real, Taylor filmed the video at a local Nashville high school – just like the place where her flirtations with Drew had originally taken place.

Knowingly or not, the character in the video seems to tease Taylor, asking her, "Are you gonna go to the game on Friday?" She responds that she was thinking about it, before he disappoints her by passing off his question as friendly curiosity. Immediately afterwards, he changes the subject by telling her about a beautiful girl he had met. Later, he approaches her in a laboratory, causing her to spill the liquids she was mixing.

The scene was an intriguing replica of Taylor's real-life embarrassment in a high-school chemistry lesson, when her impatience led to the contents of a test tube spilling out all over her desk. In this case, however, the spillage is a metaphor for the emotional mess made by the relationship that nearly but never was. Taylor's agony is further revealed when Drew teases her with flirtatious smiles, before falling into the arms of his girlfriend and kissing her instead. All the while, a horrified Taylor is forced to watch.

Unrequited or complicated love seems to be a theme on almost every teenager's radar at some time or another – and listeners responded by welcoming Taylor with open arms. The song became Taylor's highest-charting single from her début album, hitting the number-one spot on the *Billboard* Top 100. It would go on to sell over 2.5 million copies, hitting the double-platinum mark.

The excellent sales also highlighted Taylor's crossover appeal. She was an authentic country singer, but the pop world was equally quick to claim her as its own. *About.com* claimed: "Remove the twang of soft country guitar and 'Teardrops On My Guitar' is the best teen-pop ballad for quite some time." Alternatively, by not removing it, she could make the track a hit in both camps.

Reviewers began to compare her work to David Bowie, The Cranberries and Shania Twain at her most commercial. Meanwhile, *Billboard,* the USA's best-known mainstream music magazine, asserted: "The straightforward conversational quality in her lyrics is like hearing the love-lorn confessions of a dear friend. The longing in this song is relatable and makes the heartbreak palpable in a moving performance. It's tender, sweet and destined to be another hit."

Taylor was also cementing her status as a crossover artist in her live shows – and when she played a bittersweet homecoming show in Reading on April 6, many of the pop fans who taunted her musical tastes back at school were in the audience cheering her on. "They showed up wearing my T-shirts and asking me to sign their CDs," she revealed to *Teen Vogue*. "It made me realise that they didn't remember being mean to me and that I needed to forget about it too. Really, if I hadn't come home from school miserable every day, maybe I wouldn't have been so motivated to write songs. I should probably be thanking them!"

However, one of Taylor's bullies countered that, telling the author: "Oh, everyone remembered. We did make [her] a laughing stock. You don't torment and ridicule someone every day and then forget about it in a matter of a few years. I mean, people were still at the same school where it happened! Reading doesn't have amnesia. I was embarrassed to show up at the gig, knowing how bad things had been. I can only assume for the others it was convenient to forget because they wanted to brag about being friends with a superstar."

Whatever their motivation for trying to get close to her, for someone who had been the epitome of uncool a few years earlier it was a triumph to finally win her detractors over. She started off proceedings at the show, one of her first headlining performances, by announcing that she had been born nearby in Reading Hospital. Taylor then combined a mixture of traditional country tracks, brought to life by a five-piece band playing fiddles and banjos, with some pop favourites.

At one point, she took the microphone to paraphrase Eminem, confiding, "When I left three years ago, I had one shot, one opportunity to seize everything I ever wanted. Y'all think I did alright?" She then broke into 'Lose Yourself', the Eminem song that had inspired her words.

Pairing America's good girl with the words of a tough-talking rapper who seemed to eat, breathe and excrete profanities didn't seem like the most obvious choice; but the lyrics of the track mirrored Taylor's own struggle for survival in the music business. Eminem tells of a nerve-wracked young performer desperate to prove his skills, but when it comes to the crunch time, he starts sweating, trembling and even vomiting down his clothes. He talks of someone who was "chewed up, spat out and booed off-stage" but who eventually triumphs, seizing his chance in spite of nerves and declaring that failure is not an option. In Taylor's eyes, Eminem shared one important trait with her above all – when it came down to it, he was fearless.

She went on to surprise the crowd by performing the John Waite track 'Missing You', along with her opening act and video actor Tyler Hilton, as well as a solo snippet of Beyoncé's good-riddance ballad to an ex-boyfriend, 'Irreplaceable'.

From R&B to rap to country to pure pop, the set list was a diverse one. Yet there was an abundance of heartbreak anthems and it seemed as though relating tales of love and inevitable loss was what Taylor did best.

Taylor's ballads had attracted some famous admirers too – young country star Brad Paisley warmed to her work and invited her on tour with him in April 2007. "For her to have written that record at 16, it's crazy how good it is," Brad raved to *Blender*. "I figured I'd hear it and think, 'Well, it's good for 16,' but it's just flat-out good for any age."

He also insisted that her talents could knock the average accomplished country singer off their pedestal, continuing, "She is operating at a level I will never reach – already – in the ground-breaking way that she has taken a new audience and said, 'I'm a country music singer,' and they love it."

Coming from a multi-million selling artist, the prediction boded well for Taylor. Finally, he added, "I was looking at a lot of artists to come out on tour with me, but as soon as I downloaded her album, I knew we had to have her – I was floored by the songwriting."

So the deal was sealed. And Brad's 2007 tour also happened to be the place where she met her soon-to-be best friend in the industry, Kellie Pickler. The pair were opposites – while Taylor's background was one of love, affection, wealth and privilege, Kellie's could barely have been more different. Born to a drug-addicted father who flitted in and out of prison during her formative years and a neglectful mother who abandoned her at age two, Kellie's chances of just leading a normal life, let alone becoming a renowned celebrity, seemed slim.

Her mother was first convicted of accepting a forged prescription for the highly addictive sedative Valium at the pharmacy she worked and then she disappeared altogether, leaving Kellie with her grandparents. She returned when her daughter was nine and was granted custody, in what would turn out to be among the most miserable era in Kellie's life. After two years of extreme physical and verbal abuse, a court placed her with her grandparents again. It would be the last time Kellie ever saw her mother.

A natural beauty, Kellie grew to be a cheerleader and pageant queen, even participating in Miss America one year – but underneath the model smile, she was desperately unhappy. Her middle-school life story was just like that of the girl Taylor had brought to life in 'Tied Together With A Smile'.

The rest of her life, unfortunately, was something to which Taylor couldn't relate. Kellie's grandmother, her primary carer throughout her childhood, died of lung cancer while Kellie was still in her teens, leaving her devastated and emotionally homeless. To make matters worse, there wasn't even a single phone call of condolence from her mother.

Things started to look up in 2006, when she took part in the talent show *American Idol*, with music mogul Simon Cowell earmarking her as a favourite to win. She was eventually eliminated the week before her father was released from prison for his role in a stabbing. Yet this defeat wouldn't be the end of Kellie, who went on to record her début album.

Due to the trauma of her early life, she had struggled through education, something that would see her hopelessly humiliated on a charity edition of the show *Are You Smarter Than A Fifth Grader?* When asked, for $25,000, what European country Budapest was the capital of, she replied in confusion: "I thought Europe *was* a country!"

In spite of her shortcomings, Kellie proved highly successful with music – something which Taylor did share with her. Brad's tour saw the pair build a fond friendship, first breaking the ice over a cuddly kitten. "I was 17 and she was 20, we were both on our first albums and one of our first tours," Taylor revealed to *Tiger Beat* of their first meeting. "The way that the Paisley tour worked was that he had three opening acts and we would alternate in rotation every night. One of us would go on first, one of us would go on last. So, one of the first things that bonded us was she got a kitten – the cat she has now, Pickles – and she needed someone to look after her kitten when she would go on to play. She would leave the kitten with me or my mom. Then we started hanging out all the time, talking about boys, and just became fast friends."

Although Taylor later described Kellie as "the older sister I never had", it seemed at times as though the same was true in reverse. Despite being six years her junior, Taylor was the sensible, grounded one in the relationship, who encouraged her friend to stay out of harm's way. "I'm crazy, she's sane," Kellie later told *People*. "She keeps me in line. She takes care of me!" It seems eerily prescient that the coded message Taylor had picked out in the lyrics of 'Tied Together With A Smile', which might have been about Kellie's early struggles, was the phrase 'you are loved'.

But Taylor's surrogate sister did turn out to be a perpetual partier. In fact, she would later joke, "When I'm with Taylor, I never get into any trouble!" But she was also guided by a no-nonsense Andrea, who – as well as being Taylor's parent – would become the mother Kellie had never had. "My mom looks at Kellie as a second daughter," Taylor confirmed. "It's a family thing at this point."

Kellie accompanied Taylor to the CMA Awards in April, where she won her first trophy for Breakthrough Artist of The Year, and she was right beside her friend for the Academy of Country Music (ACM) Awards on May 15, too.

Taylor had been looking forward to the ACM Awards for months, since it would be her first opportunity to sing in front of Tim McGraw and Faith Hill. She had told *Nashville Lifestyle* magazine that Faith was her "favourite person" in the city and, as for Tim, she had longed to see him since a live radio phone conversation the pair had weeks earlier.

Taylor had set her sights on joining his hugely successful Soul2Soul II tour, and the only problem was that she hadn't been invited. Not to be defeated, Taylor audaciously tried her luck live on air.

The chat had originally been engineered to get Tim's feedback on her song about him and for the two to exchange thoughts about music. The DJ's first question to Tim was how he felt about Taylor's début single bearing his name. "It's awesome… except I don't know if I should take it as a compliment or I should just feel old!" he groaned.

A thrilled Taylor pledged to Tim: "I swear I'm not a stalker!" before confessing that she dreamed up the melody in a high-school maths class, to which Tim responded, "*Now* I feel old!"

Taylor tactfully threw in a genuine yet carefully placed compliment, assuring him that all her favourite songs were Tim McGraw songs, before moving in for the million-dollar question, "When are you going to start bringing out opening acts again?" Met with a stuttering "I don't know," she continued, "I have someone who I think will be really perfect for it." When Tim enquired, "What would their name be?" she joked, "Uh, um, I think Taylor something!"

Then she set back and pondered what the odds would be of getting a rejection live on air. It was a heart-pounding few seconds, before he answered, "I'll be more than happy to have you out with me." Meanwhile, the incredulous radio DJ spluttered: "You're pretty fearless, Taylor Swift, I'll tell you that!"

Perhaps it was a prophecy – two years later, she would show the world exactly what her definition of fearless was. For now, though, Taylor was preparing for her very first meeting with the man who would help propel her to global fame.

The ACM Awards was an annual ceremony which saw all of the top names in country gather for one occasion. That year, Taylor would be mingling with Miranda Lambert, *American Idol* winner Carrie Underwood, Kevin Chesney and Reba McEntire, to name but a few. And she would be performing her short set just two feet away from Tim and Faith, who had front-row seats for the event. What was more, she was doing it solo, just her and her acoustic guitar, with no band to hide behind. "I've never met Tim and he's going to be sitting in the front row," she had commented. "I think right afterwards, I'll be like, 'Hey, I'm Taylor!'"

On the night of the ceremony, she did exactly that, walking up to the couple while she was on stage to shake hands, introduce herself and give both of them a hug. The moment would prompt one blogger to comment witheringly, "The cheese factor just shot up ten-fold." Reba McEntire responded by jokingly hinting that she would love a teenage boy to write a song in her name, too.

Although Miranda Lambert rivalled 'Picture To Burn' with her own vitriol-loaded track, 'Crazy Ex-Girlfriend', directly afterwards, and Reba McEntire added the pop factor to the event by performing with Kelly Clarkson on 'Because Of You', Taylor was still the talk of the town the following day. It would prove hard to top singing a track titled 'Tim McGraw' to the king of country himself – although she had walked away with the trophy for Best New Artist, too.

That summer, alongside touring with Tim, Taylor and Kellie Pickler made their acting débuts in Brad Paisley's music video, 'Online'. The storyline is of a spotty geek on minimum wage who transforms himself into a handsome, desirable male model on his MySpace account.

In reality, he works in a pizza restaurant – although, judging by his appearance, he spends more time eating them than serving them. Yet on MySpace, he adopts the persona of a model who strips off for *GQ* and Calvin Klein. In his profile, he adds over a foot to his height, relocates to California, parties around the clock and drives designer cars, when he actually spends time at home watching science fiction movies and borrowing money from his parents to live on.

Taylor and Kellie were cast as Brad's backing dancers. Ironically, after appearing in a video about people misrepresenting themselves online, Taylor then joined forces with Delete Online Predators, a charity aimed at dissuading children from meeting strangers from the internet or becoming the victims of internet sex crimes.

Appearing in person at one Tennessee school, Taylor told a class, "When you meet somebody online, you can never really know them. If there are maybe two or three of you here that maybe would get lonely after school and somebody randomly instant messages you and says they're a 19-year-old college student at Yale and does modelling work on the side, they're probably 45 years old and live in the basement of their parents' house – and they're probably an online predator."

As Taylor took her first steps into philanthropy, her third single – 'Our Song', released on August 22, 2007 – had made the number-one spot in the country charts, a position which it held onto for six weeks. It would be her first time on the top spot – all inspired by a mere two-week relationship with Brandon Borello. "I wanted a song that would make people tap their feet," recalled Taylor to *The Washington Post*. "I got that and a whole lot more! A number-one single for six weeks! Whatever! No big deal!"

Then, in October, Taylor made country music history when, at 17, she became the youngest person ever to win the Nashville Songwriters Association's Songwriter/Artist of the Year Award. Soon afterwards, on October 14, a mini-album followed, titled *Sounds Of The Season: The Taylor Swift Holiday Collection*, which combined Christmas classics with two of her own creations.

The album included George Michael's 'Last Christmas', a slow acoustic take on the carol 'Silent Night' and Irving Berlin's 'White

Christmas' – best known as Bing Crosby's 1942 version, which is still the best-selling single of all time. Taylor also followed in Kellie Pickler's footsteps after her friend released a rendition of 'Santa Baby', originally recorded by Eartha Kitt, on a compilation album the same year. The track had been covered by a myriad of artists including Kylie Minogue, Madonna, Shakira, The Sugababes, The Pussycat Dolls – and now Taylor.

In new track 'Christmas Must Be Something More', Taylor led a campaign against materialism. She felt too many defined Christmas as an excuse for a spending spree, while to her it was less about money, mince pies and mistletoe, than about Jesus – "the birthday boy who saved our lives".

Meanwhile, 'Christmases When You Were Mine' was a melancholic tune featuring a lonely Taylor begging those around her to take down the mistletoe so she can reminisce on times past with a lost love.

She got into the Christmas spirit – not to mention adding her name to the list of country icons who had played Nashville's historic Ryman Auditorium – when, on November 19, she joined a Christmas for Kids charity show there. The organisation raised funds for children from poverty-blighted families to give them a Christmas they couldn't otherwise have afforded.

She followed the fundraising show with a string of festive performances, including playing America's biggest mall in Minnesota on December 8. She even appeared on national TV on Christmas Day, serenading *The Today Show* with live renditions of 'Silent Night' and 'Christmases When You Were Mine'.

The workaholic got a very special Christmas gift of her own when her management surprised her with a Barbie pink Chevrolet truck. The country equivalent of socialite and heiress Paris Hilton's candy-pink Bentley, it was a combined Christmas and 18th birthday gift. However, the garish gift had some of the media aghast, with the Celebrity Carz blog sneering, "Just because she is a girl does not mean she wants a pink car, and just because she is a country singer does not mean she wants a truck."

Taylor may well have thought the same, since within days of receiving it, Taylor had given the truck away to Victory Junction Gang, an organisation that provided free summer camps for terminally ill children. "My label was so awesome to give me this amazing truck," Taylor praised. "The moment I saw it, in all its pink glory, I knew that the kids would love it." She added, "They have camps all over the country for kids who are sick. It's one week each summer they forget they're sick and just have a blast and hang out with other people they can relate to. They look forward to it and I love that cause."

On January 29, 2008, Taylor released her fourth single, 'Picture To Burn' – three-and-a-half minutes of fury and light feminism. The song sees Taylor retaliate to complaints that she is obsessive by promising to tell her friends her ex is gay. It was a tale of rebellion and infantile yet irresistible humour, but it was also a classic tale of a woman scorned and had the feel of Rihanna's 'Breaking Dishes' and PJ Harvey's 'Don't You Wish You'd Never Met Her'.

However, it was a long way from the full-on murder fantasies of fellow country singer Miranda Lambert, as seen in tunes like 'Crazy Ex-Girlfriend' and 'Gunpowder And Lead'. "I love Miranda, but I don't do, like, an 'I'm going to kill you!' kind of thing," Taylor reassured *The Washington Post.* "At least right now I don't – but I can't make any promises!"

That said, Taylor knew there was a whole market of furious females waiting to be catered to. Her live shows had shown her that this was the song that inspired the most riotous crowd reaction, seeing her fans "scream along" to the lyrics. A demonic, vengeful persona might have seemed out of character for her, but she wanted to share her miserable moments with fans, the times when she had sat alone with her guitar, quietly raging.

Although she had never so much as kissed the object of her resentment, she was still wounded – and she felt there was no better way to portray that in the song's video than with pyrotechnics. It starts with Taylor looking at a photograph of her with her man and wondering out loud how she could have thought they were so happy together, when he turned out to be so worthless. Taylor's real-life best friend, Abigail, is sitting beside her in the passenger seat of Taylor's car, playing up to her role as bunny boiler by watching through a pair of binoculars as Taylor's former sweetheart pulls up in a truck with another woman.

To add insult to injury, Taylor's love rival is at the wheel, whereas he had never allowed her to drive. The scene rapidly switches to a room where Taylor is performing with her guitar, with a blaze of flames burning behind her. At the time she frantically quipped, "My hair could very well catch fire!" before being reassured that not only were the flames at a safe distance, but there was also a fire extinguisher at hand.

After the performance, Taylor and Abigail are seen sneaking into her ex's house in the dead of night to throw toilet paper over his furniture, spit in his mouthwash, lick his cutlery and trash his belongings in any way that they can think of. The only limit is their imagination.

Using a walkie-talkie, Abigail helpfully informs their victim – who is hot on their tracks and approaching the house fast – that they are already there. As the pair leave, Taylor realises she is finally over him – and the final frame shows the photo of them together that she had been gazing at earlier bursting into flames. "The storyline of the video is, if you break up with me, my band will ransack your house," Taylor joked later, warning off any prospective admirers in advance.

In fact, the video showed a different side to the formerly demure Taylor – one her fans had never seen before. The lyrics to the song even came across as potentially promiscuous, featuring claims that there was nothing to stop her having vengeful rebound affairs with all her ex's closest friends. She was also wearing some uncharacteristically sexy fetish-themed, thigh-high leather boots.

Or was she? The wardrobe department had scoured the shops for the perfect pair of thigh-highs, but was forced to give up when Taylor's long legs and 5-foot 11-inch frame made it impossible to find any long enough. Instead, some black fabric was stitched to high-heeled shoes for a customised finish.

Although the sexier outfits and dominant persona might have given the impression that Taylor had come of age, looking back, she felt she might have dealt with her emotions more maturely had she been a little older. Yet, despite having evolved as a songwriter and being less inclined to fly into fiery rages when relationships didn't go to plan, she insisted she had no regrets about showcasing her anger on CD.

"The way I feel that kind of pain [now] is very different," Taylor confessed to MTV. "Years from now, I'll look back and go, 'I didn't know anything back then' [but] I got to immortalise those emotions that when you're so angry, you hate everything. It's like recording your diary over the years – and that's a gift."

Indeed, it was a gift, and one that would see Taylor nominated for an award at the 2008 Grammys. At a pre-show event, when the nominees were announced for Best New Artist and she heard her name called out, she couldn't contain herself. Rushing over to Dave Grohl, front-man of The Foo Fighters, and his band mate Taylor Hawkins, she gave them both a warm embrace, only to be told by Dave, "Don't worry, Taylor, you got it in the bag!"

"I've always been a hugger," Taylor would later tell *People* of her dramatic reaction. "I honestly did not think I was going to get nominated, so when they said my name, I felt like hugging somebody. If we all hugged more, the world would be a better place!"

The mood was a little more chilled on February 10, the night of the award ceremony. Despite Dave Grohl's prediction, it wasn't to be. Taylor lost out to Amy Winehouse. However, she had learnt to be stoical about defeat, shrugging, "I've come to terms with the fact that I can control what I say, I can control how I act, I can control what I do on a stage – but I can't control award shows."

However, just two months later, her luck changed. On April 14, she appeared at the CMT Awards for the second year running, this time claiming the prize for Best Video of the Year and Best Female Video of the Year – both for 'Our Song'. The awards were especially important to Taylor because they were voted for not by industry executives, but entirely by the fans. As she took to the stage to accept her awards clad in a raspberry-coloured Balenciaga dress, she looked picture-perfect from her head to her ankles – but where were her shoes?

She had strutted towards the audience bare-foot, brandishing a pair of lethally high heels in one hand and her microphone in the other. What was more, she couldn't blame the fashion *faux pas* on a few too many drinks – as always, Taylor was stone-cold sober. Her bare-foot guise allegedly had unforgiving stylists all around the room grimacing in disgust. "If it was Amy Winehouse or Joss Stone, I wouldn't have blinked an eyelid, but Taylor Swift?!" one said. "She looked like a tramp!"

However, she had an excuse – it was on the command of someone who, to Taylor, was almost the manifestation of God on earth – Faith Hill. "I had these gorgeous hot pink heels on and they were awesome, but they really hurt so bad," Taylor confessed. "I was limping up the stairs. I walked by Faith Hill and I was like, 'This hurts so bad'. She was like, 'Take them off!' And so at that point I just took off my shoes and did not put them back on – and actually accepted an award barefoot, but Faith Hill told me to. So I did it."

Meanwhile, Taylor's live shows continued, in which she played 16-song sets armed with a pink guitar, before ordering her band offstage as she broke into impromptu acoustic solo versions of songs like Rihanna's 'Umbrella'. When the media quizzed her on the implausibility of adding a pure pop song to her repertoire, she fought back. "You say bizarre," she challenged. "I say interesting."

As she continued to tour the country, she was now able to call herself a multi-award-winning, chart-topping artist – and she had bullies and cheating boyfriends to thank. Before 'Picture To Burn' had left the charts, it was time to release her final single from the album – 'Should've Said No'. It débuted on May 19 for a storm of chart success, becoming her second number one on the country chart. She also hit the record books by becoming the first female artist ever to see five singles from her debut album make the Country Top 10.

Naturally, Taylor was delighted. "The truth of the matter is that when somebody is a jerk to you and you write a song about it and it becomes a Top 10 hit, that's good for you," she revealed mischievously. "It's totally, completely sweet!"

That wrapped up promotion for her first album, but inundated with a deluge of fan mail all with one common question – when the next instalment would be – Taylor decided to release a six-track teaser to "tide them over". The EP, *Beautiful Eyes*, which was released on July 15 in Walmart stores only, contained an alternative version of 'Should've Said No', a radio edit of 'Picture To Burn' and an acoustic version of 'Teardrops On My Guitar'. Finally, there were three new tracks, 'Beautiful Eyes', 'I'm Only Me When I'm With You' and 'I Heart Question Mark'.

The EP sailed straight to number one in the Country Albums chart, upstaging Taylor's first album, which slipped into second place. That made her the first artist to own the top two chart positions together since LeAnn Rimes in 1997 – who had also been a teenager at the time. It was official – no matter what cynical Nashville executives might have said, young female country artists really were in vogue.

One of the fan favourites on the EP was 'I Heart Question Mark', which urged a past partner to get over her, since she had moved on and had another man in her life. Given her past candour, Taylor was unusually coy about the identity of the characters in the song. But perhaps this was fitting, as she was by now in a new relationship that was shrouded in secrecy.

In fact, she was dating singer Joe from popular boy band The Jonas Brothers; but – allegedly because his management wanted him to appear young, free and single – he refused to appear in public with her as a couple. "When someone's not allowed to go out with me in public," Taylor later stated, "then that's an issue."

Joe was one of four brothers, the three oldest of whom performed in the group. They had released two albums when Taylor first met them, been involved in the Disney Channel show *Hannah Montana* and even tried their hand at movies. However, their Christian values set them apart from most other boy bands on the circuit.

The brothers were deeply religious. Their father had been an evangelical pastor, and their mother had home-schooled them to protect them from the "negative" influences of their peers. They had also made a vow of chastity until marriage and, to prove their point, all three wore purity rings as a "promise to ourselves and God that we'll stay pure".

A family of hormonal teenage boys abstaining from sex might have raised a few eyebrows but, by September 7 of that year, the blushing boys' beliefs would be reduced to a laughing stock by English comedian

Russell Brand. Hosting the 2008 MTV Video Music Awards, Brand took to the stage claiming that he had already relieved one of the brothers of his virginity – a serious *faux pas* for a family whose religion forbade homosexual acts altogether. As the crowd watched with bated breath, Russell continued: "Well done, Jonas Brothers! God bless those boys! In case you're wondering, each wears a purity ring to show their commitment to God. I would take them more seriously if they wore it around their genitals!"

Warming to his subject, he added, "It is a little ungrateful to be able to have sex with any teenager in the world, but they won't! They're not going to do it… It really is a weird way to control a boy band!"

In some ways, Taylor sympathised. Sex wasn't on her radar either, so Joe's abstention wasn't going to be a problem. It was his refusal to commit to a relationship that worried her. Those around Joe seemed keen to portray him as a man who loved God more than girls, but they also believed that presenting him as "available" would appeal to his female fans. Although Taylor wanted to use a slice of her trademark honesty to stake a claim, she agreed to go along with the secrecy.

In early August, Joe was put on the spot about his relationship with Taylor by Ryan Seacrest on his radio show. Joe's religious beliefs obligated him to tell the truth at all times, but it didn't commit him to transparency – he got around it by replying diplomatically: "She's a great girl. I think anybody would love to go on a date with her." It was a line that he and Taylor had clearly worked out together, since her answer was very similar: "He's an amazing guy and anybody would be lucky to be dating him."

The relationship didn't become public knowledge until later that month, when a cautious Joe stepped out to watch Taylor's show – supporting Rascal Flatts again – at the West Palm Beach Cruzan Amphitheatre in Florida. A watchful Mishelle Rivera of Miami's Y100 Radio revealed: "He was trying to hide from the crowds by kicking in between a few people – he was wearing a baseball cap and real casual dress so he wouldn't stand out."

Joe crept to the soundboard to watch the show alongside Taylor's father and then, instead of staying to watch Rascal Flatts, he immediately headed to the backstage area to find his new beau. "When he saw people start to recognise him, he hid," revealed Mishelle. "It was real obvious he didn't want people to know he was there to see Taylor."

In spite of the secrecy that surrounded her trysts with Joe – which Taylor may even have seen as romantic – the relationship seemed to be solid.

Taylor had scorned the notion of *Romeo And Juliet* as a young and bitter schoolgirl back in English classes, but for the first time she understood the intensity of a hidden affair. While Taylor's situation wasn't as serious as belonging to a rival group at war, it was a *Romeo And Juliet* scenario: they had Taylor's disapproving father to contend with, as well as Joe's management and possibly his family standing in their way. When it came time to release some new material, the choice of the first single from her forthcoming album *Fearless* was easy. Taylor picked the Joe Jonas-inspired 'Love Story'.

The relationship had changed Taylor from a songwriter who couldn't abide writing about missing someone to someone who was using it as the central focus for her work. "I didn't want to write songs about being on the road and being in hotels and missing your family and missing your friends," Taylor had once insisted. "When I was like 14 or 15, I would hear these things on an album... being alone, living out of a suitcase... I was always like, 'Ugh, skip!'"

Fast forward a few years to age 18 and Taylor was writing about exactly that. Her arduous life on the road, combined with a relationship that could not make itself known, meant that she felt lonely at times and also related to the theme of forbidden love.

"I used to be in high school where you see [a boyfriend] every day," Taylor lamented to *The LA Times*. "Then I was in a situation where it wasn't so easy for me and I wrote this song because I could relate to the whole *Romeo And Juliet* thing!"

In the song, she talks of sneaking out for clandestine meetings, outwitting paparazzi and parents, and the impossibility of ever being alone together. It was the reality of superstardom – but it was also the life she had chosen. Taylor also struggled when, one by one, her friends started to turn against the man she loved.

From a father's perspective, a chaste, God-fearing, sex-abstaining boy for whom honour was all-important couldn't have been a safer or more pleasing prospect for his daughter's affections. Yet both Scott and many of Taylor's friends still felt there was something about Joe that they just didn't like but couldn't put their fingers on.

"I was dating a guy who wasn't exactly the popular choice," Taylor elaborated. "His situation was [also] a little complicated, but I didn't care... When I wrote the ending to this song, I felt like it was the ending every girl wants to go with her love story. It's the ending that I want. You want a guy who doesn't care what anyone thinks, what anyone says."

The single was released on September 12, and Taylor gave an even clearer indication that the song related to Joe when she revealed: "It's about a love that you've got to hide because for whatever reason it wouldn't go over well. I spun it in the direction of *Romeo And Juliet* – our parents are fighting [but] I relate to it more as a love that you cannot really elaborate on, a love that maybe society wouldn't accept or maybe your friends wouldn't accept."

Taylor was being more vague than ever. But it was clear that things with Joe were heating up fast. "I was really inspired by *Romeo And Juliet*," she told *The LA Times*, "except for the ending. I feel like they had such promise and they were so crazy for each other and if that had just gone a little bit differently, it could have been the best love story ever told. And it is one of the best love stories ever told, but it's a tragedy. I thought, why can't you make it a happy ending and put a key change in the song and turn it into a marriage proposal?!"

Unfortunately, the fact that the story ended in tragedy reflected the harsh realities of life – and in real life, things didn't always go according to plan. While Taylor might have been craving her very own happy-ever-after ending, it wasn't to be. Within weeks of the release of 'Love Story', the ending wrote itself when Taylor and Joe split for good.

Joe might have been a virgin, but that didn't stop him lusting after seemingly limitless numbers of female celebrities. He refused to talk about his relationship with Taylor and yet in almost every interview he gave, he seemed to be confessing to a crush. Whether it was singer

Cheryl Cole or actresses Natalie Portman and Emma Watson, he had all bases covered. Not content with publicly humiliating Taylor, it also seemed that he had given into temptation with the then 25-year-old actress Camilla Belle.

When *OK* magazine cornered her at that year's Country Music Awards in April, Taylor finally confessed to the relationship and, show-stoppingly, implicated Camilla in their split. "They've been together for months," she revealed simply. "That's why we broke up."

Taylor's life had taken an unfortunate turn for the worse ever since. Gruellingly long tours and numerous personal commitments gave her little time to grieve for her relationship and when she finally made it home for some "me time", she spent it "talking to my cat and making play-lists of sad songs".

She then found herself facing rumours that she was pregnant – perhaps with Joe's child. She took to MySpace to defend herself: "I read a very creative rumour saying I'm pregnant, which is the most impossible thing on the planet. Take my word for it – impossible!"

By November, Joe found himself in defensive mode too, when he wrote an open letter for the benefit of his fans – and presumably Taylor – denying the accusations of infidelity. "Several things I will state with all my heart," he began. "I never cheated on a girlfriend. It might make someone feel better to assume or imply I have been unfaithful, but it is simply not true. Maybe there were reasons for a break-up. Maybe the heart moved on. Perhaps feelings changed. I am truly saddened that anything would potentially cause you to think less of me. Anytime you are in a relationship for any length of time, there are going to be issues. Sometimes they resolve. Other times, they lead to a change of heart. This was the case recently."

His letter sparked feverish debate among fans of both parties. Had Joe cheated? Did he have anything to hide? No one knew that apart from the man himself – and, of course, his alleged partner in crime. With the truth still untold, it seemed as though Joe had had the last word verbally, but Taylor made note, moved on – and wrote a song.

Whatever the reality of her relationship with Joe, it had taught the romantic, idealistic Taylor an all important lesson about viewing love with rose-tinted glasses. With all the optimism of youth, she entered a relationship innocently and with expectations of a future, only for it to end in a way that caused her great hurt.

She learned that a guy could be deceptively perfect on the outside, but his charm could be merely an illusion. Love could fade, die or become twisted – and that was what had happened.

"I'm very fascinated by the differences between reality and fairytales," Taylor would later admit. "When we're little, we read these books and we see cartoons and the bad guy is always wearing black. You always know who he is. But in real life, the bad guy can be incredibly charming and have a great smile and perfect hair. He says things that make you laugh and he's sweet and he's funny, but you don't realise that he's going to cause you a lot of pain."

Chapter 8

A Fearless Fairy Tale

After her breakup, Taylor's first line of defence was to humiliate Joe on CD – and she had more than enough ammunition. "[He] broke up with me over the phone," she revealed later on *The Ellen DeGeneres Show.* "I looked at the call log – it was like 27 seconds. That's got to be a record."

Needless to say, Taylor's song of catharsis was considerably longer. 'Forever And Always' saw her lash out at Joe for destroying her innocent fantasy and shattering her illusion of perfect love – one which, in this case, turned out to be as fragile as glass.

"It's about when I was in a relationship with someone and I was just watching him slowly slip away," Taylor lamented to *That's Country.* "I didn't know why because I wasn't doing anything different. I didn't do anything wrong. He was just fading. It's about the confusion and frustration of wondering why. What changed? When did it change? What did I do wrong? In this case, the guy I wrote it about ended up breaking up with me for another girl."

According to Taylor, Joe had promised her they would be together forever, but – as much as she tried to avoid turning her life into a romantic tragedy – she had to submit to the inevitability of the *Romeo And Juliet* ending. In this case, the death hadn't been of a person, but was the metaphor for closing the door on a dead relationship.

Sensationally, Taylor would also allegedly take a swipe at Joe's new beau when she made a catty reference to an actress who was more renowned for her skills in bed in 'Better Than Revenge'. Meanwhile, there were rumours circulating that the relationship had crumbled because Taylor had come across as "cold" and "frigid". The contrasting tales of a sexually adventurous actress and a young ice-queen made for interesting love rivals – especially considering that the object of their affections had never had sex.

Eager to put her side of the story across, Taylor had contacted her label just as *Fearless* was about to be mastered and "absolutely begged" for them to stop and make room for 'Forever And Always'. In a way, she found that kind of pressure a thrill. "I think it's fun... knowing that two days before you're scheduled to have the last master in and everything finished and they're ready to go print up the booklets, I can write something, call my producer, we can get in the studio, put a rush on it, get an overnight mix and that can be a last-minute addition to the record," she confessed.

The song, which saw Taylor "basically screaming because I'm so mad", exorcised her unhappiness with Joe and enabled her to move on – but not before she delivered one last kick where it hurt. In a video on her MySpace page, which saw her brandish a Joe Jonas plastic doll, Taylor joked, "This one even comes with a phone, so he can break up with other dolls." Then she turned to another plastic figurine, which looked suspiciously similar to herself and warned, "Stay away from him, OK?"

Another song that nearly didn't make it onto *Fearless* was 'White Horse'. Taylor had originally felt that the album had enough melancholy on it already. "I really felt like we had the 'sadness' represented on the record," Taylor told *That's Country*. "Then my agency out in LA set up a meeting with executive producers Betsy Beers and Shonda Rhimes at *Grey's Anatomy*, because that's my favourite show.

"It would just be a dream come true to have a song on it, so I played them 'White Horse'. It was just me and my guitar and they freaked out and they loved it! If it wasn't going to be on the show, then we weren't going to put it on the album. Then they called and said they were very interested [so] we recorded it right away."

The song expressed Taylor's sad realisation that fairy tales were called that for a reason and rarely reflected real life. The lyrics spoke of the superficial, larger-than-life glamour of Hollywood and the idealised version of beauty it marketed. As the heart of the big-screen movie world, few people were seen without a full face of make-up – and, sometimes, breasts that seemed to weigh more than their body weight. Yet underneath the make-up and the perfectly packaged fantasy they sold, the faces of Hollywood weren't really like that. Taylor has grown to prefer the safe option of a small town. She claims to be no princess and, despite her dreams of meeting a real Prince Charming, has come to think no such man existed outside of movies or the pages of a book.

"'White Horse' talks about falling in love and the fairy tales that you are going to have with this person – and then there is that moment when you realise that it is not going to happen," Taylor clarified to *Billboard* magazine. "That moment is the most earth-shattering moment."

She added, "It's the most heart-breaking part of a break-up. That moment when you realise that all the dreams you had, all those visions you had of being with this person, all that disappears. Everything after that moment is moving on – but that initial moment of 'Wow, it's over' is what I wrote 'White Horse' about."

Taylor found herself wondering if she had even known her partner. Did the relationship she saw in her mind ever exist – or had she just been blinded by love? Recording the track helped her to come to terms with her disappointment. However, the icing on the cake was finding out her song was going to feature in the *Grey's Anatomy* season premiere, broadcast on September 25 to millions of householders across America. "You should have seen the tears streaming down my face when I got the phone call," Taylor confessed. "I've never been that excited. This is my life's goal, to have a song on *Grey's Anatomy*. My love of *Grey's Anatomy* has never wavered. It's my longest relationship to date!" Clearly, for Taylor, some fairy tales did come true.

Ironically, however, for someone who had been subjected to a higher dose of reality than recommended on the bottle – and who seemed to have sworn off love altogether for the moment – her faith in the male race seemed to have been restored all over again the day she wrote 'Fearless'. In this song, she described the joy of a flawless first kiss, a relationship where she could forget all of the angst and pain. Although she had been hurt along the way in her search for love, she firmly believed that the best love affair possible was still yet to come.

But, while Taylor insisted on respect, her childhood fantasies of perfect romance had rapidly matured – without losing their essential innocence. "I think the coolest way to have a first kiss is when you're in the middle of a sentence and you're rambling on about something and the guy looks over and just kisses you and you're not expecting it," Taylor explained to CMT. "That's not underneath a terrace, underneath the moonlight of a shooting star running across the sky and everything's perfect. I think the perfection of love is that it's not perfect."

So Taylor had come full circle. The album was bringing to life a two-sided fairy tale. On one side she was angry and pessimistic about men, expressing her sentiments in songs like 'Forever And Always' and 'White Horse'. On the other, she was the eternal optimist of 'Love Story', a believer in true love. With 'Fearless', Taylor brought both these sides of her personality together, explaining that no matter how many times she had been hurt or how badly, she would never let a bad break-up jade her or close her heart to love – she knew that the pain would fade and, hopelessly romantic as she was, she would one day find love again.

Meanwhile, the quest to find it provided her with the inspiration for one album track after another. 'You Belong With Me', for instance, had first taken shape in a packed school corridor, back in the days when Taylor was still a regular pupil at Hendersonville High. She had been chatting to one of her male friends when the two were interrupted by a furious call from his girlfriend. Taylor heard the words, "No, baby… I had to get off the phone really quickly… I tried to call you right back… of course I love you. More than anything! Baby, I'm so sorry."

While her friend struggled to please a high-maintenance, emotionally needy partner, Taylor found herself wishing she could be with him instead, resolving that she would treat him much better if given half the chance. "She was just going on and on at him because he called her back

154

10 minutes late," Taylor revealed to *The Useless Critic*. "I was thinking to myself, 'Wow, if she is going to get upset over something as trivial as that, maybe you don't belong with her!' I went to one of my co-writing sessions with Liz Rose and we turned it into this whole 'You belong with me, she's popular and I'm the geek' type of scenario."

Taylor emphasised the difference between them lyrically by summarising that, while she wears casual T-shirts, her cooler rival is always in mini-skirts. Yet could she dare to hope that one day she would be the type her friend would choose? "It's basically about wanting someone who is with this girl who doesn't appreciate him at all... girl-next-door-itis," Taylor groaned to MTV. "You like this guy. You know him better than she does. But somehow the popular girl gets the guy every time."

Meanwhile, 'Hey Stephen' was about a more recent crush – this time Stephen Barker-Liles, one half of country duo Love And Theft. The pair had first met backstage at a 2007 event, and Love And Theft had then gone on to become a support act for her in 2008. In the song, Taylor makes a sales pitch for her love, cataloguing all of the reasons why Stephen should forget his other admirers and pick her. After all, would the other girls write him a song? "This guy has absolutely no idea I had a crush on him," revealed Taylor to *Teen Vogue*. "It's going to be kind of interesting when he finds out."

In fact, Stephen's initial reaction was anything but interesting. Far from a romantic, he responded to *Yahoo Music* with a lacklustre: "It probably was just a crush, or lack of people to write about."

However, he changed his tune a little later when he revealed that not only had she penned a track about him, but he had simultaneously written one for her. "Taylor genuinely loves people in a way only the Lord would," he gushed to *Planet Verge*.

What had prompted Stephen's sudden change of heart? It sounded unusual that the two had unwittingly penned tributes to each other without the other's knowledge – especially as Stephen hadn't mentioned his own song the first time round. His loved-up reaction now was miles apart from his original, less-than-romantic claim that Taylor had used him as a song topic simply because she had run out of ideas.

Was the apparent songwriting coincidence a mark of fate or a carefully constructed publicity stunt?

No one knew, but one thing was for sure – Taylor had no shortage of ideas or people to write about. The list of people who offended her, in particular, was growing by the day.

'Tell Me Why', for example, was about a boy Taylor had never officially dated, but who infuriated her just the same. "It's the hardest thing when you have all these dreams of dating [the person] and you're getting close, but it doesn't work out," Taylor explained to *That's Country*. "He would say things that would make me go, 'Did you just say that?' It bothered me so much because he would say one thing and do another and do one thing and say another. Because he didn't know what he wanted, he would just play all these mind games."

When Taylor had turned up "ranting and raving" at co-writer Liz Rose's house, Liz took on a role of part-therapist, part-producer, channelling Taylor's self-destructive energies and aggravation into a song. "She goes, 'If you could say everything you were thinking to him right now, what would you start with?'" Taylor told the Associated Press. "I would say, 'I'm sick and tired of your attitude, I feel like I don't even know you…' and I just started rambling and she was writing down everything that I was saying and we turned it into a song."

Taylor then used the same approach to expose a deceptively charismatic liar who had cheated his way into her life under false pretences for 'You're Not Sorry'. Some might say Taylor was turning on him in just the same way the popular girl at school had done in 'You Belong With Me' – but in this case, she felt her actions were justified.

"This guy turned out not to be who I thought he was," she told *That's Country* in indignation. "He came across as Prince Charming. Well, it turned out Prince Charming had a lot of secrets that he didn't tell me about – and one by one, I would figure them out. I would find out who he really was. I wrote this when I was at the breaking point of 'You know what? Don't even think you can keep on hurting me.' I had to walk away."

However, was walking away that simple? Another song, 'The Way I Loved You', documented Taylor's frustrating tendency to fall for bad guys. She might have substituted the "beautiful liar" for someone much more suitable – a perfect gentleman who would buy her flowers, wine and dine her (in Taylor's case, without the alcohol) and hold doors open for her – but something was missing. In other words, she was addicted to self-destructive relationships.

Taylor was keen to share writing duties on the song with a real-life bad guy, John Rich. "He was able to relate to it because he *is* that complicated, frustrating, messy guy in her relationships," Taylor joked to *That's Country*. "I wanted to see what it was like to get in a room with John because I know I'm a very opinionated writer. So I knew this was either going to be the best thing in the world or was just going to be a complete train wreck."

While nice guys seemed to leave Taylor dead inside, it seemed as though she wasn't the only one with the same problem: another song, '15', was about the similar experiences of her best friend Abigail. Abigail's tribulations were enough to bring Taylor to tears – even when her own break-ups left her dry-eyed. "I'm not likely to cry about something I've ever gone through, even if it's the worst break-up ever," she told CMT. "Maybe I haven't had that break-up yet. Maybe there will be a break-up where I'll just cry every time I think of it – but the things that make me cry are when the people I love have gone through pain and I've seen it. 'Fifteen' talks about how my best friend Abigail got her heart broken when we were in ninth grade and singing about that absolutely gets me every time."

Then there was 'Breathe', Taylor's first recorded collaboration that would see her team up with Californian pop singer Colbie Calliat. In 2008, Colbie had recorded a duet with Jason Mraz, 'Lucky', that ended up winning her a Grammy award, so her vocals were like gold dust. On a day off, after a concert in Nashville, Colbie recorded her song to voice sadness about the ending of a relationship. "It's about having to say goodbye to somebody," Taylor confessed. "Sometimes that's the most difficult part, when it's nobody's fault."

There were two more songs on the album – but, unusually, neither was about a romance. 'The Best Day' was a Christmas present for her mother, reminiscing over her early childhood and thanking her mother for being there for her. The best day Taylor refers to was the evening back in seventh grade when her so-called friends made excuses not to go to the local mall with her – only for Taylor and her mother to run into the entire group of them shopping together. 'The Best Day' was Taylor's way of showing her mother her appreciation for how she handled a potentially explosive situation. Using her video-editing skills to make a montage of childhood home videos to accompany the track, Taylor then surprised her mother with an impromptu screening.

"I recorded it secretly," she told *That's Country*. "[My mother] didn't even realise it was me singing until halfway through the song! She didn't have any idea that I could possibly write and record a song without her knowing about it. When she finally got it, she just started bawling her eyes out." That was a pattern that would continue every time she played it. In fact, Taylor would later have to remove it from her concert set list because it would prompt her mother to break down in tears every night – and her fans were almost as emotional.

Finally, 'Change' expressed Taylor's impatience in regard to climbing the career ladder. "I began to understand that it would be harder for me on a smaller record label to get to the places and accomplish the things that artists were accomplishing on bigger record labels," she vented. "I realised that I wouldn't get favours pulled for me because there weren't any other artists on the label to pull favours from. It was going to be an uphill climb and all I had to encourage me was the hope that someday things would change – that things would be different. After so many times of just saying that to myself over and over, I finally wrote it down in a song."

Taylor had joked many times about passing up the chance to be on a worldwide major label in favour of a tiny company that barely had any furniture, let alone capital, to its name, but that would finally allow her the creative control she craved. The sacrifice that she had made for her artistic freedom, however, was to start small. While she didn't doubt that she had made the right decision, she sometimes felt side-lined by fellow artists with more money and promotional tools behind them.

The change Taylor had been waiting for finally came when her second album, *Fearless,* was released on November 11, 2008. Sales of over half-a-million copies in the first week surpassed her debut album's first week sales nearly 20 times over. She also made her first serious impact on the pop market with *Fearless*, débuting at number one on the *Billboard* chart.

The lead single, 'Love Story', also saw Taylor's appeal move outside of the USA – an unusual feat for a country singer. Many of her contemporaries rarely stepped outside the USA and Canada for a show, but it looked as though the Taylor Swift brand was about to go global. 'Love Story' reached number three in New Zealand, number two in the UK and number one in Australia. What was more, she hadn't neglected her duties Stateside either – and fans had reciprocated her attention by keeping *Fearless* in the Top 10 for over a year, an achievement she would share with Michael Jackson's *Thriller* and Shania Twain's *Come On Over* to name but two. Her fame had reached such a level that a Taylor Swift doll had even been released.

'Change' also became part of the *AT & T Team USA Soundtrack*, an album full of patriotic songs intended to cheer on the American team in the 2008 Olympics, and became the backing track for the TV highlights of the events. "It's interesting how you can apply the lyrics to the Olympics and to someone who got beat a few times and is really hoping things will change," Taylor commented. However, the biggest change of all had been her own.

The same month her album was released, she teamed up with British hard rock group Def Leppard – cue gasps of astonishment from the country camp. A heavy rock band with album names like *Pyromania* and *Hysteria* and a self-confessed appetite for debauchery and self-destruction didn't seem like the most obvious musical partners for Taylor. But, courtesy of her mother Andrea, her passion for hard rock was in the blood.

"She's been a fan since she was in the womb," joked Def Leppard lead vocalist Joe Elliott. "Her parents are responsible for her Def Leppardness. They were big Leppard fans so, obviously, she heard the records growing up and, rather than resent her parents' music, she's embraced it."

It might normally have been the other way round, with rebellious teenagers blaring metal music from their stereo speakers while their more conservative mothers grimaced, covered their ears and tried to hum along to a gentler, more demure country melody instead.

However, Taylor's early exposure meant that when the country music channel CMT contacted her to take part in an episode of *Crossroads* – a series which paired up traditional country stars with bands from other genres – she knew instantly who her partners would be.

Unfortunately, Def Leppard didn't reciprocate her familiarity. "The first thing we did was google Taylor Swift and we were like, 'Whoa! She's only a kid!'" Joe Elliott told *People* magazine. Taylor had heard that reaction before. It was a tense moment – would her idols look beyond her age, something she saw as just "a number on my birth certificate", or would they shun her?

Her albums featured candy-coated, sugar-sweet anthems, chronicling life for a young woman coming of age, discovering both the joys and disappointments that love had to offer. Def Leppard, on the other hand, had a very different outlook on life. To see an example of a star shunned by the rock world, she had to look no further than one of her favourite pop singers, Rihanna. She had sought a guitarist for her video, 'Rockstar', but one nominee after another had turned her down, fearful of the effect it might have had on their hard-as-nails reputation and rock credibility. Nikki Sixx from Mötley Crüe, for instance, had implied he felt embarrassed to be associated with a "bubblegum pop" act.

Fortunately for Taylor, Def Leppard were instantly enthusiastic. "You start listening to the songs and it's like, 'Why wouldn't we want to do this?'" Joe Elliott continued. "I mean, she's one of the biggest stars in America right now."

So Taylor paired up with them – just as Faith Hill had paired up with rock group The Pretenders before her – and combined songs like 'Love Story', 'Teardrops On My Guitar', 'Picture To Burn' and 'Should've Said No' with Def Leppard tracks like 'Photograph', 'Hysteria', 'Pour Some Sugar On Me' and 'When Love And Hate Collide'.

"I was singing Def Leppard songs and they were singing my songs," Taylor later enthused to *Time*. "It was just a complete out-of-body experience."

On stage at New York's Madison Square Garden, Taylor sports an eccentric Victorian era dress a la Lady Gaga, but underneath the over-wrought ruffles, she remains a wholesome all-American girl. JASON KEMPIN/GETTY IMAGES FOR ERICKSON PUBLIC RELATIONS

A heart-pounding moment: as Taylor receives the Best Female Video award at the 2009 Video Music Awards, rapper Kanye West storms on stage to sabotage her acceptance speech. JEFF KRAVITZ/FILMMAGIC

Beyoncé saves the day: following her own award win for Best Video of the Year, the 'Single Ladies' singer hands the microphone back to Taylor. CHRISTOPHER POLK/GETTY IMAGES

ackstage at the 2009 Academy of Country Music Awards, aylor poses for a picture with Nathan Chapman, the producer ho brought much of her music to life. GETTY IMAGES

Taylor's biggest idol, country music star Faith Hill poses with her at a charity concert for the Country Music Hall Of Fame in Nashville. LARRY BUSACCA/GETTY IMAGES

t's a moment of mutual celebration as Taylor invites her backing band on stage to share the love at the 2009 CMA Awards.
ONY R. PHIPPS/FILMMAGIC

Look At Me Now: dueting with Miley Cyrus at the 2009 Grammy Awards, Taylor sends a clear message to ex-boyfriend Joe Jonas about what he's missing. ROBYN BECK/GETTY IMAGES

Spot The Mannequin: Taylor poses next to her astonishingly life-like waxwork at the Madam Tussauds museum in New York. MARCEL THOMAS/FILMMAGIC

Taylor arrives at the 2010 American Music Awards in LA, hoping to bring a taste of country music to the mainstream. VERA ANDERSON/FILMMAGIC

Dressed in a purple plaid skirt and blue woollen hat, Taylor is hardly the height of fashion on *the Late Show With David Letterman*, but in spite of her casual 'preppy' style, she still exudes star quality. JEFFREY UFBERG/GETTY IMAGES

Taylor performs from behind a grand piano on stage at the 2010 American Music Awards. LESTER COHEN/GETTY IMAGES

A Group Effort: Taylor takes to the stage with her band at the 2011 Academy of Country Music Awards in Las Vegas.
CHRISTOPHER POLK/GETTY IMAGES FOR ACM

In the name of philanthropy, Taylor transforms the final dress rehearsal for her Speak Now tour into a free-for-all charity concert to raise funds for victims of tornadoes. The show, held in Nashville on May 21, 2011, raised more than $750,000 for the cause.

Taylor takes part in a nationwide broadcast of the 2011 CMA Awards. RICK DIAMOND/GETTY IMAGES

Taylor sports a look of astonishment and disbelief as she wins the trophy for Favorite Country Female Artist at the 2011 American Music Awards – and this time, there's no Kanye in sight to gatecrash the stage. CHRISTOPHER POLK/GETTY IMAGES FOR AMA

Repeat Offender: Back at the Grammys again in 2012, Taylor clutches two award trophies as she poses in the press room.
MICHAEL TRAN/FILMMAGIC

The unlikely collaboration led to some interesting moments, seeing Joe duet with Taylor about princes and princesses. However, unlike many of his rock contemporaries, he claimed to be in touch with his "feminine side" and comfortable with it.

"We've never really had a problem doing the cross-genre thing," he added to *Rolling Stone*. "It's fun to do and it takes you off the beaten track… it gets you out of your homogenised bubble, expands your brain and expands your musical horizons."

Taylor agreed – and wouldn't rule out the chance of writing a rock song of her own one day, no matter how unlikely it might have seemed. "I'm inspired by all kinds of different sounds," she told *Rolling Stone*, "and I don't think I'd ever be someone who would say, 'I will never make a song that sounds a certain way, I will never branch outside of genres,' because I think that genres are sort of unnecessary walls."

However, Taylor would soon return to her favourite genre with the release of the second single from *Fearless*, 'White Horse', on December 8. For the video, Taylor mischievously changed the context of the song slightly to reflect her experiences with Joe Jonas. The plot featured a man involved with both Taylor and another woman, both of whom are implicit in infidelity without even realising it.

To portray her loved one, Taylor chose actor Stephen Collett for his good looks, his acting skills on *One Tree Hill* and his charisma on reality TV show *Laguna Beach: The Real Orange County*. He had model looks; next to him, Taylor seemed shy and awkward and – in spite of her beauty – almost geeky. That was exactly the dynamic she had hoped for – not to mention that Stephen was adept at playing the smooth operator.

"This girl falls in love with this guy and he's perfect. He's adorable. He's charming. He's endearing. She falls in love with him," Taylor revealed of the video's plot. "Then she comes to realise that he's been leading a double life. He was already in a relationship a year before he ever met her… I'm the one that was ruining a relationship without even knowing it!"

On the day of the shoot, there were torrential rain storms, which added a heaviness to the atmosphere on set. It was also a fitting metaphor for the tears Taylor might have cried when the love of her life betrayed her. By February 9, 2009, the moment arrived that Taylor had been dreading: she would have to come face to face with Joe Jonas – the inspiration for the video, if not the song – for the first time since their split. The occasion was the 2009 Grammy Awards, and Joe was set for a live collaboration with Stevie Wonder on his song 'Superstition'.

To make matters worse, Joe knew that Taylor hadn't earned a single nomination at that year's ceremony. However, determined to steal the show, Taylor took to the stage with a duet of her own – singing 'Fifteen' with Miley Cyrus. It was an awkward moment – Miley had previously dated Joe Jonas's brother Nick and broken up with him a matter of weeks before Taylor's own relationship hit the rocks – and now the brothers would have to watch their exes duet together. Taylor wanted to meet Adele and M.I.A. that night; Joe clearly wasn't on her list.

As it happened, however, her biggest revenge was her success. It was still taking the country by storm when, a couple of weeks after the Grammys, the film *The Jonas Brothers: The 3D Concert Experience* arrived in cinemas. Shot during the brothers' 2008 tour, the film also included a performance from Taylor herself, singing 'Should've Said No', but even that couldn't save it: its first-week profits were less than a quarter of what the boys' management had hoped.

Meanwhile, on respected film website IMBD, the movie scored just 1.4 out of 10 from a sample of over 15,000 users. Comments such as "torture", "it reeks of failure" and "it's terrible that music has sunk so low" summed up the viewers' experiences. One more inventive reviewer blasted: "Another joylessly choreographed gig from pop stars so squeaky clean they probably leave their internal organs soaking in buckets of Persil overnight... [and] a tour called Burning Up suggests only one thing – we are in Hell!"

As if to add insult to injury, Taylor's own performance inspired one journalist to comment, "Perhaps Disney would have had better luck starring Swift in a concert movie and leaving the Jonas Brothers second on the bill." It would be a while before Taylor would hear from Joe Jonas again.

The same week his concert film opened, she was filming in Nashville for Kellie Pickler's video, 'Best Days Of Your Life'. The plot focuses on a cheating boyfriend who is on the brink of settling down and marrying his new lover. The experience is bittersweet for Kellie – she feels she has had a lucky escape by discovering his infidelity before she got in too deep – and she even sympathises with his new partner because, while she can move on to better things, the cheat she left behind seems apt never to change.

Taylor's involvement brought the song to a wider audience and it became Kellie's biggest hit to date, as well as the first to impact the Top 10 on the country charts. For the first time, downloads also exceeded the one million mark. Taylor was happy too – she enjoyed a glimpse into someone else's life instead of the heartbreak she wrote about perpetually being her own. "It was so cool jumping into someone else's feelings for a minute and writing from their perspective," she recalled to *Elle Girl*. "It was like I was writing my very first song. Exhilarating!"

Taylor would also get a second opportunity to see the world from another person's eyes when it came to her acting début – a role in her favourite crime thriller series, *CSI*. While many singers longed for little more than chart success, her to-do list included a desire to die for the entertainment of the nation. "I've always joked around with my record label and my mom and everybody," Taylor told CBS. "All my friends know that my dream is to die on *CSI*. I've always wanted to be one of the characters on there that they're trying to figure out what happened to."

However, Taylor's throwaway comment happened to have been on a TV show – and that took it out of the realm of a joke straight away. "We reached out to Taylor Swift because one of the CBS executives had told me, 'Taylor loves your show!'" *CSI* producer Carol Mendelsohn revealed. "So Taylor came in to meet me and we talked about the character, [but] I said, 'It's a very edgy part – this may not be what you want.'"

Her trepidation was understandable. The part they had in mind for Taylor was that of Haley, an aggressive troubled teen with a penchant for piercings, an anger-management problem and a drug addict for a boyfriend. Not surprisingly, she was later described by critics as "the complete opposite of [Taylor] herself".

So was Taylor up for the challenge? "I love it!" she told them.

The show, which aired on March 5, 2009, was the 16th episode of the ninth series. It began with the macabre image of a girl lying dead in the car park of her parents' motel. Taylor – as Haley – had finally got her wish.

The crime of her murder was then solved through a series of flashbacks, which showed Haley to be a rebellious teenager with little conscience, hell-bent on a life of crime. The differences between Taylor and her character quickly became apparent. Haley was no stranger to piercings, whereas way back, when Taylor promised to replace the fake heart tattoo on her ankle with a real one if she sold more than two million albums, her father memorably retorted that if she did that, he would remove it for her with a belt sander. Haley also had the tell-tale signs of someone promiscuous: her crystal meth-addicted boyfriend comes into her life as a sociopathic stalker, but – far from that being a deterrent – it isn't long before she is kissing him. He tells her at one point: "I can tell there's a vicious bad girl inside [you] waiting to claw its way out" – presumably the motive for continually stalking her – but Taylor got a chance to show her real self in the show too, with a snippet of 'You're Not Sorry'. The CSI remix of her song became one of YouTube's most played videos the day after the show.

Meanwhile, the murder mystery was finally solved when viewers learned her mother had accidentally stabbed her to death with a pair of scissors. "When I'm really old and can only remember one story about my life to go back and relive and tell over and over again to the point where my grandchildren roll their eyes and leave the room – that's the story," Taylor wrote on MySpace of her gory death. "When I was a youngster, I got to guest on *CSI!*" But wouldn't selling millions of albums also be part of the tale?

Taylor's next acting venture was on the big screen, playing a cameo role in *Hannah Montana: The Movie*. Adapted from the hit Disney Channel series of the same name, the film features Miley Cyrus as Miley Stewart, a former small-town nobody who has risen to become a glamorous pop star. She becomes entwined in a double life of secrets and lies because no one knows her true identity. She gets the shock of her life when a watchful journalist heads to her hometown and interviews residents to dig up the gossip. Meanwhile, Miley is being swept away by the seductive qualities of fame and is struggling to live up to two very different images.

Her father – played by real-life dad Billy Ray Cyrus – is a traditional man with old-fashioned Southern values, and he is devastated when her public slanging match with supermodel Tyra Banks over a pair of designer heels makes headline news. He worries that Miley may be getting caught up in a fantasy and forgetting where she came from. He tricks her into flying back to Tennessee by telling her the plane is headed for New York, where she'll make a celebrity appearance at an awards show.

Lured back home under false pretences, she falls in love with a local boy – someone calm and quiet who is the polar opposite of the love interests she meets in Hollywood – and she spends time with him horse-riding, building a chicken coop and reacquainting herself with the farm life of her youth.

The twist comes when she lies to her boyfriend that she is a friend of Hannah Montana in a bid to impress him. Eventually, she finds herself switching between the two personas several times a day to maintain her lie. She is finally exposed when she realises that he likes the real her more than her alter ego, Hannah – and, having seen how much she has hurt him, she tries to stop leading a double life.

The storyline was suspiciously similar to Miley Cyrus's own life, blurring the lines between fiction and reality. Miley was once a small-town Southern girl herself, living on a farm before she rose to fame through the TV series *Hannah Montana*. Within less than two years, she would release her third album and sell out tickets for a 70-date tour. According to Ticketmaster's reps at the time, there hadn't been "a demand of this level or intensity since The Beatles or Elvis".

A devout Christian like Taylor, Miley's behaviour in the wake of her success began to surprise some people. In 2007, photographs implying a lesbian kiss were posted on MySpace and, a few months later, provocative pictures of Miley in her lingerie also emerged. She apologised profusely for the "inappropriate" pictures and claimed it was a mistake. However, almost as if to prove it hadn't been a mistake, she then agreed to pose for some risqué, apparently topless photographs in high-brow fashion magazine *Vanity Fair*.

Gary Marsh of the Disney Channel had to issue a stark warning to Miley about her raunchy behaviour, telling *Portfolio*, "For Miley Cyrus, to be a 'good girl' is now a business decision for her. Parents have invested in her godliness. If she violates that trust, she won't get it back."

Ironically, just two years later, Miley gave the impression that the good-girl image was false and that her father's attempts to tame her had failed, when she starred in *LOL*, a film about a bad girl with a drug habit, but whose mother "has her on this perfect pedestal". Miley was reported to have "fallen in love" with the story.

Miley's early upbringing shared much in common with Taylor's. Both had spent their early years living on a farm – Taylor in Pennsylvania and Miley near Nashville. In fact, the farm in *Hannah Montana: The Movie* was less than 200 miles away from the one where the real-life Miley had grown up. Both girls were deeply Christian and had vowed to remain celibate until marriage.

Both she and Taylor had experienced the frustration of being "too young" to pursue their dreams – at 12, when Miley first auditioned for *Hannah Montana*, she – like Taylor at the same age – had had the door slammed in her face. Plus both had turned around an unpopular, small-town upbringing to be propelled into the world of fame. Their humble upbringings had made them identifiable to ordinary teenagers.

Ironically, the farmhouse in the movie had been mouldy and in a state of disrepair when the film crew first discovered it – a fitting metaphor for the transformation from troubled teen to superstar, something both Taylor and Miley had experienced in early life. They could relate to youthful uncertainty, so found themselves meaning every word of their roles – but they were also related to the normal girls who were watching.

"It's basically a superhero movie for girls," producer Al Gough said of the film. "Miley is a normal high-school student by day and pop star by night. So she's dealing with identity issues, family issues, relationship issues. Most kids and adolescents who deal with the same issues feel as if they don't have any power, so the idea of putting on a wig and costume and being a powerful superhero is teen wish fulfilment."

However, as Taylor already knew, fantasies weren't always what they seemed. She had discovered a similar blurring between fiction and reality in her own life, when she found romance didn't always have a perfect Hollywood movie ending. The lyrics of 'White Horse', where she tells her lover that she's not in Hollywood now, but is from a small town so he can't come in on his white horse to save her, could have been made for the movie.

However, Taylor was given the opportunity to start afresh writing songs for the film. She co-wrote 'You'll Always Find Your Way Back Home', combining a fantasy life of fame and fortune in LA with the real-life roots and sense of belonging of Tennessee. "[Miley's] kind of lost herself, the little girl from Tennessee. [Her father] decides the best medicine would be to go home," explained Billy Ray Cyrus of the emotions surrounding the song. "Always be looking forward and know where you want to go, but, most importantly, never forget where you came from."

He added that, when filming in Tennessee, Miley had regressed back to the country girl she had been as a child, "out climbing trees and riding horses". She seemed to have learned a lesson from the experience too, concluding of her film role, "When audiences walk away from the movie, I hope they feel like they've been to my home. I hope they feel like they understand Nashville because Nashville is my everything. Nashville is who I am." Taylor felt exactly the same – and perhaps that was why the two bonded and became such firm friends.

The other piece of music which Taylor wrote for the film was a song to describe "the moment of falling in love". "When I got an email from Disney saying they wanted a song that was perfect to fall in love to and sort of a country waltz, I sent them 'Crazier'," Taylor revealed, "and they loved it."

Although Taylor's role was a very small one, playing a concert in a tiny Tennessee town as part of a fundraising day to protest against the demolition of a local park at the hands of developers, she was able to sing 'Crazier' on camera. This seemingly throwaway performance, with little relevance to the bigger picture in the plot, nevertheless saw critics almost unanimously declare that Taylor had stolen the show. *TV Guide* praised, "When genuine teen star Taylor Swift shows up to perform, she demonstrates all the spontaneity and authenticity that Miley Cyrus lacks," while *The San Francisco Chronicle* claimed, "Swift is so talented that she makes Cyrus seem bland in comparison." *All Music* called 'Crazier' "the best song on [the film]", adding: "Arguably, the movie's biggest mistake is having Taylor Swift perform a song, since she can sing, and the comparison is not flattering to the movie's star."

Yet it was no mistake in the eyes of the film's director, Peter Chelsom, who raved, "I've made a very big mental check to work with her again."

It was while on the set of *Hannah Montana* that Taylor discovered the actor who would play opposite her in next single 'You Belong With Me'. The video had a "revenge of the nerd" theme where a geek with conservative clothes and "Clark Kent glasses" manages to win over the school's most sought-after boy, in spite of his relationship with the most popular girl. Taylor played both female roles, "the nerd who is pining away for this guy that she can't have" and "the popular girl who's horrible and scary and intimidating and perfect".

The plot echoes Avril Lavigne's 'I Don't Like Your Girlfriend', where a nerd persuades a boy that he needs to ditch her love rival for a new partner – namely her. Like Avril, Taylor had a body double so that both versions of her could appear together in the same shot. It also had traces of Katy Perry's 'Last Friday Night (TGIF)' where, after a makeover, the school nerd turns heads and attends the season's hottest party and sees a fellow nerd get into a fight with the school's Mr Popular over who will be hers.

While Taylor had recruited one of the most handsome actors from *Hannah Montana*, to play her love interest, she was keeping it real too, just like in the movie – several scenes were filmed at Pope John Paul II, her brother's high school. "When I'm playing the mean girl cheerleader and I'm flirting with some other guy on the football field, that other guy is just one of my brother's friends," Taylor revealed to *Rolling Stone*.

The single achieved the number two spot on the *Billboard* Hot 100, making it her highest charting song so far. It gained the largest cross-over radio audience and the most pop music fans since Faith Hill had released 'Breathe' back in 2000. Plus the song saw her make a serious impact on European charts for the first time, achieving Top 50 positions in Belgium, Denmark and Sweden – as well as in the UK.

Taylor hadn't just conquered the charts and won over the most popular guy in high school – she had also won over one of the best-known men in American music, guitarist and singer John Mayer, whose work appealed to both young pop fans and the serious rock fraternity. He announced on Twitter that he had a song in mind just for her. "Waking up to this song idea that won't leave my head – three days straight now!" he wrote "That means it's good enough to finish. It's called 'Half Of My Heart' and I want to sing it with Taylor Swift."

Taylor couldn't resist responding to such flattery – and before long she won a competition on Twitter, judged by John, for conceptualising her life story in just a few words. According to John, Ernest Hemingway had claimed that only six words were needed to write a "great story" – so he invited people to contribute their own six-word autobiographies. Taylor was the triumphant winner with the simple: "My diary is read by everyone."

The two soon got together to record the song John had visualised, a track about someone torn between ending a relationship and regaining his freedom or giving in and surrendering to love. Both sides of his heart seem to struggle with a split personality – the monogamous partner and the liberty-loving lone soul. The track would later appear on John's subsequent album, *Battle Studies*, released on November 17.

In the meantime, the two got together for an explosive performance when John joined Taylor on stage at her May 22 show at the LA Staples Center. He sang on 'White Horse', while Taylor added her vocals to his track 'Your Body Is A Wonderland' – an erotically charged song John had once claimed was about "lady parts" and which was rumoured to have been inspired by a fling with the actress Jennifer Love Hewitt. Onlookers from the front row reported tell-tale signs of sexual chemistry between Taylor and John, but was it for real or part of an elaborately constructed showbiz fantasy? Only time would tell.

Meanwhile, Taylor had more than enough man trouble to deal with from past relationships. The Jonas Brothers' new album, *Lines, Vines and Trying Times*, hit the shops on June 16, 2009 – and it seemed that a certain someone had borrowed his ex's trademark tendency to spill the beans on previous lovers. While the lead single, 'Paranoid', was cryptic, making only the vaguest of references to being "caught in a nightmare", the full album was a bit less discreet.

The brothers revealed in interviews that the vines in their lives were "the things that get in the way of the path you're on" – and, according to one track, 'Much Better', Taylor had been one of those vines. Joe claims in the lyrics that he has had it with superstars with tears on their guitar, before claiming that his new partner is a much better prospect. The reference made it only too clear who the song was about.

It might have been a pass-the-sick-bag moment for both Taylor and Camilla Belle – the better girlfriend – when the two were referenced together in the same song. But, in an added twist, Camilla was already facing a cheating scandal of her own when she was reported to have been unfaithful to Joe with *Twilight* star Robert Pattinson. Perhaps Joe would have to replace her with someone much better, too!

To add to all the confusion, Joe's mother had told *Star* that, in spite of being a pastor's wife, she didn't hold things like infidelity or sexual affairs against her children if they had given into temptation. "They are men, they have desires, they have testosterone," Denise Jonas declared. "If they make a mistake, I'm not going to hate them. I don't think they're above or beyond being seduced." Taylor kept a dignified silence concerning all of the allegations. One thing was for certain, though: she was above and beyond the failed relationship.

The same day that The Jonas Brothers' album hit the shops, Taylor's *CMT Crossroads* DVD was released in Walmart stores featuring the songs and interview snippets from the TV show she and Def Leppard had appeared in together. It became the supermarket's highest selling DVD of the week.

Meanwhile, just three days later, Taylor was at the CMT Awards on June 19. It was a tale of three Swifts that night, seeing her embrace rap, rock and country personas one after the other. Multiple personality disorder wasn't normally worthy of an accolade, but it might have been that night. Even before the awards started rolling in, Taylor started off the ceremony in style when a pre-recorded video was shown of her and notorious gangsta rapper T-Pain – together.

"The CMT Awards asked me, 'Do you want to be part of our intro?'" Taylor explained to *Rolling Stone*, "and one of the first things that came to my mind was that I really, really want to be able to rap and go to the mall and go to those kiosk things and go buy bling and experience rapping in front of a car with spinners for the first time. T-Pain agreed to it and flew to Nashville and we were in a sweltering hot 90-degree parking garage for an entire day's shooting."

While many singers might have grimaced at the memory, Taylor was undeterred by the heat, calling the afternoon "unforgettable".

The video, entitled 'Thug Story', saw Taylor taking on the persona of T-Swizzle and bragging in true rapper style. T-Swizzle boasts she is 8-foot 4-inches, has blonde hair down to the floor and surprises her followers with dreams of gangsta rapping. She blings it up, showing off a mouth packed full of diamonds, and playfully pokes fun at her good-girl image when she reveals her penchant for baking cakes and knitting. She says she has barely stepped foot inside a nightclub, doesn't own a gun and still lives with her parents – but, in her eyes, she is still a bona fide thug.

When the clip aired, the audience was divided between bubbles of laughter, gasps of amazement and mesmerised silence. Taylor had teasingly taken to Twitter at the time of recording the video to ask, "If I said I was in the studio with T-Pain, would you believe me?" In reality, few people probably had done.

With her tough demeanour and blonde curls beneath a baseball cap, Taylor looked like an early days Beyoncé – but, ludicrously, a little edgier and more street. *Rolling Stone* raved that the skit was "worthy of a *Saturday Night Live* short". Most importantly, it had fulfilled Taylor's life-long wish to collaborate with a rapper, just as Tim McGraw had done with Nelly – and notably, she looked more comfortable in the duo than a slightly awkward-faced T-Pain.

Taylor later revealed she was a huge fan of his genre, telling *The*

Useless Critic, "I'm really into rap at the moment, Nicki Minaj, Diddy, Dirty Money, T-Pain, Tupac... I've always said that I'll listen to any music regardless of who it's by or what genre, as long as I think it's good."

She added, "I don't think you should limit yourself by deciding you aren't going to listen to country music because you like pop, or you aren't going to listen to pop music because you like rap music, you know. I think you should keep an open mind when it comes to music and just because it's different doesn't necessarily mean it's bad."

After that short interlude, Taylor was back to business as a country star, performing 'You Belong With Me' and picking up awards for Best Video Of The Year and Best Female Video for 'Love Story'. "I want to thank CMT for letting me live out so many of my dreams this year!" Taylor claimed, referring to earlier skits where, as well as being a rapper, she had appeared as a Vulcan in the *Star Trek* movie, as well as a member of local American football team the Tennessee Titans. "I also want to thank Shania Twain for always making such theatrical videos, and I want to thank Garth Brooks for always putting his fans first. I take my cues from you! And I want to thank my little brother Austin for agreeing to be my date tonight!" she concluded.

By the end of the show, it was time for her third personality change of the night – to a heavy rock musician. She ended proceedings by performing 'Pour Some Sugar On Me' with Def Leppard. According to CMT, the rock-country crossover was "the most watched part of the entire evening". As both bands were stand-out contenders in their genre, dictated by boundary-breaking, rule-defying album sales, it made sense for the two to appear together – and they were even nominated for two awards, Performer Of The Year and Wide Open Country Video Of The Year.

For Taylor, the collaboration was "the most amazing thing in the world", while Def Leppard singer Joe Elliott reported, "We brought the house down... Taylor's such a bundle of energy!" Finally, for the fans, the performance showed her versatility. But while Taylor enjoyed her foray into two new genres, her first love would always be country.

By July, she was filming again – this time for *Valentine's Day*, a movie about make-ups and break-ups around the most important day of the year for lovers. She played opposite *Twilight* star Taylor Lautner as his new girlfriend, and alongside such high-profile actors such as Jessica Alba, Jessica Biel and Julia Roberts.

It seems that Taylor also contributed to her character's storyline. When her character Felicia gives her on-screen partner a T-shirt, she customises it with the number 13 for "good luck". As the date of her December birthday, Taylor had often claimed that, unlike most, she saw the number as auspicious. In fact, by this point she was taking her acting so seriously that it began to overlap with real life – and romance was about to heat up between the pair off-camera too.

In the midst of their mutual crush, however, she was interrupted by tour dates with Keith Urban, who – contrary to his name – was a fellow country star. Not content to be merely the supporting act, Taylor and her band gate-crashed the stage during his headline show in Kansas City on August 8, dressed from head to toe as members of hard-rock band Kiss, renowned for their use of extravagant make-up and wild costumes. Complete with a wig, spangly clothes and full-on white face paint, Taylor took the part of guitarist Ace Frehley. Explaining that it was the last night of the tour, she tweeted, "Pranking is a must!"

She had a mind full of harmless mischief, but the next prank was on her – and this time it wouldn't be quite so funny.

Chapter 9

Sticks And Stones

Taylor had successfully fended off almost all criticism of 'You Belong With Me'. *The Observer*, for example, had accused the track of "needling British ears", but when it reached Number 30 in the UK charts, the numbers spoke for themselves. It was another unprecedented victory. However, shaking off Kanye West was another story. It all began at the 2009 MTV Video Music Awards.

It had been less than a year since *Fearless* had exploded around the world and mainstream fame had come as a shock for Taylor. She was thrilled just to be invited to the ceremony – an event which was packed to the rafters with pop celebrities – let alone win a trophy. That night, on September 13, 2009, when she was announced as the winner of the Best Female Video Award, Las Vegas's Radio City Music Hall erupted with a deafening wave of applause. Taylor was grinning broadly – but the sound wasn't music to everyone's ears.

Backstage, a fuming star's temperature was rising. Kanye hadn't won a single award. Earlier that night, when it emerged he had lost out in all of the categories he was nominated for, Kanye had stormed off, shouting, "That's two years in a row, man! I have the number-one record, man!", repeating his stunt from the previous year. According to insiders, the string of profanities that followed backstage had to be heard to be believed.

Yet his biggest *faux pas* of all was launching a stinging attack on one of his fellow nominees. It hadn't been his night, and when Taylor took to the stage, he could contain his fury no longer.

"Thank you so much! I always dreamed about what it would be like to maybe win one of these sometime," she began tentatively, "but I never thought it would have happened. I sing country music, so thank you so much for giving me a chance to win a VMA Award."

She could go no further. A nanosecond later, Kanye had taken possession of the stage. "Yo, Taylor!" he bellowed. She turned with visible excitement and gave him a shy smile, clearly believing he was there to offer congratulations. She was wrong.

"I'm really happy for you and I'm 'a let you finish, but Beyoncé has one of the best videos of all time!" he raged. "*One of the best videos of all time!*"

Taylor's face fell, Kanye's face was contorted with disgust, while Beyoncé visibly cringed from her seat in the audience. Beyoncé was a certified success – she had sold more than 75 million albums and was now in her second decade at the top, plus her former group Destiny's Child had won awards that declared them the best girl band of all time. Yet Taylor had beaten Beyoncé's video, 'Single Ladies (Put A Ring On It)', to the trophy, and Kanye – for reasons best known to himself – was incandescent with wrath.

Taylor was stunned into silence – and her time on the stage was soon up, leaving MTV to handle their tight production schedule by switching straight to a video. It left a mortified Taylor with little choice but to shuffle off the stage, her tail between her legs.

Backstage, fellow rapper P. Diddy had simply shrugged: "It's rock 'n' roll" – and it certainly was. Within seconds of her rival's outburst, Taylor was ushered out through the VIP exit to begin a performance of 'You Belong With Me' atop a taxi cab outside the venue. It was a celebratory song for her win – except a shell-shocked Taylor no longer felt like celebrating any more. Tearful, shaking and on the verge of forgetting every part of the routine she had painstakingly memorised and rehearsed, she resolved instead, difficult as it was, that the show must go on.

However, as soon as the last notes had rung out and she was back in the safety of her dressing room, she let down her shield and the tears began to flow.

Comforted by Beyoncé's father and manager Mathew Knowles, she was seen wringing her hands and sobbing hysterically. It was a moment of raw emotion – her perfect night had just turned into the type of public humiliation nightmares were made of. When Taylor's mother approached Kanye to defend her daughter and demand an explanation, he allegedly repeated the same insult – that Beyoncé's video had been better by far.

However, most people were in Taylor's corner. The audience had given a standing ovation to show their sympathy, while Pink had shook her head disapprovingly before being led away by security, who feared a fight. Yet the biggest show of support had come from Beyoncé herself.

When it came time for her to accept the Video Of The Year Award, she sacrificed her own acceptance speech to invite Taylor back to the stage. Recalling how special it was to her to win her very first VMA at 17 with Destiny's Child, she said she wanted Taylor to get the opportunity to "have her moment" too.

Taylor tentatively joined her on stage and the two – both wearing dresses in matching shades of crimson – exchanged hugs, before Taylor joked, "Maybe we should try this again." She went on to thank the video's director, its actors, her brother's high school and, of course, the fans. Thankfully, she regained her composure completely by the time it came to her red-carpet interview with *Wonderwall*. "I thought it was so wonderful and gracious of Beyoncé," she explained. "She's always been a great person before anything else. I thought that I couldn't love Beyoncé more and then tonight happened and it was just wonderful." Admitting that she had also been a Kanye fan before that night, she added: "I was really excited because I had just won the award and then I was really excited because Kanye West was on the stage – and then I wasn't so excited anymore after that."

Asked whether she harboured any hard feelings towards the rapper, she insisted, "I don't know. I've never met him." Yet many people knew more of him than she did – and his chequered history revealed a track record of gate-crashing the stage at award ceremonies and coming to blows with other artists.

He had stormed out of the 2004 American Music Awards when he discovered the trophy for Best New Artist had been allocated to country singer Gretchen Wilson instead of him. "I was robbed," he claimed. What was more, it wasn't merely a moment of champagne-fuelled bravado and bitterness – he meant it. When reporters quizzed him on the incident afterwards, they expected to hear a contrite apology, but he simply repeated, "I was the best artist" before telling open-mouthed journalists that there was a racist conspiracy at work, preventing black artists from being recognised for their success.

The following year, at a charity concert to benefit victims of Hurricane Katrina, Kanye launched into a sudden attack on George Bush live on NBC TV, claiming the President "doesn't care about black people". Then, at the 2005 Grammys, he warned there would be "a real problem" if he failed to secure an award. He dismissed others' attempts at modesty as being in bondage to "clichéd media training", before offering a full-on war cry against the show's organisers.

By the time of the 2006 MTV Europe Music Awards in Copenhagen, his behaviour had, needless to say, made him quite unpopular. However, public disapproval didn't stop him – and this time, he objected to being beaten to the trophy for Best Hip-Hop Artist by Justice vs. Simian. He interrupted proceedings to yell in indignation, "'Touch The Sky' [his video single] cost a million dollars. Pamela Anderson was in it! I was jumping across canyons!"

The following year, at the 2007 VMAs, he staged a tantrum because his performance would be in a luxury suite at the Palms Hotel instead of taking place on the main stage. Of his five nominations, he won nothing – and again insisted he had been marginalised due to the colour of his skin. By this point, his rants were becoming so commonplace that it might have been more shocking if he had managed to sit through an entire ceremony without gate-crashing the stage.

Kanye's inflated sense of self-importance – together with his penchant for "a little sippy sippy" – made for a dangerous combination.

Kanye was undeniably successful – his last four albums had made it to number one in America – but he was also immodest. Google the words "Kanye West" and "arrogance" together and you will find well over a million hits. He regarded himself as a "super hero", an "icon", a "fashion reference" and, whenever he ran out of superlatives, "simply the best".

He told the press, "I am the tree and the people are the branches" and, "I will go down as the voice of this generation and of this decade – I will be the loudest voice!" The problem was he seemed to be going down for reasons that weren't necessarily flattering to him, prompting his father Ray to admonish, "That's not how you were raised!"

Yet Kanye's last words on the matter? "I still think I am the greatest."

Even after winning 14 Grammys and a plethora of other awards, it wasn't enough. Kanye had seemed intent on destroying the night for a girl who was picking up the very first VMA of her life. How would he react in the aftermath of that moment – would he maintain his position or be forced to back down and apologise?

First of all, Taylor received some support from President Obama, who reportedly called Kanye a "jackass" for his actions. Unlikely support later followed from short-fused Liam Gallagher, who raged on MTV, "If I ever win any more fucking awards, I'd personally invite him to get up and fucking take my award off me! That was rude, what he did to that girl, that Taylor Swift. So yeah, give me an award and see where it goes. It will roll out of his fucking arse!"

Then it was Kanye's turn to speak. He posted a public apology on his blog, claiming: "I'm *so* sorry to Taylor Swift and her fans and her mom. I spoke to her mother right after and she said the same thing my mother would've said. She is very talented!"

However, what came next, although it was an outwardly innocent compliment, seemed to poke fun at Taylor's retreat from the stage without finishing her acceptance speech that night. He wrote: "I like the lyrics about being a cheerleader and she's in the bleachers!" Was it a jibe about how he had been Beyoncé's cheerleader, sidelining her, with the reference to the bleachers as a metaphor for how Taylor had backed away from the stage?

If any more evidence was needed that Kanye was not sorry, he continued by combining an apology with a reiteration that Beyoncé had deserved to win. "I'm in the wrong for going on stage and taking away from her moment," he admitted. "Beyoncé's video was the best of this decade. I'm sorry to my fans if I let you guys down... everybody wanna boo me, but I'm a fan of real pop culture... I gave my awards to Outkast when they deserved it over me." (The reference is to the 2007 BET Hip-Hop Awards when he had attempted to give his trophy to Outkast, who politely refused it.) "I really feel bad for Taylor," he continued, "and I'm sincerely sorry!"

But he later added cryptically that Taylor "had nothing to do with my issues with awards shows", perhaps alluding to his earlier allegations of white supremacy and racial discrimination in the music world.

The day after the award show, he appeared on *The Jay Leno Show* to make amends a second time. Asked by the host when he realised his actions were wrong, he claimed, "When I handed back the microphone and she didn't continue." Controversially, Leno then asked what Kanye's recently deceased mother might have made of the situation – only for him to dissolve into tears. He finally claimed that his actions were driven by his "dream of what award shows were meant to be".

Taylor then appeared on TV the following evening to give her side of the story. She appealed to sympathisers' heartstrings when she recalled her joy at seeing Kanye approach her and how that emotion had quickly diminished into sorrow. "I think my overall thought process went something like, 'Wow, I can't believe I won. This is awesome. Don't trip and fall. I'm gonna get to thank the fans, this is so cool! Oh, Kanye West is here! Cool haircut! What are you doing here?' And then, 'Ouch.' And then, 'I guess I'm not going to be able to thank the fans.'"

"I'm not going to say I wasn't riled by it," Taylor added of the experience. "[But] there were a lot of people around me backstage that were saying really incredible things and just having my back. And all of the other artists that came and showed me love in the hours following and all the people tweeting about it and the fans... I just never imagined that there were that many people out there looking out for me."

In the end, seeing how many people were willing to stand up and show solidarity for her had been a validating, confidence-boosting moment for Taylor. Yet in the midst of that, rumours began to emerge of a fix. "I call this whole thing staged," read one blog entry on *The Guardian* website. "Swift comes out of this more vulnerable and loveable than ever, Beyoncé gets props for her grace and generosity after she brought Swift on to complete her speech later in the evening, Leno gets a boost to his brand new, five-times-a-week chat show." As for Kanye, he simply seemed to thrive off all the attention.

However, his extensive history of misdemeanours and public outrage at award ceremonies suggested that it was anything but a fix – and more a case of Kanye's poor impulse control.

The day after Taylor's TV appearance on *The View*, it emerged that Kanye had also phoned her to offer a personal apology, which she had accepted. At a New York costume ball the following week, reports even indicated that they had warded off a potentially awkward face-to-face moment by giving each other a high five.

However, Kanye's words of contrition were soon shown to be empty as, the following year, he waged a verbal war against Taylor again on at least three separate occasions. On New York's Hot 97 radio station, he claimed that his attack on Taylor was not wrong, but merely badly timed. "I made a mistake," he acknowledged. "My timing was definitely extremely off and the bigger plans, the bigger fight – how do you go about it? How do you go about getting it done?"

In the same interview, he expressed irritation at Taylor, who had told him privately that she always defended him when people asked her about the event when she was out shopping. She should go on air to defend him publicly, he said, not just in her local grocery store.

He went on to claim that storming Taylor's acceptance speech was an act of selflessness caused by an innocent desire to see Beyoncé appreciated. "What was arrogant about that?" Kanye queried. "That's completely selfless. That's like jumping in front of a bullet. I lost an arm. I'm walking around, I'm trying to put up my album with a missing arm right now. Every time I try to perform a song, everybody's like, 'Well, what's up with that missing arm, though?'"

Later that year, he had the "missing arm" on show when he interrupted his own concert at New York's Bowery Ballroom for a 10-minute rant about his media persona. Referring to the decision to give Taylor a VMA, he said: "When you do things like what happened last year, it's disrespectful to everyone who's creative. It's a slap in the face to everyone who tries to do something real. If I wasn't drunk, I would have been on stage longer!" He added, "Taylor never came to my defence in any interview – she rode the wave and rode and rode it."

That same month, he stormed out of an interview on national TV when they screened a clip of the moment. He subsequently blogged, "I feel very alone, very used, very tortured, very forced, very misunderstood, very hollow, very, very misused. I don't do press anymore... I don't trust anyone but myself!"

Finally, in the clearest indication yet that he was not sorry, he taunted Britney Spears in an identical manner when she made the number-one spot for her single 'Hold It Against Me'. "Yo, Britney, I'm really happy for you and I'm 'a let you be number one but me and Jay-Z's single is one of the best songs of all time!" he tweeted, before sarcastically adding, "LOL".

Taylor eventually moved on from the experience, next lending her vocals to the rock group Boys Like Girls for the song 'Two Is Better Than One'. Front man Martin Johnson revealed, "Taylor's such a versatile artist – she can go from country to pop to rock to anywhere!"

However, it wasn't long before the bad luck she had had with Kanye started to spread to other areas of her life. Excitement was initially high when Taylor announced a re-release of *Fearless* complete with six new songs. The internet exploded with tweets from delirious fans after she revealed the news, including bizarre claims such as "My ovaries just exploded!" However, not everyone was as happy. While Taylor wanted people to see the evolution of her life from year to year by providing them with a snapshot through her latest songs, some people criticised the decision, labelling it cynical and profit-hungry.

Yet new material wasn't in short supply – not only had Taylor recorded new versions of songs from the old days such as 'Superstar' and 'Come In With The Rain', and added a piano version of 'Forever And Always', she had also written new songs such as 'Jump Then Fall', 'The Other Side Of The Door' and 'Untouchable'. Meanwhile, the additional DVD contained interview snippets, concert photos, behind the scenes footage of Taylor, her 'Thug Story' collaboration with T-Pain and previously unreleased promotional videos for songs like 'Change' and 'The Best Day', as well as all the official singles.

In spite of the criticism, the album – which had already sold over five million copies in its previous format – sold like hot cakes. Consequently, when her birthday came around that year, instead of having a lavish bash and inviting the celebrity crowd over, she gave away part of her fortune. She donated $50,000 to the schools she had attended in her youth, even including her pre-school.

Her birthday, Christmas and New Year's Eve all fell within a period of three weeks, so there was no shortage of reasons to celebrate. Yet anyone who was expecting a night of hard partying and riot-girl posturing was to be disappointed, as Taylor was still tee-total. In fact, when the clock struck midnight to mark the beginning of 2010, she wasn't stumbling out of a nightclub, wild-eyed and crazy, nor was she even enjoying a glass of wine with friends. She was at home alone.

"I was texting Hayley [Williams, of Paramore] to let her know I got home from dinner and that my paranoid thoughts of getting in a car wreck were unwarranted," Taylor told *Rolling Stone* of how she spent the midnight hour. "I think I texted her something like, 'Don't worry about me, I'm not dead' and I looked at the clock and it was midnight. So I actually got to experience looking at the clock when it struck midnight and that was a really fun moment for me. It was the most unconventional New Year's Eve I've ever had." Taylor had vowed to herself and to the media that she wouldn't become another casualty of hard living and end up in rehab. It might not have been rock 'n' roll, but that wasn't the image Taylor was representing.

"I've never been a party girl," she clarified to *The Washington Post*. "I'd rather sit at home and bake on a Friday night than go to parties. In my high school, all my friends would go out drinking and stuff, but

I never, ever wanted to let my parents down – and I never want to let my fans down. I never want to let those little girls I see in the front row down by doing something stupid that's completely preventable and completely my fault. When people go through drug problems and alcohol problems, everyone points their finger at them and says, 'You did this to yourself.' I don't want to be that girl... My career is the only thing I think about. It's stronger than any alcohol, stronger than any drug, stronger than anything else you could try, so why should I do those things? Every night, I'm in a different small town and I see those little girls and their moms and it's a constant reminder of why I want to live this way."

She added defiantly to *Seventeen,* "If somebody wants to criticise me for not being a train wreck, that's fine with me."

Indeed, with Taylor's blemish-free record, the worst criticism anyone could throw at her was that she was a little strait-laced. Even her mother had been incredulous at her abstention, exclaiming, "I had my first drink when I was 18!"

Suddenly, however, new evidence emerged that cast doubt on her squeaky clean image – and the backlash she had experienced the previous year began all over again. Public MySpace messages had been unearthed from early 2005 from a girl purporting to be Taylor – and, for someone with her spotless reputation, they were scandalous.

In one, she spoke of getting "drunk as hell and crunk [crazy drunk]", while in another she made jokey references to "deep throating" lollipops. In a third, littered with profanity, she showed her mischievous side by threatening to wind down her car windows and shoot her enemies with a paintball gun.

Many fans collectively rolled their eyes upon hearing the news, assuming the messages had been penned by an imposter. However, there were some indications that they might have been authentic. They dated back to a time before Taylor was famous, when – as an anonymous artist – there would have been little reason for someone to impersonate her. She also signed off each message with her distinctive and widely recognised signature featuring "lovelovelove" at the end. There were also references to her favourite film, *Napoleon Dynamite* –

in which one of the central characters paints cross-bred creatures called "ligers" – when she wrote, "What's the difference between a lion and a tiger? A whore!"

All of this suggested that if it wasn't Taylor who wrote the messages, it was probably someone who knew her and her tastes very well.

In any case, the revelations spelt a nightmare for Taylor's public image. Not long before, her record label boss Scott Borchetta had insisted to *Elle Girl*, "Taylor really is the girl next door. She hasn't been drunk at a party, hasn't been in any crazy photographs. In this moment of total madness in culture, Taylor's fans know they can count on her. I think parents just go, 'Oh, thank God, my kids love Taylor Swift!'"

However, they might not have felt that way anymore. Scott – as well as a wide variety of magazines – had tagged her as the anti-Britney: someone who provided an alternative role model for young people who wanted to sidestep the craziness. Yet Taylor then confessed to a passion for the woman many people saw as her polar opposite and even seemed to admire some of her more outrageous antics. "What I love about Britney is that in every awards show performance, you're going to be surprised," she mused, "whether she's doing a costume change on stage, kissing Madonna or walking out with a snake around her neck. I think there's always a surprise element to what she does and that's what keeps the audience entertained."

Intriguingly, Catholicism forbids expressions of sexuality with a partner of the same sex, and Britney's kiss with Madonna certainly came under that category. Could the Catholic Taylor have idolised Britney's party-loving image and saucy routines on stage more than she had previously been willing to admit?

As for the talk of drink and drugs, Taylor now faced a new backlash over whether her promises of being teetotal had been entirely truthful. Previously, she had said that the hardest drug she was addicted to was her guitar, telling *Glamour*, "For me rebelling is done with words. I love to write honest songs that name real people, then get up on stage and live out those emotions in front of 15,000 people. Pencilling in a night to get wasted is not something I want to do." She elaborated to

The Reading Eagle: "It's great when a mom comes up to me and says, 'You're what I hope my daughter grows up like.' I'm very careful about that. I'm not a partier. It's just not who I am. I've been raised to be who I am."

Yet did a few MySpace messages really invalidate her right to be a role model? They were written long before she came into the public eye, at a time when she was much younger and still trying to find herself. Perhaps at the time she felt obligated, under pressure to keep up with her friends, after her poor record of fitting in. Perhaps her career had changed all that.

Tellingly, in an interview with *Seventeen,* she seemed to pinpoint her success as one of the reasons she shunned alcohol and a party lifestyle. "It's not a priority for me," she said. "I have to get up early and do interviews. I have to sing every night. I don't have any interest in going out to clubs right now."

It was clear that, whether or not Taylor had kept her promise to stay dry, she had a drive and focus that alcohol wouldn't dilute – that of someone whose first love was music.

However, it had been a stressful time for her. She had gone from being America's sweetheart and the poster child for innocence to enduring an inquisition about who she really was. It was ironic that her next single, released on January 4, was 'Fearless': something she needed to be to face the war of words against her. "Fearless doesn't mean that you're completely unafraid and it doesn't mean you're bulletproof," she told MTV. "It means that you have a lot of fears but you jump anyway."

Taylor also admitted that, despite her love affair with it, one of her biggest fears was of the music industry. Those fears were proved correct at the end of January when she attended the 2010 Grammy Awards. It was a night that should have been one of the highlights of her career, but instead it turned into yet another ill-fated awards ceremony. She must have thought it couldn't have got worse than her run-in with Kanye West the previous year, but while, on that occasion, she had been inundated with support and offers of shoulders to cry on, this time she would receive little sympathy.

Although she opened with new track 'Today Was A Fairytale', little did she know that that night would be anything but. It had started out positively enough – Taylor had eight award nominations, beaten only by Beyoncé with 10 – and it wasn't long before she started raking in the trophies. Following a 3D Michael Jackson tribute from a plethora of artists, Taylor took her first Grammy, Best Female Country Vocal Solo for 'White Horse'. Talking of contenders she beat to the trophy such as Miranda Lambert and Carrie Underwood, she claimed, "I live in awe of the people I was nominated against."

Just five minutes later, 'White Horse' triumphed again as Taylor took to the stage a second time to accept the award for Best Country Song. Calling upon co-writer Liz Rose to receive some of the applause, she explained, "She started writing songs with me when she had absolutely no reason to do so. I didn't have a record label. I didn't have anything to offer her."

Her third win, for Best Country Album, saw her describe the moment as an "impossible dream". While Beyoncé had shocked fans with a spirited performance of pop-rock artist Alanis Morissette's 'You Oughta Know', crawling on all fours across the stage like a true rock goddess, Taylor challenged her rival's crossover crown by engaging in a surprise of her own, a medley of 'You Belong With Me' and Fleetwood Mac's 'Rhiannon' with Stevie Nicks singing alongside her.

"Country music is my home," Taylor declared later. "Country music is my love – but to have it organically cross over this year, it's been fantastic. I think the healthiest thing you can do when making music is to remove stereotypes from it!" That cross-over was what led to Taylor picking up the final honour of the night – Album Of The Year – and it was a mainstream one.

"I hope that you know how much this means to me and all my producers that we can take this back to Nashville," she said, eyeing the trophy admiringly. "This is the story that when we're 80 years old and we're telling the same story over and over again, this is the story we're going to be telling – that in 2010 we won Album Of The Year!"

However, there was another story to be told of that night – and, as disgruntled journalists rushed back to their newsrooms with acid tongues and poison pens, they had already mentally formulated it.

By the next morning, the criticism started coming. *Entertainment Weekly* claimed, "The last thing I want to do is ruin another awards ceremony for Taylor Swift, but there's no doubt that someone was badly off-key." Meanwhile, *Sign On San Diego* described her duet with Stevie Nicks as "alarmingly under-rehearsed" and claimed that Stevie was "annoyed by her young partner's eyebrow-raising warbling", before concluding that she "might really benefit from lip-syncing or using [pitch-correcting software] Autotune". *The Washington Post* denounced her performance as "off-key caterwauling", too. Almost everywhere Taylor looked, someone had a negative word to say.

Some blogs dripped with sarcasm, including *The Borowitz Report*, which wrote spoof news headlines such as "Satan chooses Taylor Swift Performance As Ringtone" and "God Hoping Taylor Swift Does Not Thank Him".

Even fans had some harsh words to say. One astonished mother commented, "My eight-year-old daughter absolutely worships Taylor Swift, so it pains me to say this – but that girl cannot sing outside of a recording studio. Even my daughter asked me why Taylor was singing 'so funny'."

There were countless calls for her to get a vocal coach, while one tweet read, "Taylor Swift has given me hope. If she, who can't even sing, can win a Grammy, I can do anything!"

While the performance was almost universally condemned, perhaps the most painful words of all came from *The LA Times*, which sniped, "What Beyoncé may as well have been saying to Taylor Swift – 'So you think you're a crossover artist? You ain't seen nothing, kid.'" After all, Beyoncé was the very artist Kanye West had insisted should have received her VMA. Did this mean the media agreed that the older female artist was more deserving of the fame?

Despite calls for Taylor to get a vocal coach, it turned out she had already done that. "I have had vocal training since I was little," she explained to *Access Atlanta*. "I'm constantly working on improving my singing style."

Another of Taylor's loudest critics was music industry blogger Bob Lefsetz. Ironically, her first negative review from him the year before had been a blog entry accusing her of using Autotune to polish her live performance. Taylor's father had emailed him to deny the accusation and, weeks later, Taylor herself had followed up with a phone call, insisting she was "all natural all the time". Bob blogged in response, "It frustrated her to think that I believed she used Autotune. She denied it. Emphatically... but it still didn't address the underlying issue. Could she sing?... I'm convinced she's vocally challenged."

Three months later, after watching her Grammys performance, he took to the keyboard again to pen incendiary headlines such as "Poor Taylor Swift showed everyone she can't sing." First accused of faking a flawless pitch with Autotune and then criticised for not using the technology at all, it seemed that no matter what Taylor did, she couldn't win.

"People seemed desperate to do Taylor down," observed one friend. "It was any excuse to bash the starlet who'd had mammoth success at such an early age. That success didn't sit well with people – it intimidated them. So they turned against her."

Scott Borchetta agreed: "It's that classic thing that critics do of building something up and then wanting to tear it down."

Was it true that her most vocal opponents simply resented her success? There was certainly cause to envy Taylor. She was young, beautiful and already had songs that millions of fans adored – something that was demonstrable by millions of album sales. However, the sheer volume of complaints about her voice on the night of the Grammys was too great to be ignored.

In the nick of time, Scott Borchetta came to her rescue. Telling *The Tennessean* that the criticism was "just over the top", he blamed an inner-ear volume problem for her failure to hit the right notes. According to him, Taylor didn't want to be cold, calculated and soulless – she wanted instead to convey the emotion of the song, even if it was at the expense of perfection. Taylor's emotions might have come spilling out haphazardly, but weren't all passions in life equally uncontrollable and messy?

"This is not *American Idol*," Scott defended. "This is not a competition of getting up and seeing who can sing the highest note. This is about a true artist and communicator. It's not about that technically perfect performance. Maybe she's not the best technical singer, but she's probably the best emotional singer because everybody else who gets up there and is technically perfect, people don't seem to want more of it."

Taylor clearly agreed – just a few months before she had told *The LA Times*: "It's really more about portraying the song in a way that gets the feeling across, rather than every phrase being exactly perfect. I think it's the writer in me that's a little more obsessed with the meaning of the song than the vocal technique. All that stuff is like math to me. Overthinking vocals and stuff – I never want to get to that point."

To one sound engineer, Taylor's unwillingness to rely on Autotune showed commendable bravery. "Almost every A-list recording artist uses this technology in the studio and most use it live without apology," he challenged. "Does this mean your favourite country star can't sing? Not at all. It means he/she believes you want the concert to sound just like the record, which was brushed, polished and Autotuned in the studio. That's the nature of record making today. Taylor chose not to have her voice tuned at the Grammys. Then she delivered a less than convincing performance… is she a talentless fraud? Of course not. She makes records using the same technology and methodology of anyone else in town."

In other words, how many artists who had seen their Grammy performances celebrated by the press would have had as much reason to crack open the champagne over their media reception if they too had dared to discard the Autotune and let their voice speak for itself on the night?

Round one to Taylor. But she and Scott hadn't counted on the wrath of former *American Idol* winner Kelly Clarkson, who believed Scott had unnecessarily belittled the show that earned her success. "I understand defending your artist obviously, because I have done the same in the past for artists I like, including Taylor," Kelly began in an open letter to Scott which was published on her blog. "So you might see why it's upsetting to read you attacking *American Idol* for producing simply vocalists that 'hit the high notes'. Thank you for that 'Captain Obvious' sense of humour, because you know what, we not only hit the high notes, you forgot to mention we generally hit the 'right' notes as well. Every artist has a bad performance or two and that is understandable, but throwing blame will not make the situation at hand any better."

She added, "I have been criticised left and right for shaky performances before (and they were shaky) and what my manager or label executives say to the public is 'I'll kick butt next time' or 'every performance isn't going to be perfect'. I bring this up because you should take a lesson from these people and instead of lashing out at other artists (that in your 'humble' opinion lack true artistry), you should simply take a breath and realise that sometimes things won't go according to plan or work out and that's OK. Sincerely, one of these contestants from *American Idol* who only made it because of her high notes."

That was just the beginning of the backlash. Public conversation swiftly turned to whether Taylor's wealthy parents had brought her a record deal and paid her way to the top. Industry insiders were hearing rumours that Taylor's father had invested funds to enable Scott to set up his record label, provided that Taylor was the star attraction. Meanwhile, the general public argued that her parents' money and connections had paid for recording time in the studio.

As the most expensive album produced in Nashville was estimated to be *The Woman In Me* by Shania Twain, for a breath-taking $500,000, studio time certainly wasn't going cheap. "Money can buy anything, including a recording contract," raged one blogger on the CMT website. "She can't sing and she is getting by on daddy's money, her looks and the cluelessness of the public… they are so mesmerised by her youth and looks that they ignore her very poor singing ability."

Another agreed, "Truth is, without her father's millions, investments and connections, Taylor would likely be a good-looking waitress singing her original songs on table-waiting breaks at Tilley's. The music biz *is* about money and connections, her father has the money and the connections and the rest is history. God bless her, but the days of someone coming from nowhere and being successful on talent alone are *way* over."

It was true that Scott Swift had connections – he had secured Taylor a gig singing the national anthem at a Philadelphia 76ers basketball game through his friendship with one of the marketing managers there. It was also true that her parents had given her the freedom to pursue her own dreams by emotionally and financially supporting her, not to mention making the gruelling cross-country drives to and from Nashville in her youth.

"We've always made it clear that we didn't need her to pay the bills," her mother confessed to *The LA Times.* Taylor had never denied her family's role in her success, repeatedly telling interviewers that if it hadn't been for her parents' support, she felt she might never have made it. In spite of all that, surely a head start in the industry could only have got Taylor so far?

From an industry perspective, if an artist is wrongly chosen and promoted, there would be the potential for a massive financial loss. In Scott Borchetta's case, even if Taylor's father had invested generously in the company and he had no financial worries whatsoever, there was one thing he couldn't afford to lose – and that was his reputation.

Scott's name depended on picking artists who he believed in and who could deliver on that belief. Plus, as he had decades of experience in the industry, he already had connections of his own who could be potential investors, as well as a track record that lent itself well to gaining access to finance. Surely there was no reason for him to take a chance on Taylor if he hadn't seen potential in her?

Besides, whatever might have been offered to Scott on Taylor's behalf, even if it could buy a record deal, it certainly couldn't buy success. As a fan named Alex wrote on CMT's website, "Taylor's family didn't buy her the success that she's earned. Her daddy didn't pay me to go out and buy her CD. I bought her CD and concert tickets because I identify and connect with her and I believe that this is probably also the case for the millions of other people that are doing the same."

She added, "Taylor may not vocally be an American idol, but in my opinion, she is in a league of her own."

There was clearly a chemistry between Taylor and her listeners, which had maintained itself long enough for her to have shifted millions of CDs. Even major labels, who invested millions of dollars in their singers' futures, often made mistakes. Some artists faded into obscurity before their careers had even begun and before some of the music-buying public had the chance to hear their names. Even those with massive TV exposure on shows such as *The X-Factor* and *American Idol* often fail to build careers afterwards, and are reduced to playing half-empty coffee shops within a year or two of winning.

Yet Taylor had gained fans and sustained them. One of her biggest critics, Bob Lefsetz, had claimed, "She was so horrible in the opening of the CMAs... she was so far from perfect, anywhere but on the note." However, what he declined to mention was that the CMAs had been voted for entirely by viewers. Taylor was there because they had demanded her.

Scott's comments about the Grammys might have inflamed high-profile readers such as Kelly Clarkson, but he could back them up with figures. Taylor's fans seemed to be satiated by a less than technically perfect performance – and they bought into her words, and what they represented, in their millions. After all, who better to judge talent than the fans – the very people buying the concert tickets and albums?

Finally, while not the last word on the subject, perhaps one of the most definitive points of view came from a commentator on CMT who purported to be Scott Borchetta himself. "I have had the good fortune to work with the biggest of the big in Nashville, including Reba McEntire, George Strait, Vince Gill, Toby Keith, Sugarland and now Taylor," he claimed. "I can tell you with absolute clarity that she is one of the most talented artists I've worked with some 25 years in the business.

"Also, when starting the new label Big Machine and watching every dollar, I can factually tell you we made her first record for one third of what major labels spend. There are tons of artists that come to town every year with tons of money, whether it's from investors or parents. You can't buy talent. You can't buy charisma. You can't buy songwriting skills. You can't buy a record deal at Big Machine... If you're jealous of Taylor's success and you're looking to tear her down, keep making this crap up… [but] she's likely to be a big star for a long time to come, so you might be smart to pick a fight you can win and a target you can successfully tear down – this ain't it!"

If further proof was needed of Taylor's widespread appeal, she delivered it when the film *Valentine's Day*, which featured her as both a singer and an actress, made over $50 million at the box office in its first weekend. Unfortunately for Taylor, she had no one to share the lover's season with. After a brief fling, she had broken up with on-screen boyfriend Taylor Lautner on her birthday the previous year.

The failure of the relationship, which would go on to inspire the song 'Back To December', came amid rumours that his previous partner, Disney star Selena Gomez, wanted him back. As Taylor was close friends with Selena, it could have become a tricky situation. As it was, she now faced an awkward few weeks of collaborative film promotion alongside a person she was feeling anything but romantic about. It was hardly in the spirit of Valentine's Day.

However, ironically, even her lack of a boyfriend couldn't prevent her chastity from becoming the object of close scrutiny. When Taylor said she had no comment, she was criticised for being secretive and put under pressure to reveal the truth; but when she came out and confessed she was a virgin, she was then accused of lying. Not for the first time that year, it seemed that Taylor just couldn't win.

It had started when she rebuffed *Allure* magazine's attempts to expose her sex life, claiming, "I think when you talk about virginity and sex publicly, people just automatically picture you naked, and as much as I can prevent people picturing me naked, I'm going to."

However, the questions were persistent in every form of media. Eventually she tired of the never-ending speculation and gave in, telling *Blender* that she was a virgin. She added that a partner with a promise ring, signalling his abstention from sex, was by no means a deal-breaker. "I don't ever talk about how I feel about that sort of thing because it makes people look at me sexually, which has never been a goal of mine," she told *Philadelphia* magazine coyly, "so, honestly, deal-breaker? [A guy who wears a promise ring] is actually a plus for me."

However, noting that every one of Taylor's songs seemed to bring a different man into the spotlight, *Hollywood Life* sneered, "Continue to believe that Taylor Swift is a virgin as she has relationship after relationship with sexually active men."

Taylor was rapidly learning the price of rising fame: no subject was out of bounds. To every journalist, photographer or verbal gold digger posing as a *faux* friend, her life and the stories about it were now a valuable commodity. What was more, no matter how much she tried to keep her personal life under wraps in interviews, choosing to say all that she wanted to say through her songs, it would never stay private for very long. Whatever she did – or didn't do – someone, somewhere, would be waiting to criticise it.

As long as her friends and family knew the truth about her, however, Taylor felt she would be OK. "I thought in this industry I'd have more friends than before," she mused, "but I've actually got less. It makes me value my true friends even more. I've had the same best friend since high school."

It was that same close friend, Abigail Anderson, with whom Taylor took a short break from the music world to explore what it was like to be a normal girl. She flew into Kansas City and, much to the surprise of a class full of journalism students, attended Abigail's university lectures with her.

"I keep one eye on the path I didn't choose every day," she explained. "That's why I [attended] journalism classes... because I just want to sit there and see what it's like for a day. That's why I [also] go to Notre Dame and visit my brother and sit in his dorm room. The life I choose is very different from theirs."

Her brother was in business school, earnestly studying to be a financial entrepreneur like his father, while Abigail was training to be a news reporter – and, for Taylor's part, she was simply curious. "College is the one thing that she hasn't been able to experience that everybody her age pretty much has and to some that's a big deal," Abigail claimed.

"I always thought that I would go to college, most definitely," Taylor elaborated to *Elle Girl*. "You're always going to wonder about the road not taken, the dorm not taken and the sorority not taken… but then I really thought about it and assessed the situation and I can't leave this life… there just wouldn't be enough time in the day to be on tour, do interviews, meet and greets, TV appearances and everything that I need to do… going to college would mean saying goodbye to my music career."

Therefore, while Abigail asserted, "Once you have the opportunity to meet her, you understand that she's just as normal as it gets," Taylor's experience of college would be a fleeting one to satiate her curiosity. She was soon back in the spotlight with no regrets.

When she returned to Nashville, it was back to the grindstone and, after Chris Robinson, singer of rock group The Black Crowes, heard Taylor's collaboration with Def Leppard, he certainly had an axe to grind.

Astonishingly, after seemingly enduring enough pages of criticism to strip several acres of forest for singing off-key, she was now facing complaints that she lacked emotion because she sang on key. "I find it embarrassing that adults are like, 'Taylor Swift is very talented,'" he raged to *Nylon Guys*. "She's not. She might be cute, but she's horrible. [Artists like her] have stylists who dress them, they make records with producers who play a chord into a computer and it all comes out the same… singing isn't always about being on key – it's about emotionality."

It had been a year of breathtakingly intense criticism for Taylor and, by the time September arrived, she would be returning to the VMAs which she and Kanye West were both scheduled to attend. Kanye, who had been telling anyone who would listen that he had been "suicidal" at times the previous year, announced that he had written a song for Taylor and wanted her to perform it with him.

"If she won't put it out, I will," he threatened. A dubious Taylor declined his invitation of a duet, but did show forgiveness when she sang 'Innocent', a song addressed to Kanye from her soon-to-be-released third album, *Speak Now*. It was her first performance on the VMA stage.

Kanye's song, meanwhile, was a little less innocent. It acknowledged that she had probably had enough of him and was laced with profanities.

196

A chorus inviting America to toast a scumbag left it unclear whether Kanye was referring to himself or making a sarcastic dig at Taylor.

Either way, a year of bad luck had come full circle – and almost exactly a year after she was humiliated by Kanye, she was performing again – a little older and wiser and just a little bit thicker skinned.

Chapter 10

Speak Now Or Forever
Hold Your Peace

It was August 4, 2010, and Taylor was winging her way to Japan for a promotional visit, to precede the August 16 release of 'Mine'. Ironically for a song by that name, it wasn't going to be her possession for much longer – and she ended up having to part with it earlier than expected.

"When I got on that plane, I just thought I was going to Japan and I thought it was going to be a regular flight – watch a few movies, take a nap," Taylor told *Entertainment Weekly*. "But an hour into the flight, one of my managers came up to me and said, 'Hey, so try not to panic, but how would you feel about a release of the single on August 5? So that's 8/5 and eight plus five is 13, which is your lucky number!' I said, 'It leaked, didn't it?' and she said, 'Yes.'"

By the time she landed, it felt as though there wasn't a single music fan with a computer who hadn't heard the song. Within seconds of leaving the aeroplane, her phone was already exploding with texts of congratulations.

It could have been a moment of incandescent rage, Kanye West style, with insults flying faster than a Boeing 747. It could also have been a fit of tearful histrionics on the floor of the arrivals terminal, a paparazzi photographer or gossip columnist's dream. Thankfully, it was neither: Taylor quickly resolved not to get too hung up on anything she couldn't control. There was no way she could change the past, but she could control the future – by releasing her song on iTunes straight away.

The song represented her coming of age – not only was she feeling intense emotions, but her new maturity meant she was also starting to analyse them. As a result, 'Mine' – like much of the rest of the third album – was about what made Taylor Swift tick.

For someone who claimed not to want a "constant stream of boyfriends", she had enjoyed a great number of affairs and crushes over the months, none of which had lasted particularly long. She declared on *The Ellen DeGeneres Show*, "I want to be the girl that when she falls in love, it's a big deal and a rare thing", but these wholesome desires had yet to translate into long-term love. In fact, even if it was in the non-sexual sense, Taylor had ended up quite promiscuous, something of a romantic butterfly. In 'Mine', she was addressing all the reasons why.

"Every really direct example of love that I've had in front of me has ended in goodbye and ended in break-ups," she explained to *Entertainment Weekly*, "so I think I've developed this pattern of running away when it comes time to fall in love and stay in a relationship."

Taylor had flicked to the back page of the metaphorical book in any affair, found a blank page and then, like the reader of a *Choose Your Own Adventure* story, visualised and filled it with a horrifying ending. That tendency to second-guess her lover's intentions and assume the worst, coupled with her fear of abandonment, drove her to end promising relationships before they began to protect herself from the perils of getting too close emotionally.

After recognising her problem, Taylor had rewritten the story to reflect the type of ending she would prefer. "The song is sort of about finding the exception to that and finding someone who would make you believe in love and realise that it could work out, because I'm never going to go past hoping that love works out."

Although the track was mainly about Taylor's insecurities, there was one man in particular that shared the spotlight with her – Corey Monteith from hit TV musical *Glee*.

Corey had first announced his crush on her with about as much subtlety as Taylor herself, telling the national magazine *US*, "She's lovely. I think talent is attractive." He had been just as forthright and proactive about taking the relationship a step further when they finally met, too.

However, fearful of getting in too deep, Taylor didn't warm to his advances and the relationship ended up fizzling out. "A guy that I just barely knew put his arm around me by the water and I saw the entire relationship flash before my eyes, almost like some weird science-fiction movie," Taylor confessed to Yahoo Music. "[The song] was sort of half-confession and half-prediction or projection of what I saw."

If Taylor thought she hadn't been transparent enough, she needn't have worried. Within hours of the song hitting the web, she received an email from Corey – who had cracked the code instantly. "The fact that it came across so clearly to that guy that he would email me meant that I had been direct enough," she added jubilantly.

Although the song had been leaked almost two weeks earlier than intended, the video was fortunately ready to go. It had been shot in Portland, Maine, on a private estate, and Taylor travelled back there to premiere the final cut with 800 curious fans on August 27, former President George H.W. Bush and his grandchildren included. While she was there, she treated the fans to a concert outside the local church where she had filmed the video's wedding scenes.

Why had there been a wedding? Taylor had looked into the future and reworked the wistful repetitive endings of her ill-fated relationships, this time directing the final frame to give it the ending she really wanted – one of everlasting marriage.

Her on-screen husband, however, had been chosen by much more fickle means and without much forethought. Taylor had been watching a film featuring British actor Toby Hemingway called *The Covenant* – and, after seeing the sweatshirt he was wearing, her mind was made up. "I've got this crazy lucky 13 thing," Taylor told *People*, "and he walks on screen for the first time wearing a sweatshirt with a 13 on it! That was the deciding factor. It wasn't really up to me, it was about the number."

The song itself had come to life just as instinctively. According to producer Nathan Chapman, Taylor had perfected the song in the first demo. That initial version had taken less than five hours to record, but – despite polishing the song for four months and spending $30,000 to perfect it – he claimed the demo ended up "almost identical to the record". That disclosure was a slap in the face for those who believed Taylor's sound could only have been achieved with big bucks.

Nathan and Taylor had co-produced all of the tracks on the third album – which Taylor was intending to call *Enchanted* – and they had followed a similar process. "With [the third album], we deliberately went back to our initial way of working together," he explained. "We had an unlimited budget and could have gone and recorded the whole album in the Bahamas, used any studio we liked and whatever musicians we wanted. But we decided to bring it back to the basics on purpose, because we wanted to keep it about the music and our chemistry."

Another notable point about the album was that, unlike her previous two releases, Taylor hadn't collaborated with a single songwriter. She explained it simply, on a live webcast, by declaring, "I actually wrote all the songs myself [but] it didn't really happen on purpose, it just sort of happened. Like, I'd get my best ideas at 3 a.m. in Arkansas and I didn't have a co-writer around."

However, was that really all there was to it? Or, following acid-tongued talk by journalists about her lack of ability, had she simply wanted to prove first-hand that she could stand on her own two feet and wasn't hiding behind someone else's skills?

If so, Nathan was definitely in her corner. "It's not a vanity credit, we really were a team," he explained. "She'd [even] have opinions on drum sounds and everything that we did... Taylor is a great songwriter and there's not much I have to do on that front. I'm not afraid to be OK with that. Some producers may be uncomfortable with not giving an opinion; they don't want to appear useless. I'm not like that. I want to capture her gut instinct... because nine out of 10 times, that's the right way to go."

What was Taylor's songwriting instinct on the new album? She had endured more than her fair share of break-ups in the months leading up to its production, so it was fair to predict that many of the tracks would cover her heartbreak. Perhaps, like pop singer Lily Allen, she was running short on inspiration. Lily had confessed to the *Radio Times*, "I've actually broken up with boyfriends for inspiration. When I hit a period of not being able to write music, I get up and walk away. It's pretty mean, but it's true."

For a compulsive writer like Taylor, who valued her creative output more than anything else, perhaps a little drama was necessary. "If I've just written a song, I'm the happiest you will ever see me," she told *Entertainment Weekly*, "but if I haven't written a song in a week and a half, I am more stressed than you will ever, ever see me at any point."

Whether or not Taylor really was using men as pawns to get her creative juices flowing, it was undeniably the opposite sex that formed most of the subject matter for her new album. In any case, one promise she could definitely make was: "Whatever I go through in life will be reflected directly in my music." Consequently, when the album was released on October 25, listeners were in for a bumpy ride.

'Better Than Revenge' saw Taylor dispense with all pleasantries and, in trademark frank style, aim straight for the jugular to get her vengeance. She was well qualified to speak on the subject of revenge – after all, her life thus far had been full of nerd-scorned-comes-back-laughing stories. One of the sweetest payback moments had come with Corey Robinson, who had shunned her affections back in Wyomissing. In the summer of 2007, when her début album had been storming the charts and she had been out on the highest grossing tour in country music history with her idols Faith Hill and Tim McGraw, Corey was still on the bottom rung of the ladder, spending his summer working as a poorly paid public swimming pool cleaner for the local council.

It was ironic, considering that she would once have given anything to be in his life, how quickly the tables were turned. She wouldn't be shedding any tears for the bullies she left behind in Pennsylvania either; and it was with a tinge of satisfaction that she saw the people who had dismissed her as a nobody back then turn up to shows wearing her tour T-shirts and clutching copies of her album. Now, they were not stopping by to tease her, but to clamour for an autograph.

Her revenge on Kanye West, meanwhile, had come when she had gained more support than she had known possible due to the fracas, while public opinion of Kanye had rapidly diminished – according to him, even amongst his own fans.

Taylor had covered most bases as far as getting her own back was concerned, but there was one final score left to be settled. The best revenge was yet to come and it involved finding the strength to walk away from Joe Jonas with her head held high.

Several tell-tale clues linked 'Better Than Revenge' to her relationship with Joe and, more specifically, her disgust towards the girl she condemned as a love thief. She makes reference first to an actress stealing her man when she wasn't around.

But then, in a direct reference to The Jonas Brothers song 'Much Better', Taylor urges a woman to come out and prove how much better she really is.

After dumping Taylor, Joe had originally sung that his new love was far superior to the diva with teardrops on her guitar. Even better than revenge for Taylor was that, while she had her freedom to find someone better, her previous love rival was stuck in a relationship with someone she already felt she knew to be a cheat.

There was more revenge in store on 'Mean', when she addressed all of those who had broadcast unkind words about her in the past. She used the metaphor of words as lethal weapons, ones that – without delivering a single blow – had the power to break her down. "Words are everything to me," Taylor declared to *Entertainment Weekly*. "Words can absolutely demolish me. I am nowhere close to being bullet-proof when it comes to criticism. Feeling everything is part of being a song writer. If I block out those feelings of pain and rejection, then I don't know what I'd write about. I'd rather feel pain when I read something terrible about me than feel nothing!"

In spite of that, there had come a time when reading the newspapers was far more pain than pleasure – and she felt that certain people had gone too far. "When you do what I do, which is you put yourself out there for a lot of people to say whatever they want, there's a million different opinions," she told *Entertainment News*. "I get that, no matter what, you're going to be criticised for something, but I also get that there are different ways to criticise someone. There's constructive criticism, there's professional criticism and then there's just being mean. And there's a line that you cross when you just start to attack everything about a person."

People might have stereotyped Taylor as gregarious and carefree because of her seemingly privileged position of fame, without realising that – as one of her favourite pop artists, Rihanna, said – it could be lonely at the top. Being a multi-million selling singer didn't immunise her from negative comments, and didn't bestow on her a bullet-proof suit of armour, either.

The song was Taylor's opportunity to show that her heart was far from invulnerable. Who were the main culprits that she addressed? One repeat offender was the music critic Bob Lefsetz, whose allegations on his blog had prompted direct communication from Taylor the previous year. According to his write-up of their conversation, she had told him, "I thought you got me" – and those were the very words that appeared in the capital letters spelt out on the lyric sleeve of the CD for that song. The song's references to disloyalty and to someone who kept switching sides also made more sense, given that Bob had previously praised Taylor on his blog, but, after her performance at the Grammys, had claimed that she had destroyed her singing career overnight.

If Taylor had penned the track with him in mind, her words calling upon him to stop bullying her fell on deaf ears. When he realised that he could have been the antagonist that inspired the song, he sniped, "Here am I giving Taylor Swift the publicity she desires. She wins. But she still can't sing and isn't it time to start acting like an adult? To cast off the high-school persona and fly as a woman instead of darting around like a little girl? That's what's got everyone's eyes rolling... She still can't sing – and if this song is really about me, I wish it were better."

He later commented that the part of the song where Taylor referred to a bitter, washed-up mystery subject sitting in a bar years from now, moaning about their inability to sing, was "autobiographical".

While Taylor had dreamt of the day she would be so big that she was bullet-proof, that day might never come – even for the brightest of stars. She hadn't managed to stop the criticism – and nothing that she did would please everybody. But she had made her point: "When [criticism] is constructive, I have an appreciation for it, but when it crosses a line and becomes mean, I write songs about it."

On the subject of meanness, there was still the small matter of Kanye West. The world had been expecting the queen of unapologetic, self-dramatising honesty to pen him a song – but, for a long time, she hadn't known exactly what to say.

"I think a lot of people expected me to write a song *about* him, but for me it was important to write a song *to* him," Taylor explained to *New York* magazine. She later added to *Billboard*, "It took a while to write... That was a huge, intense thing in my life that resonated for a long time. It was brought up to me in grocery stores and everywhere I went; and in a lot of times in my life, when I don't know how I feel about something, I say nothing... That's what I did until I could come to the conclusion that I came to in order to write 'Innocent'."

It took a lot to reduce her to stunned silence, but – in the days after the fracas with Kanye – a normally chatty Taylor had dissolved into just that. Her Twitter account had been unusually, conspicuously silent, and she recognised the importance of choosing her words carefully.

"It doesn't really add anything good if I start victimising myself and complaining about things," she explained. Instead, Taylor had waited until forgiveness had come to her – and she told Kanye in the song that, at 32, he still had some growing up to do – and that the future held ample time for correcting mistakes. Plus, as if to prove he was no more than a brief blip on her radar, the encoded sentence within the lyric sleeve for the song read: "Life is full of little interruptions." However, the upside was that this little interruption had provided the inspiration for a credible song.

While Bob Lefsetz had challenged Taylor for her girlish behaviour and for failing to grow up – at the ripe old age of 20, in America, she still wasn't fully legally categorised as an adult – Taylor had rebelled against such perceptions with the track 'Never Grow Up'.

Displaying some of the Lolita character traits of Katy Perry, she idealised her childhood. She had finally moved out of her parents' house in July 2009, only to find that, instead of feeling joy at having her own place, she felt only crippling loneliness. It didn't help much that her mother was the archetypal over-protective parent, once agonising to *Rolling Stone*, "Living by yourself, I mean, think about it – there's danger. There's stepping in water and hitting the light switch. There's a bath tub overflowing – just the whole safety issue." In fact, the magazine even labelled her concerns as similar to "a horrific scene out of a *Final Destination* sequel".

"It's tricky growing up," Taylor declared on her website. "Growing up happens without you knowing it… It's such a crazy concept because a lot of times when you were younger, you wish you were older!" That was exactly how she had once felt: she had been desperate to get older so she could finally gain the attention of a record label. But now that success was within her grasp, was coming of age really all it was cracked up to be? Or was the comfort, warmth and security of childhood more appealing?

"I look out into a crowd every night and I see a lot of girls that are my age and going through the same things as I'm going through," Taylor continued. "Every once in a while, I look down and see a little girl who is seven or eight and I wish I could tell her all of this. There she is, becoming who she is going to be and forming her thoughts, dreams and opinions. I wrote this song ['Never Grow Up'] for those little girls."

Taylor soon found the right balance between independence and closeness with family in her own life – but, until that day came, the song sustained her.

More melancholia presented itself on 'Haunted', depicting a heart-broken girl driven into a panic by the thought that the love of her life was slipping through her fingers. Written in 2008, it seemed to address the decay of her partnership with Joe Jonas. Taylor used a live string section on the song to capture the "intense, chaotic feeling of confusion" she was looking for.

"'Haunted' is about the moment you realise the person you're in love with is drifting and fading fast and you don't know what to do," she explained via her website. "But in that period of time, in that phase of love where it's fading out, time moves so slowly. Everything hinges on what that last text message said and you're realising that he's kind of

207

falling out of love. That's a really heart-breaking and tragic thing to go through because, the whole time, you're trying to tell yourself it's not happening."

Faced with the fact that it was happening, Taylor eventually dealt with it in the way that she knew best: getting up in the early hours of the morning, rubbing the sleep from her eyes and writing a song.

Another ode to Joe Jonas that she wrote on one of these lonely and sleepless nights was 'Last Kiss'. The code in the lyrics for this song spelt 'Forever And Always' – the title of her previous song about Joe on the *Fearless* album. The hope of a fairy tale-style everlasting romance came in stark contrast to the reality of the couple's final kiss – and Taylor used the song to pour out her frustration about the ending. The strongest hint that the song is about Joe comes when the lyrics speak of running off a plane on July 9 – it was on July 9, 2008 that she flew to Dallas to attend a Jonas Brothers concert.

"'Last Kiss' is sort of like a letter to somebody," Taylor elaborated on her website. "You say all of these deep, hopeless feelings that you have after a break-up… you feel anger and you feel confusion and frustration. Then there is the absolute sadness. The sadness of losing this person, losing all the memories and the hopes you had for the future. There are times when you have this moment of truth when you just admit to yourself that you miss all these things. When I was in one of those moments, I wrote this song."

Even worse, while Taylor wanted to be angry with Joe, in moments of loneliness or weakness, her resolve broke and she feared she might give in to the yearnings to get back in touch. She didn't want to forgive things she previously saw as unforgivable, but she had to admit she missed him, even though he had wronged her and left her behind. There was no Loveaholics Anonymous group to attend, and the only alternative to getting in touch for real was writing her letter as a song.

Another heart-breaker who played a leading role on the album was John Mayer. Few could have imagined Taylor dating him – after all, John was no college boy, but a grown man in his thirties, and there was an age gap of more than a decade between them. Not only was John much older than her – more than enough ammunition to get the gossip columnists' tongues wagging – but he had the chequered relationship history to prove it.

By the time he and Taylor met to record their duet for 'Half Of My Heart', his reputation for womanising already preceded him. Past conquests included actress Jennifer Aniston and Jessica Simpson, the pop singer with a penchant for occasional Dolly Parton covers.

Friends had warned Taylor to give him a wide berth, but he had snared her with his charm from the very first day, according to the encoded phrase in the lyrics to 'Dear John' in the CD booklet. The song itself piles shame on the nasty games he played, and expresses not only disgust that he poisoned the heart of someone so much younger than himself, but also regret that she didn't listen to the stream of advice urging her to avoid getting caught up with him.

Cunningly, although the song was unmistakably addressed to a man called John – and she later confirmed that Mayer was the inspiration – it also initially left a teasing element of doubt. The phrase 'Dear John' was known to be an archetypal way of addressing a partner in a break-up letter, no matter what their real name. There was similar confusion when it came to 'The Story Of Us', which many listeners thought referred to a more recent ex, Taylor Lautner. Contrary to popular belief, however, it too was about John Mayer.

'The Story Of Us' described the awkward moment of coming face to face with him for the first time after their final bust-up. For Taylor, that moment came very publicly at the 2010 CMT Awards, when John was making an appearance with Keith Urban. Taylor was seated just a few places away from him on the same table, but both were giving each other the silent treatment – Taylor reluctantly and John defiantly. She found herself battling her inhibitions and pride to break the ice and, in the spirit of the album's emerging theme, to speak now. Instead, she ended up in intent conversation with virtual strangers – anything to avoid a confrontation.

"I think both of us had so much we wanted to say, but we were sitting six seats away from each other, just fighting this silent war of 'I don't care that you're here'," Taylor revealed to the *New York Times*. "I remember getting home and sitting at the kitchen table and saying to my mom, 'It was like I was standing alone in a crowded room'. That's when my eyes glazed over and I got distracted and walked away to write. My mom is used to me doing that!"

When there was just a pen and paper between herself and the sea of emotions in her mind, Taylor had no hesitation about speaking. However, when it came to real life and she had several pairs of eyes on her at the dinner table, she had failed miserably. "I think I've developed, as many people do, this sense of 'Don't say the wrong thing, or else people will point at you and laugh,'" she explained. "In your personal life, that can lead to being guarded and not making what you feel clear in the moments that you're feeling it. For me, it's never really fearing saying what's on my mind in my music, but sometimes having a problem with it in life. Sometimes you lose the moment."

That night, they said just four words to each other – a cold, faked "Hi, how are you?" They were both adamant about maintaining "this horrible belligerent battle" by staying silent, a moment Taylor described as "heart-breaking". However, she made amends by saying everything she never said to his face in 'The Story Of Us'.

She told *People*, "A lot of times when people's relationships end, they write an email to that person and say everything that they wish they would have said. A lot of times they don't push send... I guess putting [this song] on the album was pushing send."

Perhaps her relationship with John had been doomed from the start. Passionate kisses with Taylor Lautner had been a professional call of duty on the set of *Valentine's Day* – which was a better excuse than the average teenager caught locking lips with another man might have. But it seemed John was still uncomfortable with the situation and his suspicions may not have been unfounded since, after they broke up, Taylor rebounded into the arms of Lautner.

In her relationship with Lautner, she did allow real life and fiction to overlap – but while she might have hoped they would turn into the loving couple immortalised by their film roles, it too was short-lived. Sources had speculated that, during her trysts with Taylor, she was still pining with unresolved grief from her last relationship. While some thought her feelings were only puppy love due to her tender age and

Taylor had been flitting from relationship to relationship, believing she was in love with each person as only a teenager can, there was no doubt both partnerships had been intense and Technicolored for her.

As if to prove that the past was no less important to her than the present, Taylor even released an old fan favourite, 'Sparks Fly', that told of a love affair dating back to the days before Joe Jonas was in her life. According to Taylor, the early 2008 track was about "falling for someone who you maybe shouldn't fall for, but you can't stop yourself, because there's such a connection".

She first performed it live in Portland, Oregon (which is why the town's name was picked out in capitals in the lyrics). Who was the forbidden fruit in this song? An older lover? A man who was already attached? A notorious womaniser? A Romeo with insurmountable cultural differences? Or simply someone that no one in her social group approved of?

Later in life, Taylor would encounter almost all these forms of forbidden love but, dating back to much earlier days, this song was shrouded in secrecy. Intriguingly, Taylor changed the lyrics in the studio version. The early live version from 2008 spoke of being haunted by her boyfriend after he left, but, in the new lyrics, it was Taylor who would haunt him when she was no longer around. The prominence of the idea that there would come a time when she was no long around suggests the song might have been reminiscent of someone in her Wyomissing school days, whose bad behaviour she repaid when she found fame and left him behind for good.

The long-term loves of her life post-fame, albeit platonic ones, were all the people who had played a part in her musical career – and it was those that she paid homage to on 'Long Live'. "This song is about my band and my producers and all the people who have helped us build this brick by brick," Taylor wrote on her website. "The fans, the people who I feel that we are all in this together: this song talks about the triumphant moments that we've had in the last two years. We've had times where we just jump up and down and dance like we don't care how we're dancing and just scream at the top of our lungs: 'How is this happening?' This song for me is like looking at a photo album of all the award shows and all the stadium shows and all the hands in the air in the crowd. It's sort of the first love song that I've written to my team."

Meanwhile, 'Speak Now' saw Taylor shamelessly gate-crashing a "white-veil occasion" – but all in the name of free speech. "Sometimes when you're caught off guard by extreme feelings, a lot of times you don't say exactly the right thing in that moment," she lamented to *Dose*. "I walk away from these situations thinking, 'Now I know what I should've said.'"

Taylor's experiences, with John Mayer in particular, had sensitised her to the regret and despair involved with not speaking her mind when she had the chance. Therefore, when her close friend came to her with a similarly sticky situation, she knew exactly how to advise her.

"She was telling a story about her childhood sweet-heart crush guy," Taylor revealed to *E!* "They were together in high school and then went their separate ways. I understood it as they were going to get back together. She comes in and tells me that he's getting married. He had met this other girl who was a horrible person. She made him stop talking to his friends, cut off his family ties and made him so isolated. I was like, 'Are you going to speak now?'"

She added, "I think it's such a metaphor, that moment where it's almost too late and we got to either say what it is you're feeling or deal with the consequences forever. I feel like that's such a metaphor for so many things that we go through in life, where you can either say what you mean or you can be quiet about it forever."

That wasn't an option for Taylor: any experience she encountered in life was fair game for inclusion in a song. "I started thinking about what I would do if I was still in love with someone who was marrying someone who they shouldn't be marrying, and so I wrote this song about what exactly my game plan would be."

She later said of her lyric about urging the groom to make a run for it, so she could meet him by the back door of the church, "I have never interrupted a wedding before, but if I did, that is how I would do it."

This assertive, no-nonsense approach no doubt left John Mayer et al making a mental note to install an army of security guards should they ever get married – and it led to *Digital Spy* producing the news headline, "Taylor Swift likes to dominate men".

However, Taylor was making no apologies for the truth – and speaking out at the right moment was turning out to be a recurrent theme throughout the album. Label boss Scott Borchetta urged Taylor to rethink the title she had chosen, arguing it didn't represent how she had grown in the years since her last album release. "We were at lunch and she had played me a bunch of the new songs," he explained, "I looked at her and I'm like, 'Taylor, this record isn't about fairy tales and high school anymore.' That's not where you're at. I don't think the album should be called *Enchanted*."

That title held a special significance in Taylor's life, though. It was the name of a song about a man who, in just one meeting, had left her infatuated and desperate to see him again. It had all begun when Taylor attended an Owl City concert in New York and was introduced to vocalist Adam Young backstage. It was the closest she had ever been to love at first sight – but, painfully for her, it never got beyond the fantasies of what could have been.

"Meeting him, it was this overwhelming feeling of, 'I really hope you're not in love with somebody' and the entire way home, I remember the glittery NYC buildings passing by and then just sitting there thinking, am I ever going to talk to this person again? And [I had that feeling of] pining away for a romance that may never even happen, but all you have is this hope that it could and the fear that it never will."

Hours later on the same night, Taylor was "home" alone in her hotel room when she was inspired to write about her encounter. "It just was this positive, wistful feeling of 'I hope you can understand just how much I loved meeting you. I hope that you know that meeting you was not something that I took lightly, or just in passing,'" she explained.

She encoded Adam's name into the lyric booklet, but – just in case he was unable to take a hint and was still unsure – she inserted the word "wonderstruck" into her lyrics. "That's a word which [Adam] used one time in an email and I don't think I've ever heard anyone use that term before." Indeed, Adam had also written it several times in his blogs and had confessed it was a word he created himself. Taylor had been very direct about her feelings for him and perhaps the song would alert him

213

to a truth she was too shy to divulge in person, as always having walked away too soon.

But changing the name of the album to *Speak Now* from *Enchanted* was more than a decision for Taylor – it was a metaphor for her taking power back into her own hands. Instead of simply being enchanted, she felt she should have spoken and been proactive in making her feelings known to stand a chance of turning her infatuation into a real relationship.

As it stood, the moment with Adam seemed to have passed, but the album title was an ever-lasting reminder to her of how to handle the situation in future. Being able to come to that conclusion, as well as recognising and learning from her mistakes, indicated that she had matured. It suggested that Scott was correct in saying she had moved beyond a life of passive *Sleeping Beauty*-style fairy tales where, young and naïve, she waited for the male to make the first move in awakening her. As she would find out, sometimes the man in the relationship was just as shy.

To prove she was now growing up fast and maturing 'Back To December' revealed – from the person who had ordinarily been too proud to apologise – her first ever public apology. It was an ode to her December 2009 break-up with Taylor Lautner, which she described as a mistake on her part. The lyrics told how he had lovingly brought her roses, which she had left to wither and die – perhaps a metaphor for how she neglected their relationship.

Sources at the time reported that Lautner had seemed keener on her than she on him. Whereas he travelled cross-country to see her – as he had done the night they split up, leaving him alone and miserable in an unfamiliar town – she had rarely done the same for him. Ultimately the love had died – and all she could do in the aftermath was offer an apology.

"The person I wrote the song for deserves this," Taylor explained to E! "This is about somebody who was incredible to me, just perfect to me in a relationship, and I was really careless with him, so these are the words that I would say to him – that he deserves to hear."

Together, all of these songs comprised *Speak Now* – which, for producer Nathan Chapman, was an indisputable success story. One of his favourites was 'Never Grow Up'. "It's just her singing and me on acoustic guitar," he reminisced. "We recorded ourselves *live*. That song probably happened in two hours... a pop artist would probably release what we had done after five hours, but country artists don't want to hear programmed drums, they don't want to hear fake stuff... the main decisions were made in the demos."

It was all about raw, authentic emotion, showcased in tracks that were as simple and natural as the emotions themselves. It wasn't only Nathan who was satisfied with the album – soon CDs were flying off the shelves. It cemented its place in not just the country world but the pop world too, by débuting at number one in the mainstream *Billboard* chart.

The first week of release saw over a million sales and the biggest profit on record since 50 Cent's *The Massacre* five years previously. It was also the largest first week of sales for a female country singer in almost 20 years and the best sales week for any female artist in any genre since Britney Spears's 2000 *Oops! I Did It Again*.

That week, *Speak Now* accounted for one in every six albums sold in America. Taylor's aches and pains had now become much-loved public property – and that really *was* better than revenge.

When it was released as a single on November 15, 'Back To December' evoked a similar response, with over a million copies sold – plus it was the first track Taylor had ever penned that, according to the pop star's Twitter account, had made Katy Perry cry.

Taylor reciprocated the compliments that the song was "absolutely stunning" by revealing that 'Thinking Of You', a Perry track, had been one of her favourite songs of all time. Interestingly, the video director for 'Back To December', Yoann Lemoine, had also worked on Katy's 'Teenage Dream'.

He decided to display the pain of Taylor's break-up with stark, cold metaphorical images. He even depicted snow in an apartment. "I wanted to work on the coldness of feelings in a very visual way, playing with the snow, the distance and the sadness," he explained. "The winter theme was very interesting to me... I even wanted [Taylor's onscreen ex-boyfriend Guntars Asmanis] to go swim in frozen lakes at some point.

That was not possible, but I wanted to translate how you feel sometimes when your heart is broken. The snow in the apartment is supposed to show how connected she is to him. He is outside, in the cold, but somehow she is connected to him."

At first Lemoine hadn't known how to relate to Taylor, claiming that her world of fairy tales, fantasies, fame and postcard-perfect idealism – all wrapped up with the ribbon of youth – was miles apart from his "culture". However, her obvious melancholy at losing her love was more of a universal emotion that her director could share – and he instantly understood. "I saw something in her that could [paradoxically] be very rough and heart-breaking," he reflected, "far from the princess glittery outfits and glam that she often goes for."

That wasn't the only indication that Taylor had changed. While her good-girl values hadn't been tarnished, she had matured and developed, leading to more diverse tastes. She still had an enormous collection of country music, but alongside it was the occasional edgy rock CD, like Kings of Leon's 'Sex On Fire'. She still had modest views on sex appeal, but she had no qualms about "making out" with someone she barely knew if a film script required it.

The one thing that hadn't changed much was her notoriously bad luck with men. Perhaps that was just as well: if her life became smooth and tension free, what would she have left to write about?

By the time *Speak Now* was released, she had embarked on a new and painfully brief relationship with movie star Jake Gyllenhaal; but before Christmas, the pair had already split up. According to reports, their age difference of almost a decade had become an increasingly difficult gap for Jake to bridge. Not only that, but her fame and the attention they attracted as a twosome were also difficult. One source claimed, "He was really uncomfortable with all the attention… he wants to keep his private life private."

Things had at first seemed serious, when Taylor was photographed deep in conversation with Jake's sister Maggie and protectively holding hands with Maggie's four-year-old daughter. The *Daily Mail* commented admiringly that the seemingly down-to-earth couple "even made trips to the grocery store look romantic". Jake had already met Taylor's parents and, in photographs at least, he and Taylor seemed more like the average carefree couple than two stars with hectic showbiz lives.

That the two looked happy seemed almost undeniable. Then there was the material proof. For her 21st birthday, Jake had spent $11,000 on a vintage Gretsch guitar signed by one of her favourite country stars, Chet Atkins. It was an inventive gift for the girl who seemed to have everything and, by all accounts, she was thrilled.

Yet by Christmas, just a few days later, the liaison was already off and Jake spent the holiday season with his family. He even visited a branch of The Spotted Pig, the same pub Kanye West had checked into moments after being ejected from the 2009 VMAs for his misdemeanours.

Jake was also scheduled to be in Sydney for work commitments such as promoting the film *Love And Other Drugs*, while Taylor was contracted to stay in America. December certainly wasn't a lucky month for Taylor as far as romance was concerned – although at least this time she didn't feel compelled to apologise. At the American Music Awards the previous month, on November 21, she had performed One Republic's pop ballad 'Apologise', which tells of it being too late for someone to say sorry, on the end of a performance of 'Back To December' – her own way of saying the magic words to Taylor Lautner.

But her faith was restored in romance when she received a public Valentine's Day message from the man who had enchanted her – Adam Young of Owl City.

"I brought the record when it came out and I was playing through it top to bottom," he revealed to *US Weekly* of the first time he discovered her ode to him. "I love the classic adding up the letters in her lyrics. I got to that song ['Enchanted'] and it added up to my name and I had to take a step back and decipher the code." It didn't take long. "I was like, 'This song has to be about me!'" Adam said.

He described the moments leading up to their first meeting, waiting for Taylor to walk through the door as "the most nerve-wracking few minutes of my life" and confirmed that he was indeed "wonderstruck" when he finally met her.

It turned out that Adam had felt the same agonising regret when the invitation to his show failed to blossom into the fairy-tale relationship he had hoped for. In fact, it had fizzled out to no relationship at all. "I'm not the most romantic and eloquent guy in the world," he added. "She's just this endearing, wonderful girl and maybe I said something wrong… She's a superstar and I'm just this kid from a small town in the middle of nowhere, so I feel like that peasant in the [presence] of a princess."

However, while he claimed to be unromantic, his Valentine's gesture to her proved to be quite the opposite. Taking to his band's website to make a public post, he wrote, "Dear Taylor, I'll be the first to admit I'm a rather shy boy, and since music is the most eloquent form of communication I can muster, I decided to record something for you – a sort of a 'reply' to the breathtaking song on your current record. This is what I wanted so badly to tell you in person but could never quite put into words. Everything about you is lovely. You are an immensely charming girl with a beautiful heart and more grace and elegance than I know how to describe. You are a true princess from a dreamy fairy tale and above all, I just want you to know I was enchanted to meet you too."

Adam then attached his own version of 'Enchanted' for fans to download, which saw the track reworked in a jazzy, soulful interpretation and the lyrics changed a little too. Taylor wouldn't make her public response until a few months later.

Meanwhile, on March 7, 2011, her album's third single, 'Mean', was released to country radio. A video followed, first depicting Taylor playing a banjo in a country farmhouse with her band, seemingly without a care in the world. Within seconds, the scene then switched to one depicting her tied up on a railway track as an old-fashioned steam train approaches menacingly. Taylor's bondage on the track was symbolic of her powerlessness to prevent herself being persecuted in the public eye.

Other scenes mimicked Taylor's own childhood, depicting a girl who eats her lunch in the school toilets after her bullies deny her access to their table in the canteen. Meanwhile, an effeminate boy is teased by the football team for following his passions and reading a fashion magazine instead of joining in with their sport. Another girl is then mocked for her low-paid job in a burger bar.

A message of empowerment follows, showing the victims achieving greater heights than any of those who bullied them. For instance, the male fashion fanatic might not have fitted in with his macho classmates, but he goes on to rise above schoolyard taunts to become a legendary designer. Similarly, the McDonalds employee scrambles out of poverty to go on to university and become a brilliant businesswoman.

Like Katy Perry's 'Firework', Lady Gaga's 'Born This Way' and Jessie J's 'Who's Laughing Now?', it was a defiant statement against bullying and alienation, providing the message that fans should simply be who they are.

It illustrates how, while in the school environment, being "weird" and different is practically an invitation to be verbally crucified, years later it can be an asset. In an adult world, all of the things that make someone different might actually set them apart and make them special.

In fact, to be a famous singer, one might argue that standing out as different was almost compulsory for success. Lady Gaga – who wore imitation lobsters on her head, gave a teacup she was inseparable from its own name, wore a dress made of raw meat and led a live sheep onto a UK talk show – was having the time of her life and had millions of fans. Had she behaved the same way in school, she would likely have been teased mercilessly and branded a social outcast – or, at the very least, referred by her headmaster to a psychiatrist.

The message of the video was not to base life plans on popularity at school and to stand tall against bullies, who may even have been insecure and jealous themselves.

The video confounded expectations, too, with MTV originally predicting a "honky-tonk type performance video in which Taylor and her band have a little fun at someone else's expense". How wrong it was – and the video that did get released was soon the subject of hot debate.

Those who didn't know Taylor's own history as a childhood bullying victim felt her problems were laughably minor compared to what those outside the spotlight were going through. For example, *Entertainment Weekly* challenged, "Is she really equating a professional critic questioning her ability to sing at an awards show to getting bullied because you're different?" However, in contrast, *The Huffington Post* believed the plot made Taylor more relatable to "underdogs and dreamers" and was therefore "effective".

Slant magazine put itself at risk of being declared as mean as the song title when it queried why, "instead of actually doing something to improve on her ability to find or hold pitch consistently, Swift has simply written a song about how it's 'mean' for people to point out that problem."

Zap2It also took issue with her accuracy about bullies rotting in their hometown, insisting that, in real life, plenty of successful people were "mean" too.

However, the song also attracted positive press. *The Village Voice* described it as "hugely compassionate and fearless", while *Country Universe* raved that it "articulates the distinction between honesty and cruelty so well".

By now, Taylor had built up an army of admirers – certainly enough to protect her from the critics around her. Unfortunately, she didn't have time either to date or to separate the real from the fake as she was about to embark on the nationwide *Speak Now* tour.

In typical Taylor style, however, even her rehearsals became available to the public: she was hiding nothing. On May 23, she turned the final dress rehearsal for the tour into a charity concert for those affected by a recent spate of tornadoes. Over 13,000 people attended the Nashville-based concert and over $750,000 was raised for the cause. She then took her philanthropy a step further by donating $250,000 of her own money to a charity that helped with the relief effort in Alabama.

The day after her charity concert, on May 24, the video for Taylor's fourth single, 'The Story Of Us', premiered on TV. During the making of the video, she had direct experience of tornadoes herself. "We had to hide," she told MTV. "All of us, we had to hide in a room where there were no windows, so that was a little bit crazy. Other than that, it was incredibly fun!"

The video, set in a library to complement the metaphors about story-books and being on a different page from her lover, does all the speaking for Taylor about why she and John Mayer might have broken up. After showcasing several awkward attempts to avoid each other, it shows a flashback image to Taylor's onscreen boyfriend cheating on her with another woman.

Meanwhile, Taylor sailed her way through an intensive six-month tour of North America, missing just a few dates due to an attack of bronchitis. While she was on the road, her own personalised scent, Wonderstruck, hit the shops, as part of a special deal with perfumer Elizabeth Arden. The name came from the lyrics to 'Enchanted' – with a little help from Adam Young. "A fragrance can help shape someone's first impression and memory of you," Taylor wrote. "It's exciting to think that Wonderstruck will play a role in creating some of these memories."

While Taylor's hectic tour schedule saw her rarely stay in one city for more than a couple of nights and left her too pressed for time to reignite her romance with Adam Young, the perfume was an answer of its own to his Valentine's Day letter and song. Perhaps one day they would try again to get together – but until then they would both be left with the tantalising promise of what could have been.

Either way, it seemed unlikely that it would be the last Taylor's fans would hear on the matter – through song, it had become a true-life story, not just to the two as a prospective couple, but to the world.

'Sparks Fly', the fifth and final single from *Speak Now*, quickly followed suite, and served as a montage of the best video clips from the tour. Taylor finally revealed the answer to the mystery about the song's origins, explaining that she wrote it at the age of 16 and had first played it in smoky bars containing as few as 40 people.

To her, it was like an embarrassing teenage diary entry that she felt she had moved on from, but she also felt compelled to respond to fans' opinions. "The fans just kept saying over and over again, 'Sparks Fly', we want it on the record,'" she recalled, "and so I went back and revisited it and I kind of rewrote some things and updated it. It's been one of the fastest rising songs we've had on the record."

221

Taylor's willingness to factor in her fans when making decisions was one of the things that made her attractive to them. No matter what heartaches she went through, she had vowed to share the truth with her fans without sparing the slightest detail, insisting: "I owe it to them to let them in on everything from day one."

She also answered fan mail on MySpace personally from time to time, which is almost unheard of in the music world. Unlike many manufactured acts, Taylor had always claimed that she was her own manager and made her own business decisions, instead of hiding behind a network of corporate employees – something that helped her stay close to her fans and keep in touch with their needs.

Fame didn't seem to have changed her either. "Fans are my favourite thing in the world," she insisted. "I've never been the type of artist who has that line drawn between their friends and their fans. The line's always been really blurred for me. I'll hang out with them after the show. I'll hang out with them before the show. If I see them in the mall, I'll stand there and talk to them for ten minutes. I don't care. I [was] just a senior in high school who has a better job. Who am I to think I'm better than talking to people?"

Sometimes Taylor could take this to extremes. While most artists had to dodge the over-zealous attentions of obsessive fans at some point or another, they weren't just stalking Taylor – at times she was stalking them.

"I was driving near the mall [one day] and I saw this girl with my tour T-shirt on," she revealed to *Parade* of one encounter. "She was probably 11. I made a u-turn and tried to follow her. I really had to do some manoeuvring. I found her in a video game store and just kind of walked up to her and said, 'Oh hi. I wanted to meet you.' She had no idea what to say for about three minutes. Then her mom walked over, burst into tears and proceeded to tell me that they'd driven all the way from Austin, Texas, just to see where I was discovered."

Taylor wasn't the type of greater-than-thou celebrity whose ego was bigger than her over-stuffed, walk-in wardrobe. Her followers weren't simply an irritating inconvenience or a temporary roadblock on her way to fame and fortune – they were sharing her journey with her.

"I never get tired of it," she claimed. "I remember when I was a little kid, I used to sit there and think about how lucky I would be one day where people cared about the words I wrote or how lucky I would be if someday I was just walking through the mall and saw some little girl walking by with my face on her T-shirt. When you spend so much time daydreaming about things like that, when that actually happens, you don't ever complain about it. When I go to a restaurant, yeah, I know that a line is probably going to form in front of the table, but didn't I always wish for that? Yeah, I did. So it's like, I never want to be the girl who wanted something so bad her whole life and then gets it and complains about it. I'm not going to be that girl."

There were two Taylors: the queen of country who soaked up the attention of an arena who screamed louder than she could sing, and then the girl ordinary high-school students could relate to because she seemed so similar to themselves. Link those two personas together and Taylor became a role model for millions of young women with a dream. By being honest in her songs, she let her fans into her mind, her heart and her life.

What was more, no matter how many albums she sold or how acutely she experienced showbiz life in the fast lane, she hadn't changed fundamentally from the 11-year-old walking up and down Music Row, someone for whom nothing meant more than for the world to hear and appreciate her music.

As one reporter who had seen her both in the early days and on the *Speak Now* tour commented, "It seems like she hasn't changed. The numbers have. The money has – and maybe the love life has. But she has not... altogether Swift has sold more than 20 million albums. But the fame still hasn't gone to her head – and I don't think it ever will."